SHAPING UP FOR TODAY'S BUSINESS WORLD

Tomorrow is too late. There is a new breed of employees in every level of business today, and a new generation of technology. Unless a company reshapes itself to take full advantage of both, it does not have a future. This book was written to help business leaders retain or regain the spirit that will propel their organizations toward competitive success in the year 2,000 and beyond.

ENTREPRENEURING IN ESTABLISHED COMPANIES

"Incisive and mind-expanding. As I read the book I developed a list of 15 ideas I couldn't wait to share with my colleagues."
—Sam Ginn, Group President, PacTel Companies

"In my industry, we expect innovation. . . . We deal constantly with 'turbulence.' Brandt captures these issues concisely and effectively. His book is outstanding . . . easy to read and most important, easy to use."
—S. Rubenstein, President,
    Space Systems Division, Rockwell International

STEPHEN C. BRANDT is currently Senior Lecturer in Management at the Stanford School of Business. Dr. Brandt is an experienced CEO and corporate director, and is the author of *Entrepreneuring: Ten Commandments for Building a Growth Company* (also available in a Mentor Executive edition).

ENTREPRENEURING IN ESTABLISHED COMPANIES

Managing toward the Year 2000

Steven C. Brandt

A MENTOR BOOK

NEW AMERICAN LIBRARY

NEW YORK AND SCARBOROUGH, ONTARIO

To my wife, Wooly, and the fresh wave of corporate entrepreneurs of all ages who are starting to break onto the establishment beaches of the world

NAL PENGUIN BOOKS ARE AVAILABLE AT QUANTITY DISCOUNTS WHEN USED TO PROMOTE PRODUCTS OR SERVICES. FOR INFORMATION PLEASE WRITE TO PREMIUM MARKETING DIVISION, NAL PENGUIN INC., 1633 BROADWAY, NEW YORK, NEW YORK 10019.

© Steven C. Brandt, 1986

This is an authorized reprint of a hardcover edition published by Dow Jones-Irwin.

Library of Congress Catalog Card Number: 86-063376

MENTOR TRADEMARK REG. U.S. PAT. OFF. AND FOREIGN COUNTRIES
REGISTERED TRADEMARK—MARCA REGISTRADA
HECHO EN CHICAGO, U.S.A.

SIGNET, SIGNET CLASSIC, MENTOR, ONYX, PLUME, MERIDIAN and NAL BOOKS are published *in the United States* by NAL Penguin Inc., 1633 Broadway, New York, New York 10019, *in Canada* by The New American Library of Canada Limited, 81 Mack Avenue, Scarborough, Ontario M1L 1M8

First Mentor Printing, April, 1987

1 2 3 4 5 6 7 8 9

PRINTED IN THE UNITED STATES OF AMERICA

Acknowledgments

I wish to convey a heartfelt thank you to the many people who have been helpful in the development of this book. The list is a long one. First and foremost are the men and women participants in the Stanford Executive Program (SEP) and the Stanford Sloan Program the last five years. These practicing executives and managers have brought the challenges of established businesses from all around the world to the crucible of pointed, and frequently insightful, discussion—both inside the classroom and out. These quality people have been instrumental in opening up the range of possibilities in management's "art of the possible" which this book has sought to address. Second, it has been my pleasure to work closely in several different roles—mostly as a catalyst—with some of the senior people in a cross-section of truly engrossing companies. From them I have learned. My respect and appreciation go especially to the people at Tandem, Saga, SAI, Touche Ross, NZI (New Zealand), Bechtel, Fafco, Tektronix, Pacific Telesis, GE, Carlise, Syntex, Triad, Teledyne, First United Bank Corporation, Paxus, Bernina (Switzerland), Peat Marwick, Heart Federal, Conoco, Theo Davies, and American TV & Communication. Finally, the book would have languished in the land of wishful thinking had it not been for the probing of ever-alert MBAs, the encouragement of stimulating colleagues, and the help of a masterful staff—particularly my secretary, El Vera Fisher—at the Stanford Graduate School of Business.

S.C.B.

Contents

Introduction

This book is written to be used. It reflects a growing awareness that traditional gargage entrepreneurs and venture capitalists and high-technology whiz kids in emerging companies cannot alone produce a healthy economy and a gratifying worklife. The future, in business, will go to established companies of all shapes and sizes as well—*the ones that adapt*. Staying in the game means playing by the rules. And the rules are changing in important, discontinuous ways. All of us who manage now know from direct experience that economic viability is a moving target. This book is about what it takes to keep on hitting the bull's-eye in what social-trend researcher, Daniel Yankelovich, calls "a world turned upside down."

In May 1984, *Fortune* magazine in a cover article labeled the 1973–84 period, "The Ten Years That Shook the Fortune 500." The statistics support that label. Sales, earnings, returns, jobs—the composite curves for our largest companies plateau and drop over the decade. Why did this happen when other teams in the league, i.e., other companies in other countries, kept on winning over the same period? The answer is, of course, complex. Enough has been written about the web of economic, political, technological, and social forces at work in our world. Not enough has been written about our aging management practices—the ways in which we organize, train, plan, lead, motivate, budget, promote, and so forth. Robert Hayes and William Abernathy raised the corner of the tent for a swift peek in a provocative *1980 Harvard Business*

Review article, "Managing Our Way to Economic Decline." It is time for a more complete look.

The fact of the matter is that many, many of us in positions of management responsibility are managerially obsolete. We preside over decisions that depend on technologies we only half understand. We manage by objectives in organizations that can only be managed by consent. We weigh capital investment issues to four decimal places and depend on focus groups to delineate our markets. We preach the virtues of leadership, quality, and dedication but cut corners to make our quarterly numbers. We are unsure of just what entrepreneurs are . . . and who they are in our own enterprises. We worry about making big mistakes instead of big breakthroughs. We actually do want to do good while doing well, but we are not sure exactly what the words mean today—digital managers in an analog world. We unknowingly resist in a thousand ways the reorientation in our thinking necessary to move our enterprises into alignment with reality. The resistance is natural; you and I got to where we are by moving along a certain set of rails of our own unique design. It's tough to shift to roller skates for the next segment. It appears easier to bet on "technology" to keep our firms vital. That bet, done alone, is a bad one. Technology may be necessary, but it will rarely be sufficient to make a company a continuing winner as we wrap up the 20th century.

In two earlier books, *Entrepreneuring* and *Strategic Planning in Emerging Companies*, I attempted to distill the best from academia and the real world into some workable, usable ideas. My intent is the same here. Right now, from towns and cities to the Congress and the media, startup ventures, innovation centers, and young enterprises are in vogue. Newly minted entrepreneurs have become national heros; venture investors are now accepted members of the establishment; sweat equity and seed capital seem to be more hallowed than church; the MBA courses on new enterprise management are overflowing with men and women seeking the fast lane with the satisfying scenery. Small biz is in. But the reality is that ten thousand successful start-ups a year will, in aggregate, neither budge the balance-of-payments deficit nor have a perceptible impact on youth unemployment, U.S. productivity, or world peace. There is a limit to what chocolate chip cookie and microcomputer software companies can do. Only the established businesses that together constitute the country's core can make the necessary, sustainable difference . . . in a world turned upside down. To do so, they must become more entrepreneurial *in the broad, adaptive sense of the word*. To become more entrepreneurial, our aging management practices must grow to fit these times.

Steven C. Brandt

PART ONE

In Part One, the reader is invited to quickly solidify a framework of understanding on why managers and executives tend to do what they do as they pilot their respective charters through the agitated waters of the late 1900s. From the analysis, action guidelines emerge for practices to tap deeper into people's potential for new ideas and for committing themselves to winning as part of a tough-minded business enterprise. Part One contains the notes for the music that follows.

In Part Two, the reader is asked to consider specific suggestions on what it takes to retain or regain productive, entrepreneurial behavior across the mainstream population of a going concern.

Chapter One

Perspective

Americans in their 30s and 40s are old enough to have experienced the dominant culture of the post-World War II era . . . and yet young enough to have received, full blast, the new cultural meanings.

DANIEL YANKELOVICH, *NEW RULES*

Entrepreneuring has an aura about it. The word implies a host of desirable attributes like innovation, creativity, flexibility, and sensitivity to customers. If a company has the attributes, an important management challenge is to keep them as the enterprise grows larger and more complex. If management has let the attributes atrophy over time, a high-priority management task is to get them back . . . to "fix the culture" as it is currently called. In either case, perspective is helpful on what has happened to companies as the business world along with the country have matured since World War II. Without such perspective, there is great tendency to try to put new wine in old bottles.

MAJOR ERAS

Below is a bird's-eye view of the major eras of business development over the past 100 or so years.

The mid- and late 1800s were a time of explosive development in the United States. A series of basic inventions—breakthroughs in technology—fueled an innovation revolution to sit atop the industrial revolution of 100 years earlier. There was certainly business activity before the mechanical miracles of the industrial revolution. A wage system was used by profit-making enterprises in the Roman Empire; accounting was highly developed by the Italians in the 15th century; insurance was used by Dutch business enterprises in the 16th century; and the Bank of England was formed in 1694.[1] But this early business activity did little to leverage human potential—mental or physical. The industrial revolution gave the world power-driven machines and, thereby, cracked

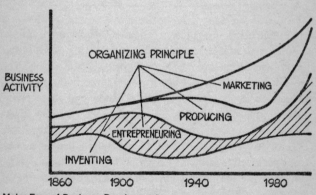

Major Eras of Business Development

open the door of opportunity to thousands of latent entrepreneurs—people who could commercialize ideas. Then the first *innovation* revolution brought forth electricity, flight, internal combustion engines, and other rousing ventures that truly unleashed the Entrepreneuring Era depicted on page 4.

The advent of technological invention in the late 1800s iterated with progress along another dimension—the social invention and acceptance of the corporation. The corporate form of organization for human endeavor facilitated the purposeful pooling of talent and capital. The combination of technology (electrical/mechanical), social form (corporation), and evolutionary, instinctual ambition (entrepreneurs) produced the surge in the flow of human events that cascaded into America, and later into other countries, culminating in the 20th century that business leaders know today. The figure that follows depicts the elements in-

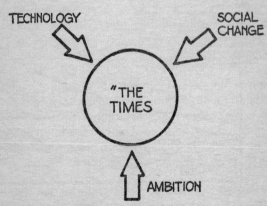

A Concurrent Meeting of Forces

volved. *This exact same concurrent meeting of forces is reappearing as society approaches the 21st century.* As Peter Drucker notes in his book, *Managing in Turbulent Times,* between 1856 and 1914, "a new invention, leading almost immediately to a new industry, was made on average every 14 to 18 months." He goes on to observe that "between 1947 and 1975, only two truly new industries emerged: computers and systemic drugs." And, most important for the purpose of perspective, he speculates that "The next 20 or 25 years are almost certain to be more akin to the years before 1914 than to those between 1947 and 1975."[2]

By the early 1900s, an economic and communications infrastructure was in place. Railroads and telegraph poles and waterways tied the U.S. common market together. More and more people wanted a piece of the progress. The management challenge was to become efficient in the production of goods and services—and particularly goods. Henry Ford's dictum to (mass) produce cars at a low unit cost so everyone could have one captures the spirit of the Producing Era. If the price was right, an item could be sold. There was little marketing, only selling. Each industry had plenty of its own, very green grass to chew. Executives, managers, and employees of that era were "in" steel or autos or packing or rubber. "Do more of what you do, better" represented the primary mode of thinking for those at work in the rapidly growing cities. An introspective industry and production orientation dominated the business scene even in the most progressive companies.

Carl Sandburg's famous poem, "Chicago," published in 1916, gives a glimpse of and feel for those times:

Hog Butcher for the World, Tool Maker, Stacker of Wheat, Player with Railroads and the Nation's Freight Handler; Stormy, husky, brawling, City of the Big Shoulders . . . [3]

Following World War II, progressive management teams inaugurated a third era in the 100-year period under review. Competitive success in those halcyon days was no longer purely a function of manufacturing efficiency; increasingly, product differentiation grew in importance. While General Motors had introduced the notion of a market—rather than a production—orientation in the 1930s, the concept was not widely adopted even in the early 1960s. Ted Levitt's famous article, "Marketing Myopia," was published in the summer of 1960. It remains a classic and one of the all-time best-selling reprints from the *Harvard Business Review*. The opening paragraph still rings true:

> Every major industry was once a growth industry. But some that are now riding a wave of growth enthusiasm are very much in the shadow of decline. Others which are thought of as seasoned growth industries have actually stopped growing. In every case the reason growth is threatened, slowed, or stopped is not because the market is saturated. *It is because there has been a failure of management*. (Emphasis added.)[4]

The Marketing Era of the mid-1900s period coincided with, and no doubt contributed to, the growing affluence of the population. Incremental product changes, cosmetic differentiation, fancy packaging, and merchandising represented the arsenal that was aimed at smaller and smaller market segments. In many respects, management teams faced linear problems: Find new holes and fill them. Use energy (fossil fuel) and intensive capital improvements to keep unit costs in line with the other domestic competitors. Nourish the historic hands-off attitude that characterized business-government and, as a practical matter, business-society relations. In short, use yesterday as a guide to tomorrow. This formula worked well deep into the 60s; then modern times began.

7

It is not necessary for the purposes of this book to recount the many causes and characteristics of what has variously been called the Age of Discontinuity (Peter Drucker); the Postindustrial Era (Daniel Bell); the Affluent Society (John K. Galbraith); and The Third Wave (Alvin Toffler). Whatever the causes, the cumulative net effect has been and is one of turbulence and unpredictability. Most important, the business challenges are truly new; they are not readily or adequately met using approaches that worked in the past. And just as managers at all levels resisted (and resist) the shift from a production to a marketing focus, many managers will (and do) resist the inevitable shift from a functional, production/marketing orientation to an innovation orientation. It is, once again, natural to deny reality when it is strange. Any alteration in a success pattern introduces uncertainties, threatens power structures, and muddles turf boundaries for the incumbents. But new skills and practices *are* required. Most managers can accept this notion intellectually. The trick is to reduce the strangeness, the ambiguity, and the threat to moving on and altering habits. An understanding of the old practices and the new realities can help individuals digest the unknowns and build the bridges to the needed new approaches to managing enterprises. "Discontent is the first step in the progress of a man or a nation," according to Oscar Wilde.

NEW VALUES

In a pioneering, 1983 report entitled, *Work and Human Values: An International Report on Jobs in the 1980s and 1990s,* a task force of authors from the Aspen Institute for Humanistic Studies and the Public Agenda Foundation crystallized these findings:

- The advanced industrial democracies can compete most effectively in those areas that require a highly skilled and trained labor force.
- The Japanese experience has called attention to how greatly productive power can be enhanced when human dedication is added to the mix.
- Millions of young people are ready to give the workplace a great burst of energy and dynamism—if jobs can be designed to meet their new expressive values.
- Many current managerial practices in the United States tend to discourage rather than to reward work-ethic behavior.
- Technology has historically favored large-scale operations. But much of the new technology is shifting the balance to favor small-scale, decentralized operations.
- Management practices have not kept pace with the changes in both the nature of work and in the values that people bring to their jobs.[5]

In effect, the social scientists came to the same conclusions in their report that both perceptive economists and thoughtful, practicing executives have, namely, that there is a phase shift behind the current turbulence, not just an aggravated economic cycle.

So what? So it is time to bite the bullet and accelerate the growth of fresh ways of doing things in all parts of existing companies, not just in product development. Intellectual jousting in search of excellence is no longer good enough. Neither are well intended, older measures: more money for R&D; encouraging product champions; building a little flexibility into the compensation scheme; setting up a small pool of venture capital; and so forth. These actions together might raise the average entrepreneurial output in an established company a few percent—at best. What the times call for are actions that make a 30 or 40 percent dent in the challenge. To get that sort of a return between now and the turn of the century means managers have to update all those everyday practices that have an impact on the mainstream of their companies—on the warehouse people and the engineers and the sales force and the accounting staff and the tellers.

CONCLUSION

Aesop observed that "It is easy to be brave from a safe distance." The safe distance for many responsible people is the buffer that comes from the fact that what they are doing today has a long and enviable record of working. That buffer generates inertia. It is time to be brave up close. And to be brave mostly means to experiment with the day-to-day activities that constitute managing in the new order of things.

> There is nothing more difficult to take in hand, more perilous to conduct, than to take a lead in the introduction of a new order of things, because the innovation has for enemies all those who have done well under the old conditions and lukewarm defenders in those who may do well under the new.
>
> MACHIAVELLI, *THE PRINCE*

Perspective on the eras, forces, values, and truly pivotal challenges facing those in established businesses can be helpful in making those challenges inviting. For, "It's what you learn after you know it all that counts."[6]

Chapter Two

Managing Practices— Yesterday and Today

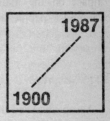

Slide rules are vanishing, victims of a calculator/computer world. Keuffel & Esser Co., once a major slide rule manufacturer, has sold three in the past three years. A group of 60 students was shown a slide rule recently; 45 didn't know what it was.

USA TODAY MARCH 7, 1985

The innovation revolution—inventing, entrepreneuring, producing—brought a whole new set of people into the world of commerce. They came off the farm, across the oceans, and out of the mines into the limelight of material progress. Their involvement coalesced into the modern corporation with its myriad of practices for getting work done through others, the classic definition of what managing is all about. Those practices have evolved over the last century with the growth in size and complexity of companies. In this chapter the reader will find diagrams and descriptions of the increasing levels of sophistication in three of the four major areas of managing practices: Organizing (activities and relationships); Planning (for the days ahead); and Controlling (what is going on). Leading, the fourth, classic subtopic of managing, will be handled separately in Chapter Eleven; it is the one area of managing practices that has atrophied over the years. The reader's understanding of just where his or her enterprise is at present in terms of organizing, planning, and controlling can pave the way for actually doing more about encouraging widespread, internal entrepreneuring in the years ahead.

ORGANIZING

Every established company today was once a growth company. Most started with a flat, family structure. For example, Ford Motor Company and General Motors were essentially proprietorships during their formative years. And both companies encountered crippling difficulties when they outgrew their proprietors (Henry Ford and William C. Durant) and their associated structures. Since the early part

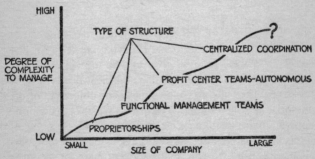

Evolution of Organizing Practices

of this century, most major enterprises have marched along the management practices road to more and more complicated ways of organizing human endeavor.

The figure on page 12 illustrates the march. The state of the art today is a company with autonomous profit centers. Each profit center serves a unique set of markets with a unique set of products and/or services, i.e., the various profit centers are in different businesses. The efforts of the collection of profit centers is coordinated by a headquarters in some way. Until recently, the coordination was done primarily by staff people with financial and/or planning skills. More recently, the emphasis is shifting toward making the profit center managers the primary planners. Reading One in the Appendix is entitled, "The New Breed of Strategic Planner." It was the cover story of *Business Week* magazine, September 17, 1984; it is included for the reader's reference.

Proprietorships

The classic proprietorship has a Main Street, USA ring about it. There is an owner-manager who puts in long, long hours. He or she is assisted either by family members or local acquaintances. To a reasonable extent, the people involved control their own destiny. Whether in retailing or manufacturing or services of some type, chances are that *successful* proprietorships are "close to the customer" in common parlance. Staffing is done unscientifically; everyone is visible to the boss at all times. The objectives of the enterprise are clear to the participants: typically, economic survival first and lifestyle or growth second. A sense of purposefulness pervades the enterprise—the same purposefulness that tends to be characteristic of many of the large Japanese corporations that have done so well in recent times. In fact, the word "proprietorship" nicely captures the essence of the culture and even the organization struc-

13

ture of many modern Japanese companies. People at all levels identify with the continuing success of their company. They are owner-employees . . . proprietors.

There were over 600,000 new corporations formed in the United States in 1983. This is 10 times the annual number of 25 years ago. To put the 600,000 new companies into perspective: In 1948, there were 8 million enterprises (sole proprietorships, partnerships, and corporations) in the United States. In 1980, the number had more than doubled to over 16 million. Proprietorships may be more American than apple pie.

Functional Teams

With success—fueled, of course, by ambition—comes the challenges of company size and, often, increased complexity in terms of products and markets served. Accompanying the new challenges is the need for more technical know-how in one or more subjects. The time comes to "get organized." Traditionally in America, some form of functional organization structure has been put into place either under duress or systematically. People knowledgeable in accounting, sales, production, finance, and so forth are identified and positioned. If the right people are chosen—from inside the company or outside—and if they work well together with the help of a competent general manager, chances are the management team will start to rationalize the business. Whereas intuition based on experience and gut feel drove the product, market, and process decisions during the proprietorship days for better or worse, these decisions now become more data driven and subject to interdisciplinary discussion.

The functional team, constituting the "professionally managed" enterprise, as it is often called, usually attempts to systematically exploit market opportunities. The team will seek to sell what it already has to new segments (market development) and/or design new products and services for the existing customer base (product development). Often higher growth companies, or profit centers, will do both, i.e., follow a compound, basic strategy for building the business.

If the team is correct in its decisions and follows through, chances are the business will become even more complex: more products, markets, and staff. At some point the "mores" strain the functional organization structure to the point of breaking. The single level of general management indigenous to the structure bogs down. Decisions are delayed; schedules and/or opportunities are missed; cash runs short; the enterprise receives some unwanted surprises; the operation falters. Since the 1920s, the standard organizational correction to this particular problem of success has been to shift to profit centers of one kind or another.

Profit-Center Teams

Divisionalization, decentralization, delegation—the three Ds—pretty much represent the state of the art today when it comes to retaining or regaining the manageability of complex companies. The hypothesis has been and is that by breaking the company into smaller pieces, the benefits of a simpler, functional structure can be achieved at the operating level. This notion has merit and has proven itself in most major companies and industries in the 40 years since World War II. However, business success under the profit-center concept may, in some respects, have lulled corporate management into inaction as the present phase-change described in Chapter One continues. In reality, reductionism—subdividing—only produces more of the same, clones, in effect. In the language of biology, established companies today need more mutations, i.e., "Sudden variations in some inheritable characteristic . . . as distinguished from variations resulting from generations of gradual change."[1]

In the early turbulent days of the late 1960s, it was the large, three-D firms which felt most acutely the need for better planning. Under the profit-center concept, the unit managers were to some degree running their own businesses beneath the umbrella of the parent corporation. However, as times got tougher, good businesses were dragged down by poorly performing ones. The umbrella developed holes. It became necessary to separate the winners from the losers—the stars and cash cows from the dogs, in planning lingo.

Centralized Coordination

The sorting and separation processes became known as strategic planning. The processes were typically driven by the headquarters staff, with or without the help of outside consultants. In the last 20 years, strategy consulting has grown into a significant industry. In terms of the national talent bank, some of the nation's best and brightest have been siphoned away from making and selling into planning activities. Today the tide appears to be turning (see Reading One), but it is important to recognize that between 1964 and 1984, a prodigious amount of corporate energy went into analysis: What is the competitive position of each profit center (planning unit)? What is the long-term market attractiveness for the unit? Which units shall be built? Held? Harvested? How shall this large, complex organization be coordinated so that the whole is greater than the sum of its parts? What is the nature of the song to which all the units of the enterprise shall be assigned singing parts?

Organizationally, there was (and is) some recentralization of power as well as tougher new criteria for allocating corporate resources. From a managing practices standpoint, corporate America moved toward a combination of headquarters and operating activities to combat the changing times. For the most part, this is *all* that has been done in response to the phase shift. Be decentralized, coordinated, lean, and mean is the current, conventional wisdom. This relatively simple formula, essentially a structural fix, is perhaps best suited to (mere) economic downturns.

What lies beyond centralized coordination of profit centers? The preceding figure shows a question mark. Chapters Three and Seven suggest specific areas of experimentation for responsible people willing to look at their organizing habits with a critical eye.

PLANNING

The term, "linear," best describes the nature of the planning methodology that was adequate until recent times. Companies were in discreet industries ("I'm in paper"); there were known and predictable competitors; population growth, energy prices, interest rates, and sex roles were fairly predictable. Tomorrow could be planned for with yesterday's experience. And so on. This has, of course, changed. And most seers do not see a return to normal in the working lifetime of those already in positions of managerial responsibility. In general, as has been said, American business management has not yet fully responded to the new realities. At best, it is stuck at the intellectual sorting and pruning level in which products and markets are rationalized. At worst, it is still extrapolating historical numbers generated in the accounting department. Most important, however, planning remains almost totally incremental, i.e., all attention is focused on changes at the margin of what the enterprise has traditionally done. It may be that the various bubble charts, experience curves, and nine-cell matrixes in the planners' tool kits actually

17

discourage really new ideas, innovation, and productive creativeness. The figure below catalogs the evolution in planning practices.

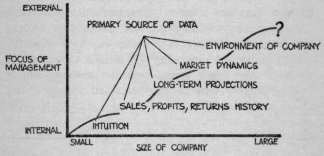

Evolution of Planning Practices

Intuition

In terms of observable sophistication, intuition as a management planning practice ranks low and early in the scheme of things. The days when you could launch a new product because your gut told you to do so have pretty well passed in companies where direction flows downward from the 18th floor. Yet, almost surprisingly, the idea of reigniting intuition is a growing one. There is a right-brain renaissance afoot as CEOs like GE's Jack Welch entreat their people to "be more entrepreneurial," "strive for quantum leaps," "look for breakouts," and so forth. But, in most companies today, planning for the future on the basis of hunches, feelings, and a quick glance at the projected payback period has become unacceptable.

Sales, Profits, and Returns History

The actual state of the art in planning, if *all* companies, large and small, are considered, revolves around sales, profits, and returns projections. Using this methodology or practice, the big decisions in the life of the enterprise boil down to which product or market or location will provide the best, long-term numbers. There are many, many fine ways to develop refined projections, discount them back, and evaluate them enroute to yes/no decisions. And the more sophisticated approaches will include a modicum of economic forecasting, some competitor analysis, and at least a cursory look at the perceived strengths and weaknesses of the enterprise. The end results are thoughtful decisions on how best to extend the business from its historic base.

Long-Term Projections

The younger sister of budgeting is, and has been, planning in which the time horizons are stretched. More often than not, the typically numbers-driven elements of the finished plan are surrounded with some prose. Today, it is even fashionable to entitle the end products "strategic" implying that a host of nontraditional factors has been taken into account in the plan formulation.

Market Dynamics

One big drawback to numbers-driven planning is that the more ethereal matters of life cycles (product and industry), sensitivities, quality, technical competence vis-à-vis competitors, and value perceptions are not automatically or typically incorporated into the process. Under the ever-present pressure of time, it is very easy to go with what you've got, i.e., hard data from accounting and sales forecasts. Market-based planning is a step forward. Proba-

19

bly the most popular form in use today is the four-cell matrix with its quadrants labeled stars, cash cows, and so forth. One axis is used to measure market share; the other, market growth rate.

Market-based planning processes, to some extent due to their simplicity, have done a lot to extricate some managements from the 1950s'-style linear thinking. To a large extent the word "strategic" as applied to planning has meant market-based during the last 10 years. The notions of a portfolio of businesses, being low-cost producers, and having different strategies for different parts of the company are relatively new news. One has but to look at many of the weak performers in the *Fortune* 500 class in recent times to find crisp examples of companies whose planning practices were (or are) of prop-plane vintage. Polaroid, Joy, Burroughs, and Storage Technology come to mind. The jet age requires a bigger view. Mike Porter, in his popular book, *Competitive Strategy*, suggests that suppliers, customers, substitute materials, and potential new competitors need to be taken into account, in addition to traditional competitors.[2] Most often, to do so, requires a higher order approach to planning.

In summary to this point, business leaders operating at the upper levels in the managing practices hierarchy in the last 10 years have generally done a good job of balancing their portfolios of planning units. The balancing, however, has generally tended to be a conservative act aimed at avoiding financial embarrassment rather than one aimed at making breakthroughs into new ground. In short, it has been asset-, rather than opportunity-, driven planning.

Environment of Company

The challenge of collapsing the environment, the whole thing, in a systematic way for analysis and discussion has been satisfactorily resolved. There are 9-cell and 16-cell matrix routines available from local consultants at competitive prices. The key point to recognize is that they are essentially mechanical ways to facilitate the asking of the right, broad band of questions that companies on the move today face. *And many of the answers are going to be intuitive.* But that is okay. "Strategic planning is a *line management activity* centered on getting *the right people, agenda, and information* together on a *timely schedule* in order to make *decisions that commit cash and people to market positioning assignments extending beyond the current operating cycle.*"[3] Normally, the competitive position and the market attractiveness are massaged for each of the various planning units of the enterprise. These broad terms hopefully encompass all the salient facts and opinions necessary to develop a comprehensive picture of the reality of the environment at a given point in time Increasingly, the internal environment is also getting attention.

In some respects, planning has become high art since the 1960s. In other important respects, as indicated earlier, the *apparent* objectivity, simplicity, and purity of the resulting visuals may have bred complacency in the management circles of many important companies.

H. Igor Ansoff, the academic father of both strategic planning and strategic management, hints at the point in his 1984 book:

> Simplicity is not a free good. While making the inside of the firm more manageable, it may cause the firm to lose touch with the complexities of the external realities. For continued success (and even survival) in a turbulent environment, there is a requisite level of internal complexity which must be maintained to enable the firm to capture the nuances and variabilities in external trends, threats, and opportunities.[4]

To summarize on planning practices, they have gravitated toward more and more abstraction which has tended to place them at a greater and greater distance from the ordinary people in organizations. At the same time, the portfolio approach has facilitated fiscal and, hence, technological conservatism. Finally, this author has yet to see a strategic planning process that attempted to incorporate any new human values that might be bubbling up in the workforce. "That's an implementation (namely, controlling) issue," so the thinking goes.

At the moment, the only response in use to the question mark at the top of the figure, Evolution of Planning Practices, is the fuzzy notion of strategic management. It implies that planning and implementation need to be more closely linked. Chapter Four ahead attacks the issue of where planning practices must go. Chapter Fourteen, "Managing with Surprises," is related.

CONTROLLING

It is natural for people to want to control their environment—to attempt to make it predictable, stable. Much of today's feverish planning activity involving analyzing data, holding meetings, writing reports, and consulting consultants can be traced to attempts by executives to get control of things. (But the case can be made that mainly they are getting an illusion of control.) The hierarchy of management practices aimed at controlling (channeling, supervising) human effort toward desired ends is relatively straightforward. The figure below illustrates the range of the practices in the modern corporation.

Personal Example, Observation, and Intervention

At the simplest level of controlling what people do and/or think on the job is one-on-one interaction. The boss

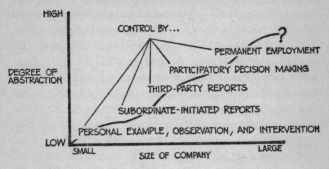

Evolution of Controlling Practices

feels, coaches, corrects, and shows with direct, continuing contact. The boss watches what is actually going on and initiates corrective action as appropriate. There is a low degree of abstraction; everything is empirical. Today, there are many sophisticated variations on this basic approach and, it seems, actually a resurgence of personal leadership (e.g., Iacocca at Chrysler) that can only be labeled entrepreneurial in style. More on this in Chapter Eleven, "Leading from Behind."

Subordinate-Initiated Reports

The next step in managing practices aimed at keeping tabs on and influencing events has historically been to have subordinates relay certain information up the line. For example, variations from the operating budget can be highlighted (managing by exception); events occurring outside certain parameters can be reported (as required by company policy); and employee-initiated performance reviews can be used to alert seniors to activities below.

These subordinate-initiated practices, when coupled with

23

a set of expectations (MBOs, strategic plans), accomplish several important ends in a growing company. First, bosses do not have to know or understand everything that is going on. They can be at least one step removed from the action. The doer will signal at least favorable information; the boss has merely to react. Second, incentives can be objectively employed to shape or influence behavior. Traditionally, incentives are given after-the-fact for past performance that exceeds agreed upon and, usually, measurable standards.

Overall, at the second step in the controlling hierarchy, reports, in part, replace direct observation; incentives and reviews, in part, replace direct guidance and feedback; and standards or objectives (as in MBO), in part, replace the need for the boss to be the visible embodiment of desired behavior.

Third-Party Reports

At some point, successful companies begin monitoring performance via the controller's office or some other staff department. Measurable events are tracked, analyzed, compared, interpreted, and fed into the appropriate slots in the management hierarchy for review and action. This practice ensures a degree of consistency across the corporation. The standardization also facilitates aggregation (by planning units, by sector, and so forth). Management information systems (MIS) represent the high art of third-party control systems. Under MIS, measurable, historic data are compiled on a continuous, rather than a batch, basis. Managers must be adept at reading. The outputs of individuals must fit in with the systems of the company. Otherwise, the output doesn't count. And, of course, people must trust the system; they must feel it is fair. Otherwise, as history shows, they will fight it in various ways. Today they fight it, in part, by withholding their commitment to the success of the enterprise, a subject addressed later.

By nature, control systems of the third-party variety tend to compartmentalize activities; such systems are fractionating rather than synthesizing. They wall off levels, departments, divisions, and functions from one another. They encourage isolation . . . in the name of operating independence and administrative efficiency. And both boss and subordinate are freed from the nitty-gritty of personal interaction. All either party has to do is look at the facts . . . the facts being whatever it is the controller or MIS people can conveniently measure.

Participatory Decision Making

No management practices have received more press over the years than those in which management attempts to involve the people of the enterprise in what is going on. Quality circles are the most recent manifestation. But the notion of influencing behavior by promoting teamwork, esprit de corps, and loyalty through various forms of togetherness goes way back, to at least the Suggestion Box days of World War II.

The rationale behind participation can run the continuum from a legitimate desire to tap into the employee talent bank to an equally legitimate desire to forestall the restrictions of unionization. Both Theory X and Theory Y managers draw upon their subordinates in a variety of ways under the heading of participation. From old-fashioned brainstorming to peer group performance reviews and Friday-night-after-work company beer blasts, an attempt is made to make people a part of the action. Management must be the initiator; and management most often is the jury on the products of the participation. Causing—or requiring—participation is a way of influencing behavior; most often it is done for very positive reasons. It is in fashion today (again). But it is not as easy to accomplish as might be expected. Donald E. Petersen, Ford CEO, stated the prob-

25

lem crisply in a *USA Today* interview. In answer to the question, "What area needs the most attention (at Ford)?" He answered:

> How we work together. The whole concept of employee involvement—particularly in a management team effort as opposed to individual effort—has many elements that are still quite fragile. This is because we come from a past in American industry that has been so fraught with bull-of-the-woods, top down, don't-think-just-do-what-I-ask-you-to-do type thinking. It is going to take time for everyone to become accustomed to participating together.

Incidentally, the title of the *USA Today* article was "Top-Down Managing Won't Work Anymore."[5] Indeed, if managing is defined in traditional terms and practices, it may not be long before an article appears entitled "*Managing* Won't Work Anymore." The post-managerial world will be here.

Permanent Employment

There are a thousand tributaries that flow together into the human resource development (HRD) river that nourishes the people in the established enterprise. HRD is today's stock answer to facilitating the permanent employment of desirable people. Personnel planning, career pathing, mentoring, management training, and so on all represent institutional approaches to building people . . . and, more recently, to cultivating a corporate culture. Why go to the trouble? Because, theoretically, members of a defined culture share a set of behavior-inducing beliefs that guide behavior. Guided behavior is controlled behavior.

Whereas the traditional corporate approach has been to manage—or attempt to manage—behavior (be on time, work hard, think straight) by means *external* to the individual, the interest today in corporate culture is that it can serve as an *internal* guidance system. So culture has become an item on the executive agenda. The models are Japanese companies as well as historically excellent companies from the United States and Europe. Distinguishing characteristics include:

- Hire only entry-level people (train the young)
- Promote from within
- Move people around the company (they develop company-specific skills rather than the more mobile, functional skills)
- Slow evaluation by multiple parties
- Considerable after-hours contact between employees

In short, at the senior level in the controlling hierarchy, permanent employment, companies socialize their staff, socialize in the nonpolitical sense of the word. The process is essentially the same as that practiced by the medical and legal professions in the production of doctors and lawyers. The end result are graduates with many planned behavioral attributes. Permanent employment, or the potential of it, is in many respects the ultimate controlling practice in use today. Ideas on what must follow or substitute for it are covered in Chapter Five.

CONCLUSION

So there you have it, a hierarchy of managing practices from today back into yesterday. Where is your company on the stairs of progress? What are the limitations of the more advanced practices? Are they in harmony with the demands of the times . . . or in conflict?

Many writers today see nothing but conflict. Daniel Yankelovich:

> Anyone who has worked for a large institution—corporation, government agency, university—can produce a bottomless supply of examples of how institutions inexorably subordinate the individual to its own rules. We live and breathe in the interstices left to us by our institutions; and they grow more constricting all the time.[6]

Other writers are less critical, even hopeful. Edward Gibbon:

> There exists in human nature a strong propensity to depreciate the advantages and to magnify the evils of present times. . . . The winds and waves are always on the side of the ablest navigator.[7]

Take your pick. There does exist a range of practices aimed at aligning human output with the needs of the enterprise. The formula may work in reverse. Today's controlling practices, along with those involving organizing and planning, have been built up over a period of 50 or more years in response to the challenge of managing increasingly large, complex companies in a relatively predictable, steady-state environment. In the chapters ahead, some general limitations of the current state of the art practices will be examined briefly. Then, specific limitations will be considered by looking at identifiable differences between smaller, entrepreneurial companies and larger, established ones. With some important differences noted, it will be time to consider what can be done to stimulate entrepreneuring throughout established companies . . . by changes in what managers and executives do as they manage.

Chapter Three

Organizing

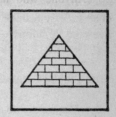

Moses chose able men out of all Israel, and made them heads over the people, rulers of thousands, of hundreds, of fifties, and of tens. And they judged the people at all times; hard cases they brought to Moses, but any small matter they decided themselves.

EXODUS 19:25–26

Nineteen eighty-five will be the year in which American business discovers what a handful of companies already know—to survive in the new information-electronics economy, they must reinvent themselves.

JOHN NAISBITT

Common managing practices have generally kept pace with the relentless growth in the size of institutions. In a relatively short time, the United States has become a nation of bigs: big companies, big unions, big government, and big universities. The people in charge of big organizations have done exactly what their forebears in the big

29

religions, kingdoms, and military enterprises of antiquity did, namely, break the bigs into littles. The efforts of those in all the littles have then been orchestrated with rules, regulations, and procedures for getting things done in an orderly fashion. Organizing practices were driven by size considerations.

THE TRADITIONAL PYRAMID

Look around. Most established companies have . . .

- A hierarchy. Vertical reporting relationships are well defined with titles, office differentials, and other trappings. Operating units and departments are separated from one another in the interest of independence, competition, sovereignty (*turf* for the unit leader), and accountability.
- Protocols. These are ceremonial forms and courtesies accepted as proper and correct in official dealings between units and levels.
- A distribution of power from top to bottom. Subordinates don't reprimand their bosses. Resources are allocated from above. Delegation flows downhill. Uppers hire/fire/promote lowers.
- Line and staff positions. The line people are responsible for results—make it, sell it, service it. The staff people advise, presumably from reservoirs of expertise.
- A reward system that favors successful, individual competitors who rise in the hierarchy, usually via one of the functional elevators.

Human resource development, equality, fairness, and minority rights notwithstanding, the above is descriptive of most modern companies. Given the pervasiveness of the organizing principles described, it is logical that the ubiquitous pyramid be an early candidate for examination and modification as perceptive managers take on the challenge of renewal and entrepreneurship called for by the times.

Since World War II, the multitiered pyramid has been the dominant organizational form. Today it is being called into question. Daniel Yankelovich puts it this way:

> For a quarter of a century following World War II, there was widespread cultural and political agreement that . . . , "If I worked hard, observed the rules and learned to keep my personal desires mostly suppressed, I might find myself well-rewarded with moral self-esteem for my self-denial, with the acceptance of others for my respectability, and with worldly goods from an affluent economy."[1]

But this ideal is breaking down. Here are some of the reasons collected from various studies.

- There are today 56 million people in the United States between the ages of 25 and 39. Many are well-educated. There are a limited number of job slots in the lower reaches of the nation's larger companies. There are even fewer, higher up. *Younger people are not keen on suppressing desires.*
- Nearly 70 percent of women aged 25–39 work. This is double the rate of 25 years ago. *Many women work for reasons other than worldly goods.*
- Software now accounts for 70 percent of all dollars spent on computing; this is one striking example of the shift from machines to minds. *Brains are more and more important in the workplace.*
- Seventy-five percent of Americans no longer find acceptable the prospect of working at a boring job "as long as

the pay is good." *Self-denial in a job setting is an aging idea*. Values are changing.

- Over 60 percent of Americans feel that an employee has a right to refuse promotions or a move to another city. *The locus of power is changing . . . away from the employer*. General affluence and education have given people alternatives.

The changing times that challenge management are not restricted to a single country . . . or even to a block of countries. The Aspen Institute report mentioned in Chapter One was done by a multinational research team consisting of scientists surveying the world of work in Britain, Germany, Japan, Israel, Sweden, and the United States. The scientists found that . . .

- The lack of a stable and predictable monetary system adds to the difficulties of recreating the climate of world-wide growth and mutual benefit that characterized the post-World War II era.
- Having enjoyed the fruits of affluence, people are now less willing to sacrifice for strictly economic goals than they were in the early years of the postwar period. In today's global economy, this new outlook means that *economic threats and incentives have lost much of their former power* to mobilize people's energies in the pursuit of strictly economic goals.
- Many young people are discovering that *work rather than leisure can satisfy their hunger* for self-expression and creative challenge.
- The meaning of work has been changing for the workforce in all of the participating countries . . . work has acquired important noneconomic meaning over and above its monetary exchange value.

- Today's reward and incentive systems, based primarily on money, are poorly matched against the contemporary meaning of work.
- Technological changes have had a significant *and favorable* impact on the workplace in the participating countries. (Emphasis added.)

So there is news. And it affects modern pyramids.

TECHNOLOGY

On the last point above, technological change, here are two tables[2] that bring home the widespread impact of technology on those at work in these times.

Perception of Technological Changes

Country	Percent Employees Who Have Experienced Technology Changes %
Germany	70
Sweden	51
U.S.A.	46
Japan	41

Effects of Technological Change

Country	Job Made More Interesting %	Job Made More Monotonous %
U.S.A.	74	22
Sweden	74	29
Germany	62	29
Japan	59	41

It is interesting to note the generally favorable impact of technology, and it is just one of the moving plates at work out of sight in the modern, established company. There are others. *The end result is that the reasons people work are shifting*. But like the grid of roads and bridges and structures on the surface of the earth, today's organization structures are essentially rigid. Moving tectonic plates ultimately result in earthquakes; moving workforce norms are pushing hard on the structures of our established companies. In geology, slight shifts in the giant plates create large, unannounced disruptions. In business, unrecognized, ongoing shifts in values are reflected in loss of organizational vitality. People issues are subtle; they are harder to address than economic ones.

The organizational philosophy behind the standard, for-profit business is essentially Darwinian in nature: promotion for the fittest. In this scheme of things, for every salesperson promoted to sales manager, three or four other salespeople are not promoted. The same formula applies throughout the company. The next figure illustrates the process in which 9 out of 10 eventually fail in conventional terms. They don't make it. Historically, those left behind at any level have either waited, accepted their lot,

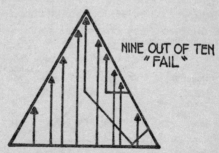

The Problem with the Pyramid

or moved on. Waiting in a slower growth world is frustrating; accepting one's lot is no longer done on the scale it once was; and moving on has drawbacks to both parties in many cases. In total, the traditional pyramid, by its form, is causing problems.

This is not an argument for eliminating meritocracy as the guiding light for promotions in the business world. It *is* the starting point for suggesting that more ways to succeed are needed. All the brainpower left behind when someone is promoted cannot be labeled as "didn't make it" in a competitive world where ideas of all shapes and sizes are needed. Smart people rebel in an unnourishing setting by withholding commitment. Strict hierarchical thinking is past its prime as the organizing principle for the talent-intensive enterprise bent on competing well under the new rules.

ORGANIZING PRACTICES—LOOKING AHEAD

So what does the progressive business person do to overcome the problem with the pyramid? Task forces? Matrix? Special committees? Or what? Purposeful human effort still needs to be organized. The main characteristics for the organization structure of the future appear to be at least four in number:

Small Number of Levels

1. Small Number of Levels The psychological, and often the physical, distance from top to bottom must be shortened. Structural compression is the order of the day. Authority and responsibility and power need to be anchored in the lowest level of the organization at which all of the variables relevant to the decisions to be made are visible.

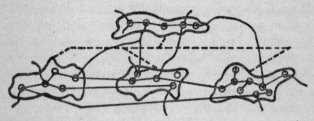

Guerrilla Profit Centers; Porous Departments

2. Guerrilla Profit Centers; Porous Departments Increasingly large companies must become federations of relatively autonomous units each of which can operate entrepreneurially, as in guerrilla warfare. And within the units, the structure must be fluid; artificial, antiquated barriers between and within departments need to be hammered down and/or made porous. Talented people should be able to float more—to move with the tide and winds and waves to get their jobs done.

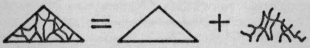

Systems Decoupled from Structure

3. Systems Decoupled from Structure Historically, most organizational structures have been essentially static, quasipermanent. And the systems—compensation, promotion, accounting, communication, and so forth—were fitted into the structures. As corporate America moves toward more flexible structures, the supporting systems must, by design, stand alone. Perhaps the key is to tailor the systems to individuals rather than to organizational units. There is also an opportunity for a philosophical shift. Systems generally exist today to protect the company from human folly. Perhaps a more useful design criterion for the future is that systems should be innovation enhancers. The test, under this philosophy, would be: Does the system liberate users, or limit them?

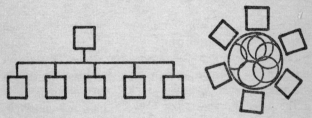

Sharing Replaces Dividing Up

4. Sharing Replaces Dividing Up Specialization has long been the sine qua non in the world of business. Individuals, departments, and even operating units are assigned certain tasks; management is the integrator, the synthesizer. Resources are allocated and only the few higher up get to work with the whole. Such an approach may have been valid when the average worker was essentially unskilled and working "just" for a paycheck. Today specialization

37

is a candidate for revision by those seeking more entrepreneuring in their companies.

These four characteristics suggest melting-pot or mixing-
bowl organizing practices rather than the reductionistic
ones prevailing since the halcyon days of scientific management and the early marvels of mechanical engineering.
Changing technology alone, once again, is sufficient reason to re-examine existing organizing practices which, by
intent, define relationships and priorities. Changing values
make it mandatory.

The Pliant Pyramid

H. Igor Ansoff pinpoints the kinds of problems being
faced (or ignored) in a common type of established company, one involved in technological intensive activities.
Professor Ansoff delineates three gaps:

- The *information gap* between technologists (knowledge
  workers) and strategists.
- The *semantic gap* that arises from the difference in
  languages, concepts, and perceptions of success factors
  between general managers and R&D managers.
- The *objectives/values gap* between those who see technology as an end (e.g., the thrill of discovery) and those
  who see it as a means to an end (improve ROI).[3]

In general, it can be said that a significant part of these
gaps is structurally sanctioned, if not induced. The challenge appears to be one of shaping—or reshaping—the
relationships in a company so as to maximize—rather than
minimize—interaction between various skilled people. Doing
so has to reflect a view of corporate life, looking ahead, in
which interdependency is on the increase. Structure must
be more fluid and plastic, a variable. John Naisbitt, in
Megatrends, suggested that the future demands both high

tech *and* high touch, a point of view with structural implications. Alvin Toffler, in 1980, was perceptive. In *The Third Wave* in a section labeled, "The Organization of the Future," he laid out this picture:

Earlier we saw that when all the Second Wave principles were put to work in a single organization the result was a classical industrial bureaucracy: a giant, hierarchical, permanent, top-down, mechanistic organization, well designed for making repetitive products or repetitive decisions in a comparatively stable industrial environment.

Now, however, as we shift to the new principles and begin to apply them together, we are necessarily led to wholly new kinds of organizations for the future. These Third Wave organizations have flatter hierarchies. They are less top-heavy. They consist of small components linked together in temporary configurations. Each of these components has its own relationships with the outside world, its own foreign policy, so to speak, which it maintains without having to go through the center. These organizations operate more and more around the clock.

But they are different from bureaucracies in another fundamental respect. They are what might be called "dual" or "poly" organizations, capable of assuming two or more distinct structural shapes as conditions warrant—rather like some plastic of the future that will change shape when heat or cold is applied but spring back into basic form when the temperature is in its normal range.

One might imagine an army that is democratic and participatory in peacetime, but highly centralized and authoritarian during war, having been organized, in the first place, to be capable of both. We might use the analogy of a football team whose members are not

39

merely capable of rearranging themselves in T-formation and numerous other arrangements for different plays but who, at the sound of a whistle, are equally capable of reassembling themselves as a soccer, baseball, or basketball squad, depending upon the game being played. Such organizational players need to be trained for instant adoption, and they must feel comfortable in a wider repertoire of available organizational structures and roles.

We need managers who can operate as capably in an open-door, free-flowing style as in a hierarchical mode, who can work in an organization structured like an Egyptian pyramid as well as in one that looks like a Calder mobile, with a few thin managerial strands holding a complex set of nearly autonomous modules that move in response to the gentlest breeze.

We do not yet have a vocabulary for describing these organizations of the future. Terms like "matrix" or "ad hoc" are inadequate. Various theorists have suggested different words. Advertising man Lester Wunderman has said, "Ensemble groups, acting as intellectual commandos, will . . . begin to replace the hierarchical structure." Tony Judge, one of our most brilliant organization theorists, has written extensively about the "network" character of these emerging organizations of the future, pointing out, among other things, that "the network is not 'coordinated' by anybody; the participating bodies coordinate themselves so that one may speak of 'auto-coordination.' " Elsewhere he has described them in terms of Buckminster Fuller's "tensegrity" principles.

But whatever terms we use, something revolutionary is happening. We are participating not merely in the birth of new organizational forms but in the birth of a new civilization.[4]

Of all the managing practices, those having to do with organizing are the most visible. Resizing the established company is the subject of Chapter Seven.

CONCLUSION

New organizing principles suggested for consideration as action items are four in number:

- Shrink the number of organizational levels.
- Nurture guerrilla profit centers; porous departments.
- Decouple systems from the structure.
- Replace dividing up with resource sharing.

Chapter Four

Planning

> But the balance between planning—which reduces the need for effective reaction—and structural flexibility—which increases the capacity for effective reaction—needs to shift towards the latter.
>
> ROSABETH KANTER, *THE CHANGE MASTERS*

Planning is to a large extent the rational manager's way of trying to understand and influence the environment. There is something comforting about pages and pages of charts, tables, and prose that tell how the future will be—best, worst, and expected case. The underlying notion is, of course, that when you can think everything through and collapse all the factors into a document of some sort, you have a useful handle on what is going on. This is an illusion, however. A satisfying illusion, perhaps, but an illusion nevertheless. Static prose, graphs, and circles may provide some feel for how things *were*; seldom will one learn from them how things *are* or *will be*. As David K.

Hurst, executive vice president of a Canadian company, put it in a provocative *Harvard Business Review* article:

> Hard box planners advocate the hard box elements and tend to be overinvested in using their various models, or "clock works" as we call them.
>
> . . . We use the models only as take-off points for discussion. They do not have to be right, only useful. If they don't yield genuine insights, we put them aside. The hardbox cannot be dispensed with. On the contrary, it is essential—but not sufficient.[1]

The entire article is included in the Appendix as Reading Two.

The issue is not whether planning is useful or necessary. The issue is that it is not sufficient in these times. Modern corporate managers may have become too plan-dependent of late. Doing so, in many respects, is like trying to pilot a racing yacht in close quarters at the starting line by looking at the tide and current tables below deck. The tables are useful, but they do not tell the whole story fast enough to do any good in establishing a leading position. (The skipper needs every crew member watching, listening, passing along information, and responding in an appropriate manner in real time. More on this later.)

TRADITIONAL PLANNING

At the high end of the planning hierarchy described in Chapter Two was environment-based planning that often results in a multifactor matrix display of some kind. By design, this methodology is supposed to take into account *all* the major relevant factors in the environment of the enterprise. But as anyone with hands-on experience knows, *all* the factors cannot be identified. And one is usually dealing with extrapolations of historical data on those that are. Net, net, tomorrow *will* hold some surprises. Therefore, once again, planning as it is practiced today is necessary, but not sufficient, for those who wish to keep on winning.

H. Igor Ansoff, once again, captures the issue well:

Just as in a radar-surveillance system, in spite of the best efforts, some issues will slip by the environmental surveyors and become *strategic surprises*.

This means four things:

(1) The issue arrives suddenly, unanticipated.

(2) It poses *novel* problems in which the firm has little prior experience.

(3) Failure to respond implies either a *major financial reversal* or loss of a major opportunity.

(4) The response is *urgent* and cannot be handled promptly enough, either, by the normal systems and procedures.

The combination of the four factors creates major problems. The previous strategies and plans do not apply, the challenge is unfamiliar, and there is a flood of new information to process and to analyze.[2]

So, in some respects, business management has come to the end of an age. It is not the end of rational management, but it may be the end of rational-only management, with strategic planning as we know it today the crowning symbol of that which is no longer adequate for the task at hand.

PLANNING PRACTICES—LOOKING AHEAD

Where from here? How are established companies to become more innovative, more robust, more entrepreneurial? Can planning be used as a lever? The answer is, yes. Planning is probably the best single ritual in a company for stimulating change . . . for making people more responsive to change . . . for helping people, "members" of the company, welcome change. No other ritual—budgeting, performance appraisal, and so forth—has so much up-side potential for actuating entrepreneurship in all facets of company life.

To accomplish such a lofty end, planning activities in an established company should have these characteristics:

Deep Participation

1. Deep Participation People like to be involved in decisions that affect them. Increasingly, managers and executives must orchestrate the participation of a higher percentage of the members of the company in working on the challenges of the times. Change is disruptive (anxiety producing) when it is done *to* you. It can be exhilarating when it is done *by* you.

One way to get deep penetration is via the structural changes hinted at earlier, i.e., reducing vertical and horizontal barriers between units of the enterprise. Another is to reconstitute the planning process itself—vocabulary, timetable, agendas, and reports—so that a large cross section, perhaps a diagonal slice, of the company provides participants.

As Reading One, "The New Breed of Strategic Planner," suggests, those who must carry out the plans of the enterprise should be active in their design.

Responsiveness Rather Than Results

2. *Responsiveness Rather Than Results* As Peter Drucker has observed, "Managing by objectives works if you know the objectives. Ninety percent of the time you don't." Think of it this way. In, say, 1990, which company will be better off? Company A (10,000 members) has a highly cultivated planning system that annually produces detailed strategic and tactical plans. The plans are developed with the full participation of the general managers of the planning units. Results against plans are reviewed at least quarterly. Compensation and other elements of the reward system are carefully aligned with the plans; so is staffing, i.e., the senior people in each planning unit are selected in view of the unit's strategic assignment. And so forth. In short, Company A has a high degree of internal consistency. It is well managed in the traditional sense of the phrase. All the pieces fit together nicely.

Company B (10,000 members) has a much less cultivated planning system. The planning meetings themselves are messy in that an odd assortment of engineers, officers, sales people, and others show up from time to time. Agendas are uncertain because a lot of people seem inclined to speak up and out on matters such as market trends, competitor strengths and weaknesses, and product feasibility ("We can't manufacture it, dammit!"). The output from the process is often garbled—just who is to do what, by when, is not always obvious. There seems to be a lot of overlap, even confusion. Good intentions seem to dominate; there is shortage of documentation. Who is boss is sometimes unclear. An awful lot of people—maybe a quarter of the company—seem to be peripherally involved in some way.

Which company will be best suited to the times in 1990? Which is more likely to land on its feet during the next economic slump? If you were a shiny (bright), young, knowledge worker, or an old, tarnished one with ideas, where would you prefer to work, A or B?

Of course, you know this writer's opinion. But the reader's own critical judgment and sense of the drift of the times are what counts. Suffice it to say that there are some compelling indicators that Company B has a better shot at the gold ring because it will be better able to attract, keep, and stimulate the folks who will make the difference in quality, productivity, service, new products, responsiveness—all the good things business must do better to be competitive as the world turns. Ideas come from people, not machines. Customer friendliness comes from people, not computers. Breakthroughs come from players, not spectators. When the times, as a practical matter, are totally unpredictable, the emphasis must shift toward people ready, even anxious, for anything. In a sense, *tactics are becoming more important than strategic matters*. Planning practices must be reoriented toward producing responsiveness rather than strictly results. The means are starting to count, not just the ends. A short reaction time may become your most important competitive weapon as the year 2000 rounds the bend.

A Longer View

3. A Longer View Much has been written about the near-term (quarterly) orientation of America's management corps. The fact is that the environment does require continuing performance, a carryover from the linear days of yesteryear, but an ever-present pressure all the same. So there is a double challenge to the signal callers of commerce: One, manage existing businesses well. This means that ideas by the bushel are needed for thousands of small, incremental improvements. Two, manage for bold moves, breakthroughs, and breakouts. Here, the required skill is more and more the ability to smell out and act on opportunity rather than to consciously plan or generate it.

Professor Robert Burgleman at Stanford has a useful perspective. He views an organization as an "opportunity structure for individual strategic actors" and sees innovations (successful and unsuccessful) as "learning events" for the enterprise. Such thinking is compatible only with a longer view of what planning is all about. A lot of what goes on today under the heading of strategic planning is actually, and totally, analysis aimed at surprise avoidance. This is essentially a defensive posture. What is needed if the entrepreneurial fires are to be rekindled is truly strategic planning aimed at capability enhancement for dealing

48

with an uncertain world. And this notion is applicable to both capital- and talent-intensive companies alike.

In a *Wall Street Journal* article on the "brain drain" in the country's basic industries over the last 20 years, three primary causes were enumerated. The reporters observed that the managements of the companies experiencing the drain were . . .

- Unwilling to adopt new technologies
- Unreceptive to innovation
- Biased against entrepreneurial risk-taking

The result of these short, time-horizon practices was "limited growth opportunities . . . impeding career development." So the brains left.[3]

In another *Wall Street Journal* article, James L. Colby, director of research and technology at Allied Corporation (114,000 employees), described the philosophy behind the company's new ventures effort: "The new ventures operate without time or earnings pressure as long as the profit potential is evident. Most operating division presidents don't look ahead much beyond three years! New ventures can take *the long view*; that's the secret of the program."[4] (Emphasis added.)

Mr. Colby was describing a special, innovations unit within Allied. This is a relatively common, organizational approach to new venturing in corporate America. In brief, known innovators (hopefully) are grouped together (compartmentalized) and sequestered from business as usual. *The emphasis in this book is on getting a substantial percentage of all the members of the company thinking innovation on a daily basis so that business as usual is subject to experimentation and change*. The principle of taking the long view fits in either case. The issue is not that of a longer view instead of a shorter one. It is a longer view as well as a shorter one: a touchdown as well as a first-and-ten in football terms.

CONCLUSION

It is fashionable nowadays to scramble to be lean and mean. In America, this often implies laying off people, starting with the mailroom clerks and working upwards—slowly. Lean and mean as a principle has its merit. In fact, in a world turned upside down, it's probably a requirement for corporate health. (Lean and agile may be a more accurate maxim, but it lacks the rhyme and cadence.) But rather than surgery, i.e., cutting off feet to lose weight, the route to leanness is probably best achieved via fat reduction throughout the corporate body. The word "fat" here suggests both physical excesses and mental sluggishness. Planning practices that elicit a high degree of involvement by the membership can be a primary regimen for getting or retaining a fighting trim.

Regarding planning practices, the next step up the hierarchy towards tomorrow would seem to require managers to:

• Push participation in planning deep into the organization.
• Focus on responsiveness as well as results.
• Take a longer view as well as a shorter one.

These elements add up to a process emphasis rather than a "finished plan" emphasis, per se. Objectives and direction and result monitering are not excluded, but the primary measure of success is not how right the plans are (or were). Whoever looks back and checks anyway? *Rather, a key measure should be how many people got involved.* Is the company moving toward a higher mode of responsiveness, even eagerness, to take on the future? Are key members of the organization thinking beyond the next raise, bonus, and budget horizon with confidence? Do they see their careers as challenges? Do they expect to have to stretch? These kinds of characteristics (feelings, attitudes) permeate the smaller, entrepreneurial company on the move. These characteristics were once descriptive of every successful company in the country.

Chapter Five

Controlling

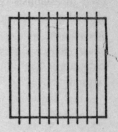

Mistakes in business are a blessing; they give us an opportunity to learn.

ED ZSCHAU, U.S. REPRESENTATIVE FROM SILICON VALLEY

Given a corporate structure with its support systems, and given a planning process that highlights milestones on the road into the future, the customary task of management has been to stay on plan. "Plan the work; work the plan." In many respects, looking back, people have been viewed as possible causes of *deviations* from plans. To minimize the deviations, control practices were developed . . . to guide the people and ensure that the assets of the enterprise were well used. Overall, assets were buildings, machinery, inventory, and cash. Plans were patterns for employing the assets in the environment. And employees, being human, were potential sources of mistakes. Control systems—whatever their level of sophistication—were put into place to monitor progress and minimize deviations from the desired patterns of asset use.

The message of this book—and others—is that the above paradigm is obsolete. In the world of now, the primary corporate assets are people. Planning must increasingly be used to establish patterns for people to interact usefully with the environment. *The environment is the primary source of mistakes.* And controlling practices should be to ensure that deviations from expectations outside the company are picked up by and/or fed into the membership at optimum speed so that appropriate responses can be formulated and executed. The members of the company *are* the new servomechanism . . . the system of control. They must monitor individual output and environmental input, intermittently compare the two, and adjust accordingly.

TRADITIONAL CONTROLLING

Clearly, perhaps for a decade now, Western management practices have been gradually moving farther and farther off the target. Budgets and performance appraisals and hiring practices and promotion criteria and leadership styles have continued to be used to channel human thought and energy rather than to excite it. In Peter Drucker's now long-of-tooth aphorism, managerial attention has been riveted on doing things right rather than doing the right things. As a class of people, management has become imbued with efficiency, e.g., minimizing mistakes, and neglecting effectiveness. Efficiency *was* the thing in a linear world. But the catalog of management practices appropriate for those days needs a big revision.

Readers can check themselves. Here is a synopsis of the rule book that dominates much of the management experience, and, therefore, management thinking, today. How do these 14 rules sound?

53

1. Division of Work Specialization of work belongs to the natural order. . . . The object of division of work is to produce more and better work with the same effort. Division of work permits a reduction in the number of objects to which attention and effort must be directed and has been recognized as the best means of making use of individuals and groups of people.

```
———————————————   ◄——— Mark a
 1   2   3   4   5              choice.
Void        Valid
```

2. Authority and Responsibility Authority is the right to give orders and the power to exact obedience. Authority is not to be conceived of apart from responsibility, that is, apart from sanction—reward or power—that goes with the exercise of power. Responsibility is a corollary of authority.

```
———————————————
 1   2   3   4   5
Void        Valid
```

3. Discipline . . . is in essence obedience, application, energy, behavior, and outward marks of respect observed in accordance with the standing agreements between the firm and its employees. . . . Nevertheless, there is deep conviction that discipline is absolutely essential for the smooth running of a business and that without discipline no enterprise could prosper. The best means of establishing and maintaining discipline are:

• Good superiors at all levels.
• Agreements as clear and fair as possible.
• Sanctions (penalties) judiciously applied.

```
———————————————
 1   2   3   4   5
Void        Valid
```

4. *Unity of Command* For any action whatsoever, an employee should receive orders from one superior only. Should it (this principle) be violated, authority is undermined, discipline is in jeopardy, order disturbed, and stability threatened.

1	2	3	4	5
Void			Valid	

5. *Unity of Direction* One head and one plan for a group of activities having the same objective. It is a condition that is essential to unity of action, coordination of strength, and focusing of effort.

1	2	3	4	5
Void			Valid	

6. *Subordination of Individual Interest to General Interest* . . . in business, the interest of one employee or a group of employees should not prevail over that of the concern. Ignorance, ambition, selfishness, laziness, weakness, all human passions tend to cause the general interest to be lost sight of in favor of individual interest and a perpetual struggle has to be waged against them. The means are:

• Firmness and good example on the part of superiors.
• Agreements as fair as is possible.
• Constant supervision.

1	2	3	4	5
Void			Valid	

7. *Remuneration of Personnel* . . . is the price of services rendered. It should be fair and, as far as is possible, afford satisfaction both to employees and employers. To arouse

55

the worker's interest in the smooth running of the business, sometimes an increment of the nature of a bonus is added.

```
———————————————
1   2   3   4   5
Void        Valid
```

8. *Centralization* Like division of work, centralization belongs to the natural order. It is always present to a greater or less extent.

```
———————————————
1   2   3   4   5
Void        Valid
```

9. *Scalar Chain* . . . is the chain of supervisors ranging from the ultimate authority to the lowest ranks. . . . Now, there are many activities whose success turns on speedy execution, hence respect for the line of authority must be reconciled with the need for swift action.

```
———————————————
1   2   3   4   5
Void        Valid
```

10. *Order* The formula is known in the case of material things, "A place for everything and everything in its place." The formula is the same for human order: "A place for everyone and everyone in his place."

```
———————————————
1   2   3   4   5
Void        Valid
```

11. *Equity* Why equity and not justice? Justice is putting into execution established conventions, but conventions cannot cover everything, they need to be interpreted and their inadequacy supplemented. For personnel to be encouraged to carry out their duties with all the devotion and loyalty possible, they must be treated with kindness, and equity results from the combination of kindliness and justice.

---
1   2   3   4   5
Void   Valid

12. Stability of Tenure of Personnel Time is required for employees to get used to new work and succeed in doing it well, always assuming that they possess the requisite abilities. If employees are moved after they've gotten used to a job (or before then), they will not have had time to render worthwhile service. If this is repeated often, the work will never be properly done. The undesirable consequences of such insecurity of tenure are especially to be feared in large concerns, where the settling in of managers is generally a lengthy matter. Much time indeed is needed to get to know people and things in a large concern in order to be in a position to decide on a plan of action, to gain confidence in oneself, and inspire it in others. Hence, it is often been recorded that a mediocre manager who stays is infinitely preferable to outstanding managers who merely come and go.

---
1   2   3   4   5
Void   Valid

13. Initiative Thinking out a plan and ensuring its success is one of the keenest satisfactions for an intelligent person to experience. It is also one of the most powerful stimulants of human endeavor. This power of thinking out and executing is what is called initiative, and freedom to propose and to execute belongs, too, each in its way, to initiative. At all levels of the organization, zeal and energy on the part of employees are augmented by initiative. The initiative of all, added to that of the manager, and supplementing it if need be, represents a great source of strength for businesses. This is particularly apparent at difficult times; hence it is essential to encourage and develop this capacity to the full.

Much tact and some integrity are required to inspire and maintain everyone's initiative within the limits imposed by respect for authority and for discipline. The manager must be able to sacrifice some personal vanity in order to grant this sort of satisfaction to subordinates. Other things being equal, moreover, a manager able to permit the exercise of initiative on the part of subordinates is infinitely superior to one who cannot do so.

1	2	3	4	5
Void			Valid	

14. Esprit de Corps "Union is strength." Business heads would do well to ponder this proverb. Harmony, union among the personnel of a concern, is a great strength. Effort, then, should be made to establish it. Among the countless methods in use I will single out especially one principle to be observed and two pitfalls to be avoided. The principle to be observed is unity of command; the dangers to be avoided are (a) a misguided interpretation of the motto "divide and rule" and (b) the abuse of written communications.

1	2	3	4	5
Void			Valid	

*   *   *

How do they sound? Chances are these rules or principles sound reasonably valid. Appropriate. But consider that they were published first in their original form (slightly paraphrased here) by Frenchman Henri Fayol in about 1916.[1]

To Fayol's credit, he prefaced his principles with a disclaimer of rigidity. ". . . for there is nothing rigid or absolute in management affairs; it is all a question of proportion. Seldom do we have to apply the same principles twice in identical conditions; allowance must be made for different, changing circumstances. . . ." Amen.

Fayol's principles, amplified and modified by others since the early part of this century, have permeated management thinking and the resulting practices generated to cope with (control) the increases in size and complexity of American enterprises. The practices did the job. But. . . .

Do responsibility and authority still go tightly hand in hand in these days of social change, knowledge workers, and technology wonders?

Is fragmentation (Division of Work) a proper philosophy regardless of company history and/or competitive environment?

Is one boss (Unity of Command) a ticket consistent with these high information flow times?

Wouldn't it be nice if there was "a place for everyone and everyone in that place?" (Order)

A quote by Ian E. Wilson of SRI International sums up the conundrum: "No amount of sophistication is going to allay the fact that all your knowledge is about the past and all your decisions are about the future."

CONTROLLING PRACTICES—LOOKING AHEAD

So what is to be done? There are already some cracks in the foundation of managing practices that supported the roadways to positions of responsibility for many, if not most, corporate managers and executives today. The new characteristics for organizing and planning were examined in the two previous chapters. The controlling practices of the future (more than half of the 14 above had to do with keeping things under control) would seem to revolve around characteristics such as these:

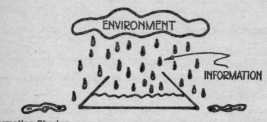

Information Sharing

1. Information Sharing "Confidentiality is the enemy of trust," states David Hurst in the *Harvard Business Review* article referenced earlier (Reading Two). When the facts of business life are kept as secrets, how does the latent creative energy of the corporation get turned on? It doesn't. One of the principal roles of middle managers is and has been that of information filtering. The person at the top knows X; subordinates "get to know" X-Y; the next soul in line gets X-Y-Z; and so on. Often, the people upon whom the future of the enterprise ultimately rests end up with an emasculated picture of what's going on.

Information has historically been a source of power.

Today, ordinary business information (knowledge) is many times more potent than in simpler times when position, connections, age, or industry experience provided organizational standing. One thing that corporate control systems do well is *control* the flow of information. Look at any established enterprise. How deep down does information on customer complaints, lost orders, gross margins, defects, new customers or competitors, employee turnover, debt service, and G&A expense levels go? How widely does information flow? Do marketing and sales people see product cost data, for example? Most companies parcel out information on some kind of a need to know basis. The underlying philosophy is that people can have and use information that affects their jobs. But given the traumas of the last 10 years, it is pretty clear that everything affects everybody! The days of labor versus management, production versus sales, and accounting versus the world are past. All the members of an enterprise are in the same corporate lifeboat. Each needs at least access to knowledge about the sea conditions. People can do something only with what they know.

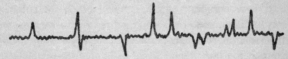

More Specials

2. More Specials Events that are unique need to be treated uniquely. And the numbers are rising. The conventional control system of today is designed on the working assumption that 80 percent of what goes on in the life of the enterprise is routine. By being routine, the events—the reasoning goes—should follow predictable patterns. Variations or exceptions are handled by the next level. In this same scheme, the remaining 20 percent of nonstandard occurrences are normally handled on an ad hoc basis. They are inserted opportunistically into the organization . . . most often in the form of something extra, i.e., in a "take care of this" mode.

What are the realities of the times? First off, the 80/20 ratio has changed. There is a higher percentage of unique events than before, a lot higher in many established companies. Predictability, therefore, is sliding. Hence the clamor for better planning. Second, the required (desired) responses more and more tend to be nontrivial, unprecedented, and unconventional. In short, unique events are increasingly the norm; at least they are common. And the correct responses are one-offs. *All the existing control systems can do in most companies is hamper the development of appropriate replies by the members of the enterprise.* Management heritage is aimed at order, not inventiveness or responsiveness.

The increase in unique events, the spikes, comes from two sources: outside and inside. The outside events have been considered in countless books, speeches, and articles. The inside ones are equally important: new plans, new CEOs, new corporate missions, new corporate cultures. These too are unique events in the life of an enterprise and in the lives of its members. A great deal has been written about resistance to change in all its human forms: rejection (of plans), procrastination, sabotage, withdrawal, and so on. Attention needs to be given also to managements' controlling practices and the no-mistake psychology they often tend to breed.

Consider, for example, any familiar established company. Is there a significant difference between the innovative, productive, customer-conscious behavior desired (presumably) and the behavior actually rewarded by the hiring, promotion, budgeting, and compensation systems of the company? Chances are pretty good that the truthful answer is, yes, for more than likely the various systems in place in the company were designed *at least* 10 to 20 years ago.

The products of turbulent times, unique events, demand novel responses. Such responses are the antithesis of traditional practices.

More Catalysts

3. *More Catalysts* To control in the corporate lexicon means to exercise authority—to check, direct, channel, curb, restrain, and regulate. For a long time now, management has been taught, with small variation, that its work is that of planning, organizing, and *controlling*. The times require an expanded view. Catalysts are needed . . . managers who see releasing energy as a vital part of their jobs. Note that the word isn't stimulators. The evidence is that people will do right when they have reasonable freedom to do so. In later chapters, some stark differences between smaller, entrepreneurial companies and larger, established ones are examined. Members of smaller companies tend to spark because they can push on opportunities unhampered—not because someone stimulated them. Frederick Herzberg stated some years ago that motivation comes "from within"; the best that management can do is to "provide the nutrients." As a minimum, management can stay out of the way.

CONCLUSION

Only a few years ago, this author routinely asked corporate leaders during cocktail conversations, "Who is your v.p. of technology?" The question was particularly revealing (and elicited a lot of chuckles—or at least smiles) when used with bankers, service enterprises, and old-line manufacturing people—leaders who considered technology a delegatable, implementation matter, at best. Today, knowledge that technology is usually also a strategic matter is reasonably widespread. The new cocktail question is, "Who is your v.p. of innovation?" Established companies have controllers; why not catalysts?! The stock answer is, of course, that being catalytic is supposed to be part of everybody's job. How true.

The characteristics of the new controlling practices suggested for consideration as action items are three:

- Share information
- Allow for more specials
- Augment controllers with catalysts.

Peter Drucker offers a pithy observation on the subject of this chapter: "So much of what we call management consists of making it difficult for people to work."

PART TWO

From analysis . . . to action. In this second part, readers are invited to generate their own proactive programs for causing more entrepreneuring to happen in the mainstream activities of their existing enterprises. As Rex Malson of McKesson puts it: "Contrary to the 'if it ain't broke, don't fix it' theory, to stay lean and mean in a mature industry calls for 'fixing it before it breaks.' "

Chapter Six

Managing by Consent

> . . . deriving their just powers from the consent of the governed.

DECLARATION OF INDEPENDENCE
JULY 4, 1776

When all is said and done, the senior question remains: What is the philosophical key or perspective needed to one, justify, and two, guide the managing practices of the future. That key is that everyone in business management is in the new ball game of *managing by consent*. People have changed; the nature of work has changed; the practices used to manage purposeful output must be updated.

THE NEW REALITIES

How have people changed? The hard data are compelling. Here is one small example. In the early 1950s, 70 percent of all households consisted of a working father, stay-at-home mother, and one-plus children. Now, a generation later, the above picture is true in only 15 percent of all households. "It is as if tens of millions of people decided simultaneously to conduct risky experiments in living, using the only materials that lay at hand—their own lives."[1]

The soft data are also compelling. Today the workforce is different in all aspects of life: eating (out), drinking (white wine), dressing (casually), playing (exercise), *and thinking*. Working people think because they have been educated to do so. The education for the many is a result of 100 years of material progress, a part of the new reality that business, in large, has fueled in this country.

What the soft and hard data add up to is an increasingly independent and talented working population with a growing immunity to being managed by directives. It is a workforce that understands the difference between human resources and human relations; and it is a workforce that has been weaned on the fruits of technology, rather than the fruits of management.

High technology has become like a force of nature: It transforms the economy, schools consumer habits, the very character of modern life. Investors pour money into it; parents urge their children to study it; communities vie to attract its factories; decorators adopt it as a style; politicians push it as a panacea. To future historians, the cultural impact of high technology on the eighties will parallel the impact of Prohibition on the twenties or that of the depths of the Great Depression on the thirties.[2]

This lead paragraph from a *Science Digest* article captures the flavor—and perhaps the driving force—behind the times. People at work no longer look solely to the higher floors for truth or wisdom. They look at technology springing up from nameless wells. In the meantime, they consent to be managed in recognition that some organization, planning, and control forms are needed to coordinate diverse, complex undertakings. There is a renaissance going on, but many managers do not seem to realize it.

It has been noted that technological innovation was responsible for 45 percent of the nation's economic growth from 1929 to 1969.[3] This statistic gives rise to the conventional wisdom that where America innovates, she leads. It has also been noted that the new idea flow in the United States (as measured by patents issued) is slowing down. According to *Inc.* magazine, "U.S. inventors account for only 15 percent of patents worldwide, a 5 percent drop in 15 years. Foreign inventors now account for [the filing of] more than half of the U.S. patents in the most advanced technologies."[4]

So the challenge is relatively straightforward. The United States must upgrade its innovative prowess. To do so, U.S. companies must tap into the creative power of their members. Ideas come from people. Innovation is a capability of the many. That capability is utilized when people give commitment to the mission and life of the enterprise *and* have the power to do something with their capabilities. *Noncommitment is the price of obsolete managing practices*, not the lack of talent or desire.

Commitment is most freely given when the members of an enterprise play a part in defining the purposes and plans of the entity. Commitment carries with it a de facto approval of and support for the management. Managing by consent is a useful managing philosophy if more entrepreneurial behavior is desired.

MANAGING PRACTICES

In earlier chapters, 10 important characteristics of new practices for the times were suggested:

Organizing

- Shrink the number of organizational levels
- Nurture guerrilla profit centers; porous departments
- Decouple systems from the structure
- Replace dividing up with resource sharing

Planning

- Press planning deep into the organization
- Focus on responsiveness
- Take a longer view, too

Controlling

- Share information
- Allow for more specials
- Augment controllers with catalysts

These are the characteristics, principles if you like, required in the upper reaches of the practices hierarchies as the world of business heads for the 21st century. In the pages and chapters that follow, the reader can test the principles by observing comparisons between smaller, entrepreneurial companies and larger, established ones. The research for this book was based on the notion that there are some subtle changes that occur to a company as it grows larger and more complex—subtle changes bred by the managing practices. By identifying these changes, they can be reversed, or at least mitigated, in an effort to *retain* or *regain* the powerful benefits of entrepreneurship.

ESTABLISHED COMPANIES AND ENTREPRENEURIAL COMPANIES

It *is* possible to duplicate the exhilaration of leading a hard-rock climb up a steep granite face in the workplace. It *is* possible to taste the sweets of an athletic victory in the successful completion of a tough project. It *is* possible to feel competitive creativity rumbling in one's mind in response to a business problem so big it seems insurmountable. The joys and the pain of a long-distance run, a solo flight, searching for the perfect color, word, or musical note, long hours, defeats . . . they are all potentially there for almost everyone in big companies. But people have to get up against the issues to experience them. You can't feel winning when there is no chance of losing. Increasingly, more of the membership of larger companies has to "work the face" as they say in mining. And the people can do it well if management will strip back some of the insulation, the systems, the procedures, and a mode of thinking aimed at minimizing human error. Looking ahead, the task is to maximize human interaction with the business problems facing the enterprise.

What is it that gives small, entrepreneurial companies their zest? Technology? Not really. A new black box of some sort may provide the enabling centerpiece around which the charter membership can gather, but technology itself most often is only that. A means, not an end. There is as much entrepreneurial excitement in a new chocolate chip cookie company on the move as there is in a laser maker with a new application.

Staffing? Are the better people in engineering, sales,

accounting, and manufacturing attracted to the go-go companies? Is everyone at Paxus or Intellisance or Lotus or Genentech or Fafco above average? Of course not. Indeed, a close look at the memberships of such companies reveals a hodgepodge of folks. The whole spectrum is there: smart, dumb; ambitious, lazy; creative, dull; opportunists and loyalists.

So where does the magic come from? . . . the zest that produces ideas and the dedication that converts them into products, services, customers, and jobs? *The magic comes from being a legitimate part of what is going on.* Each member pulls his and her individual oars, in part, because if they don't, the boat won't move. There is no backup, no system to protect the enterprise from human error or failure. Many members—not all—also exhibit what would be termed creative or motivated behavior without prodding. They do so *because it is satisfying.* They don't have to. The best ones, at least, can get a job elsewhere at any time. But they stay . . . they stay because they know they are important . . . that what they do counts . . . that they make a difference. Feedback in an entrepreneurial company is almost instantaneous. *Feedback is the single greatest reward of entrepreneuring.*

To a harmful extent, it is feedback that has been professionally managed away in many established companies. Individuals in a larger company setting don't really make a difference any more; the systems protect the company from individual actions. And, on those special occasions when an individual does make a difference, he or she doesn't know it. "Feedback is the Breakfast of Champions," say Blanchard and Johnson in *One Minute Manager.* "Feedback keeps us going. It's all because clearly the number one motivation of people is feedback on results."[5]

Bill Ouchi (*Theory Z*) gave the state of mind of many, modern, Western corporations a label. He called it ennui.

What is ennui? It is a mental state of zero. It occurs in an organization when management has created an environment too good to leave and so well organized that it usurps initiative and innovation. It doesn't take much to put the damper on initiative. Start off a new hire with an orientation program conducted by a junior person who orients the novitiate to company benefits and rules. Introduce new hires around and then leave them to fend for themselves. Keep an eye on people and point out their mistakes. (Accumulate the less prominent mistakes or less desirable behavior patterns and spring them all at once at a performance review sometime in the future.) Train people with OJT (on-the-job training) and be sure to convey the importance of productivity, new ideas, quality, service, and the like via memos, wall posters, occasional pep talks, and feature articles in the house organ. Walk around a lot so the membership knows the management cares. Emphasize results as they are measured by the accounting department. Let people know how they are doing—at least annually, and more frequently if time permits. . . .

Sounds awful doesn't it? Stifling. And it is. Over 30 years ago, Douglas McGregor introduced some new terms into the management vocabulary: Theory X and Theory Y. His research on managers and supervisors in the world of work uncovered the fact that they all seem to operate with one of two basic notions *consciously or unconsciously* fixed in their psyche:

A Theory X manager generally believes:

1. The average human being has an inherent dislike of work and will avoid it if possible.
2. Because of this human characteristic of dislike of work, most people must be coerced, controlled, directed, and threatened with punishment to get them to put forth adequate effort toward the achievement of organizational objectives.

3. The average human being prefers to be directed, wishes to avoid responsibility, has relatively little ambition, wants security above all.

A Theory Y manager generally believes:

1. The expenditure of physical and mental effort in work is as natural as play or rest.
2. External control and the threat of punishment are not the only means for bringing about effort toward organizational objectives. People will exercise self-direction and self-control in the service of objectives to which they are committed.
3. Commitment to objectives is a function of the rewards associated with achievement.
4. The average human being learns, under proper conditions, not only to accept but to seek responsibility.
5. The capacity to exercise a relatively high degree of imagination, ingenuity, and creativity in the solution of organizational problems is widely, not narrowly, distributed in the population.
6. Under the conditions of modern industrial life, the intellectual potentialities of the average human being are only partially utilized.[6]

While many people misread McGregor to favor a Theory Y approach, in fact what he suggested was that either approach will work. Now, 30 years later, what is the reality?

Here are some facts, comments, and interpretations of material included in a *Business Week* cover article on the "Baby Boomers."

• Nearly 70 percent of all women aged 25–39 work, double the rate of 25 years ago. They bring to the workplace a shift in values.

- Flexibility, autonomy, personal growth, interesting assignments, nonmanagement career paths—these are some of the new features expected out of corporate life.
- Companies increasingly must create islands within which the creative spirit can flourish.
- The boomers brought down LBJ and launched the environmental movement. They are a force for change.[7]

The *Business Week* story plus countless other efforts to describe the components of the changing times seem to converge on an emerging set of desires that are widely shared. Looking ahead, the people who will make the difference . . .

- Dislike class distinctions (labor/management; salary/nonsalary)
- Prefer variety to routine
- Like informality over formality
- Seek responsibility
- Prefer to set their own goals
- Desire feedback

In short, the world of business is becoming a Theory Y world.

The One Minute Manager closes his lecture to the young man seeking the secrets of effective management by saying, "Nobody ever really works for anybody else. I just help people work better and in the process they benefit our organization."[8]

Results *and* people; people *and* results. This is an old formula. But for a long time now, the people factor has been treated as optional. Use it if things are going really well; use it if you are dealing with a bunch of hightech prima donnas; use it if you are in a jam (union, law, product defect, out of cash); use it when you want something special. The people factor in the formula is no longer optional. The organizational behaviorists are in their ascendency! Richard Pascale (*Art of Japanese Management*), Bill Ouchi (*Theory Z*), Tom Peters (*Search for Excellence*), Rosabeth Kanter (*The Change Masters*)—they all are from the "soft" side of the house. The challenge is to translate their messages into *practices*.

When movers and shakers manage by consent, they operate on the basis that the managing job truly exists to achieve results through the membership. They recognize that the "great man" theory is dead.

That's a new mode of thinking. It can be threatening. It will occur. The only question for those already in positions of responsibility in established companies is: lead, follow, or get off the road? Results *and* people.

Volunteers

Ten to 20 years ago, it was possible to find elective courses in graduate business schools on how to manage voluntary organizations. The thrust was that such organizations—PTAs, symphonies, art guilds, and so forth took special managing techniques because volunteers required careful handling. They might at any time withhold effort, not show up, argue, and otherwise question authority . . . because they were volunteers. They didn't *have* to be there.

Isn't that pretty much the situation all around today? The best and the brightest people working for a given manager don't have to be there. They can always find a competitive position elsewhere. Therefore, they are staying with the manager and company *voluntarily*. Managers today are managing volunteers. Managers today must manage by consent.

CONCLUSION

The figures below portray the message of this book thus far. By a combination of habit, training, and oversight based on success, American business leaders have let both technology and the modern company come between individuals and the challenges of the times. Current managing practices promote this separation. They are the problem.

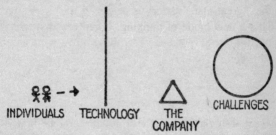

The Problem

The solution is to use the company (assets, position) as a fulcrum and technology as the lever-arm to get a multiplier impact on the application of human ingenuity directly to the big tasks at hand, i.e. entrepreneuring.

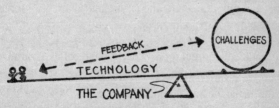

Entrepreneuring in the Established Company

Managing by consent, as well as objectives, is a keystone in the new realities of business, world wide.

Chapter Seven

Resizing

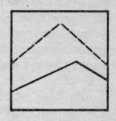

Instead of rigid conventional departments, the firm is divided into a highly flexible structure composed of "framework" and "modules."

ALVIN TOFFLER, *THE ADAPTIVE CORPORATION*

It is useful in the context of this chapter to explore three dimensions of the enterprise sizing question: vertical, horizontal, and unit diameter. The term "unit diameter" refers to the number of people grouped or pulled together to get something done. The underlying theme of the chapter is that organization structure is better thought of as a variable rather than as a constant in the life of an enterprise. To treat structure as a variable requires some fresh thinking, the results of which may well be a surgical act to resize a going concern.

VERTICAL

It is easy to see how the standard, pyramid-shaped structure came into being. Picture the general of an army in the days of old. For whatever reason, the general amasses legions in order to carry out a mission. One of the management challenges for the general is to communicate with the troops. Chances are that he would organize the army in a hierarchical manner so that he could send and receive information in an orderly fashion. He would pass the word to a limited number of people; each of them would do the same; down the line the word would go. *The intermediate levels of management are primarily information processors*. They are probably also information filters! The total number of layers in the pyramid, the vertical dimension, is a function of the width of the base.

The point is that from armies to churches to governments to more modern institutional forms like corporations, the *need to communicate* dictated a pyramid structure through which the brain and the feet were connected. Originally, the divisions into units were done by the numbers. With the march of time, the dividing up was increasingly done by specialties (cavalry, foot soldiers, and artillery) as well as by the numbers. Today, it is conventional wisdom that various specialties (e.g., R&D, sales, accounting) do, indeed, need to be managed in somewhat different ways. But, by and large, much of the vertical stratification (layers) in established companies is a carryover, and now an institutionalized form of truth from another time. The need to communicate via a limited number of individuals dictated a hierarchical structure with boundaries between subunits to preserve unity of command and, therefore, accountability. The managers in the middle did (and do) a lot of data processing and filtering. They inter-

79

pret and pass along information when they are performing the managing part of their jobs.

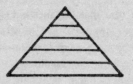

Vertical Stratification

Now two things have changed of late that should at least raise the question: Is there too much vertical stratification? Turf questions aside for the moment (see Chapter Nine), are all the layers that now exist really required to do business well, looking ahead?

The first thing that has happened is that communications willingness has improved by leaps and bounds of late. Senior managers *can be* quite visible *if* they chose to be so, regardless of the size of the organization. From Lee Iacocca to Jack Welch to Jim Treybig at Tandem, it is clear that senior people can iterate with large memberships in real time. *Business Week* in a cover article entitled, "The New Corporate Elite" put it this way:

> The new corporate elite, in many ways, is a throwback to another generation. Members have more in common with the flamboyant entrepreneurs of the turn of the century than with the colorless organization men of the postwar years. Although the barons of the 19th century often made their fortunes through predatory monopolies and trusts, they were builders, not administrators; iconoclasts, not yes-men. Similarly, most of the members of the new corporate elite are entrepreneur-founders with huge personal wealth, in the great tradition of the Gilded

Age. But many rejuvenators of old-line companies share the values and skills of the entrepreneurs and are also an essential part of the elite.[1]

It is probably true that the messages conveyed by the new wave of communicators are mostly nonquantitative. But with the ascendency of corporate culture as a legitimate management topic, the qualitative issues may be the unique contribution senior people can make anyway. The point is that from exposure via "managing by walking around" to exposure via videotape and regular small group meetings (with or without booze), the days of a few silver words in the company newsletter and Christmas party trivialities are past. Personal leadership in business is coming out of the closet. Communications willingness is headed upwards.

The second thing that has happened to encourage examination of the number of levels issue is very simply that the membership has grown smarter and increasingly wants to know "what's going on?" More media, more education, and more technology have made the membership *information hungry*. But the biggest factor punching holes in the barriers between levels is that the fallibility of management is now a recognized fact. The era of management as a science is over. There has been too much corporate carnage . . . too many big failures and loss of competitive position. "Question Authority" is no longer a bumper sticker just for teenagers. Across the land, the members of American enterprises want to know about, understand, and be a part of decisions that affect them. Storage Technology, Continental Illinois, and International Harvester have left their marks.

This writer's research on this question of sizing indicates . . .

• One of the distinguishing characteristics of the successful, emerging, entrepreneurial company is that the distance between the top and the bottom is small. *Such companies are short.*

Rx: *Shrink the number of organizational levels*

In summary, there are both methodological and sociological forces favoring the resizing of the established company along the vertical dimension. While, historically, levels were deleted to improve efficiency (cut overhead), it is now useful to think of condensing the hierarchy in search of effectiveness.

HORIZONTAL

A product of the Western love for specialization (and rational-man reductionism) has been functionalism. Today people tend to be ''in'' finance, marketing, sales, accounting, manufacturing, personnel, and so forth before they identify whom they are ''with.'' There was a time not long ago when a person was first in an industry—retailing, autos, steel, and so forth. That time was mostly before the advent of higher business education! Somewhere along the way, in part because of a Ford Foundation report on graduate business education, business schools gravitated to more of a functional emphasis. And they remain there today. When the question is raised—and it frequently is— why don't business schools teach their graduates how to *do* something?—the answer is, quite simply, that the doing disciplines lack academic rigor—so they aren't taught. For example, subjects usually left out of the *required* curriculum today include sales, production, and innovation.

Hayes and Abernathy put the situation this way in their

Harvard Business Review article, "Managing Our Way to Economic Decline."

Instead we believe that during the past two decades American managers have increasingly relied on principles which prize analytical detachment and methodological elegance over insight, based on experience, into the subtleties and complexities of strategic decisions.[2]

The complete article is Reading Three in the Appendix. Elsewhere in the article, the two Harvard Business School authors talk about the gospel of pseudoprofessionalism in which the first doctrine is that neither industry experience nor hands-on technological expertise counts for very much. And . . . "the faithful . . . make decisions about technological matters simply as if they were adjuncts to finance or marketing decisions." Professor Jim Howell of the Stanford Graduate School of Business goes even farther. He believes business schools are not keeping pace . . . that "functional fiefdoms are retarding change." Heavy words from both coasts, but to the point. Horizontal compartmentalization by function in schools and in the real world of business is an issue worthy of attention under the heading of resizing.

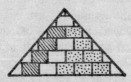

Horizontal Compartmentalization

As a practical matter, within the context of reasonably autonomous profit centers, the traditional battles between, for example, sales and manufacturing are counterproductive, to put it gently. In more innovative companies, the dividing lines are blurred and the responsibility for results are admittedly shared. In addition, there is more flow between departments—and even profit centers.

The field research on this question of compartmentalization indicates . . .

• Companies that have a reputation for innovation and creativeness promote essentially unrestricted communication between people in different functions. Such companies have *fluid activity boundaries* within the changing perimeter of relatively independent profit centers.

Why does fluidity promote entrepreneurial behavior and lead to ideas? The growing knowledge base on how the human brain works seems to indicate that new ideas come from the novel connection of heretofore unconnected pieces of information. This means that if and when energy can flow freely through the circuitry of the brain, the probability of new connections (hence, original ideas) goes up. Empirically, management has appreciated this fact for years. Brainstorming and other approaches to creative thinking all rely in part on being open, uncritical, wild, off the wall, spontaneous. Two-time Nobel prizewinner Dr. Linus Pauling said, "The best way to get good ideas is to have lots of ideas." The message is that on a personal basis, porous barriers between the chunks of data residing around the brain are good for creativity. It is a small jump to suggest that the same principle applies to a corporation . . . a big brain in many (hopeful) respects!

Matrix organizational structures have caught on to some degree in recent years. In the context of this chapter, the benefits of a matrix are easy to understand. A matrix structure provides an organization with a dual focus in its operating environment. In a matrix, some people have two bosses. In a matrix, resources are shared rather than divided up. Certain elements of a matrix make sense in turbulent times because they add up to flexibility, responsiveness, and a mix of people working on the challenges to the enterprise. Many matrixes have not worked out well, however. One key reason is a matrix structure needs to be accompanied by matrix systems—reporting, budgeting, reward, and so on. And such systems are much more complex than in a hierarchy. Messy. The free flow/sharing principles of a matrix seem consistent with the direction in which the world is going, however. In fact, the ideal structure of the future may well be a matrix with an infinite number of sides—i.e., parts of a circle. This suggests too there would be virtually *no* artificial or arbitrary barriers between members.

Idealized Structure

In summary, too many thick walls between activity centers in a company inhibit the spontaneous flow of energy and thoughts that characterize the responsive, innovative enterprise. The price companies pay for the apparent ease of administration that comes from excessive horizontal compartmentalization is high and rising.

Rx: *Nurture guerrilla profit centers; porous departments*

UNIT DIAMETER

Unit diameter, once again, has to do with the number of people grouped together to accomplish something. Alive and well yet today are notions of "span of control" in which seniors should not have more than five to ten people reporting to them. (Note the word, "reporting," as in military hierarchy.) Here too, however, current events are urging change. There are indicators that favor *both* larger and smaller unit diameters.

Smaller work groups, shrinking the diameter of an operating section, department or division, would be consistent with social trends toward individualism and autonomy, and a pluralistic society. The ultimate extension is, of course, the individual as a free unit—whether at home in an electronic cottage or in marketing on the 23rd floor. Moves in this direction display an appreciation of the uniqueness of each member of the enterprise. With the percentage of the workforce that is college-educated climbing steadily, personal independence to perform within the perimeter of the enterprise can be an innovation/productivity-enhancing event. The main difference between hippies and yuppies may simply be that the latter work for a living. And if the shared "do your own thing" mind set can be lightly harnessed (managed) in the service of the corporate mission, look out! The evidence suggests, however, that the harnesses have to be individually fitted. The unit diameter needs to be small, however, for such fittings to be performed.

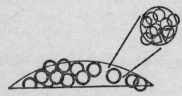

Small Unit Diameter

Now in a large organization, the small unit diameter notion may be incompatible with "delayerizing," i.e., reducing the degree of vertical stratification. As long as the principle of a hierarchy reigns, smaller units (departments and so forth) would tend to drive up the need for intermediaries, i.e., middle managers. So *new organizational configurations* are required to circumvent the impasse *if* smaller diameters fit the circumstances in which the enterprise must compete.

On the other side of the coin is the large diameter work unit: a lot of people working with one boss. Pressures here include the very human need to identify with a group, for belonging (Maslow); an increasing hunger for commitment in a more and more rootless, mobile society (Ouchi, Yankelovich); and the general march of egalitarianism that says everyone is equal anyway. The ultimate extension of this idea would be a flat, bossless enterprise with no hierarchy at all. As a practical matter, a delayerized company will tend to have larger work units. More members per boss suggests less supervision per person per day and hence, presumably, more autonomy and power for the individual—the target of resizing for increased entrepreneurship. As the legendary Viking quarterback, Fran Tarkenton, once remarked, "In the huddle, I would sometimes let the linemen suggest plays . . . because they were closer to the action than the head coach pacing up and down the sidelines."[3]

Large Unit Diameter

Historically, the unit size has been dictated by some combination of organizational design theory and managerial experience. The problem today is that much of the theory on structure is dated. And managerial experience may be less than useful as a guide to the future. The competitive challenge is to build a new experience base— quickly! *And that takes some experimentation.* When the new wave of upstart big companies is looked at closely, the word that best describes their unit diameter principles (as well as their layerizing and compartmentalizing) is flux. Pacific Telesis and McKesson are examples.

The research on this issue of work group sizing indicates that . . .

- All sizes and combinations are in evidence—task forces, project teams, committees, and solo missions. *Special assignments are common* so members often operate with two or more jobs: A regular assignment in a somewhat porous functional unit and a special assignment in an ad hoc overlay created to get something unique done.

Interestingly enough, quality circles are a good example of an overlay that has proven useful. Quality circles were and are an experiment in resizing.

CONCLUSION

Companies managed for the times have a variety of membership configurations tailored to the tasks and talents at hand.

Rx: *Share information*
Rx: *Allow for more specials*

Along all dimensions of the resizing challenge there lie creative possibilities. The shift in managing thinking from organizing in order to control people to organizing in an effort to liberate them is an idea whose time is coming in corporate America. Status, in established companies, has long been a function, in large measure, of how high one rises in the hierarchy and how many people one manages. These are old rules. Entrepreneurial companies tend to be short, porous, flexible.

Chapter Eight

Staffing for Innovation

The aim of socialization is to establish a base of attitudes, habits, and values that foster cooperation, integrity, and communication. The most frequently advanced objection is that companies who do so will lose innovativeness over the long haul. The record does not bear this out.

RICHARD PASCALE[1]

There is no way established companies can become more entrepreneurial by transfusion. There is not enough new blood to replace the old. The old has to be rejuvenated. Periodic additions of new people can help expedite the required metamorphosis; but the reality is that the behavior patterns of *existing* members have to change. PepsiCo did not suddenly become competitive vis-à-vis Coca-Cola by hiring a new breed of employees one day in 1965. It grew into competitiveness.

There is little doubt that changes in what people do can be accomplished in an established company. Another example is the remarkable transfiguration in process at General Motors (and even in Detroit) as described nicely in *The Change Masters* referenced later. And IBM continues to become simultaneously a) more aggressive and b) more relaxed of late. Other companies are trying . . . and succeeding in transforming themselves. This chapter is designed to highlight some of the areas to which attention must be paid by managements intent on truly tapping deeper into their membership to retune thousands of ears and eyes to an elastic world. But the reader should not underestimate the inertia to be overcome.

Harold Geneen paints the point of departure this way in his book, *Managing.* "Why, one might ask, do such men choose to create wealth for a large, impersonal corporation rather than try to do it alone and reap all the benefits? Many of them, as I have said, are locked into the security the corporation provides; besides, they are hardly aware of what the outside world offers. But more than that, I think, it is a matter of personality. Most corporate men are satisfied with the challenges and rewards offered in corporate life and simply do not want the sink or swim environment of the entrepreneur."[2]

Here Mr. Geneen has crystallized the conventional, if often unconscious, wisdom prevailing still today. He, in effect, says that entrepreneurs and entrepreneuring are incompatible with the modern corporation: ". . . it is a matter of personality." When one assumes that innovators are born, not made, it is no longer necessary to worry about entrepreneuring for, as Geneen puts it at the end of his chapter, "Entrepreneurs stay with large companies long enough to gain experience. Then they leave to get cash." With this point of view, there is little reason for senior people to cultivate the workforce to encourage innovative behavior. Entrepreneuring, if desired, is a hiring problem.

This writer believes that Mr. Geneen is (was) driving by

looking in the rearview mirror. Things have changed. Social research is quite clear about the fact that people (men and women) are no longer "locked into the security the corporation provides" as before. Little wonder. Life in the Fortune 500 has not been especially secure the last 10 years. And are people "hardly aware of what the outside world offers" these days? Doubtful when corporate movers and shakers have become talk show heroes and major publications carry cover stories on the new corporate elite, mostly entrepreneurs in the broad sense of the word. And is entrepreneuring outside the big company really a matter of existing on hamburger in a "sink or swim environment" as it once was? Not really. The last thing modern professional investors want is for the officers in their portfolio companies to be worrying about home mortgages and enough to eat. The worrying is okay—as long as it is directed at the challenges of building the business!

Sure, not every shiny, new, outside entrepreneur gets enlightened professional backing; some do swim on their own or sink. And a significant number do sink eating hamburger all the way down. But sink-or-swim entrepreneuring is only a small part of the bigger entrepreneuring picture that encompasses the need for new thinking in all walks of life from labor unions to health care and politics. This book is not about trying to make every corporate citizen into a swashbuckling, table-pounding, internal genius who will sell his or her mother to get to a positive cash flow. It is about revisiting and revising those managing practices that inhibit today's staffing from giving all they can and will give to make *their chosen enterprise a winner in its league,* given all the new rules that have gone and are going into effect.

Over and over again, observation in the field indicates that . . .

- When big companies in a groove are compared with smaller rivals on the move, the single most distinguishing characteristic is the lack of shackles on *talent of all kinds* in the smaller companies.

There is nothing inherently superior about 90 percent of the smaller, emerging companies except the mix of people and the depth to which those people will dig (sweat) for the cause. Normally, the cause is to build something better—product or service—and almost everyone adds discernible value. *It is an adventurous act by consenting adults.* The challenge in the established company, therefore, is to re-create or re-illuminate more of that same opportunity that is inherently present: building better products or services by adding value is indigenous to business! Such building is generally not the centerpiece of many other walks of life—law and medicine, for example. In many respects, people adding value is the heart—literally—of the matter in a business enterprise. Hence, staffing is a critical issue, more critical, than say, strategic planning. But planning generally receives a much smaller percentage of executive attention.

There are at least three, long-standing managing practices that seem to be opportunity prone for those leaders willing to challenge the staffing habits of their companies: Functional specialization; one-way career paths; and the uninspired orientation of new members to the organization.

FUNCTIONAL SPECIALIZATION

Compartmentalization was mentioned in the previous chapter as a structural characteristic that is increasingly at odds with the times in which fast information-processing is becoming more and more important (for survival). Overemphasis on functions in a company is a related anachronism. A losing football team has a *football* problem that must be understood by all the members before the specifics of what the halfbacks are to do are addressed. More often than not in a large company, people's views of the company are restricted to the perimeters of their functional areas. People are isolated, by design and by default, from the *business* problems of the enterprise. And the only path to increased visibility is up through the functional ranks. As the most popular books on Japanese management pointed out, this feature of the American corporation tends to breed functional loyalty . . . at the expense of company loyalty and perspective.

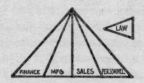

Specialization

One feature typically attributed to successful smaller companies is that everybody does everything. While there is a fair amount of folklore in this notion, the principles of flexibility and adaptability which the notion implies do have merit, particularly in times of relative turbulence. Successful smaller companies *are* faster on their feet. Bigger companies *are* trying to learn how to "make the elephant tap dance." The essence of flexibility and responsiveness is multiple skills ready and eager to go, company-wide, not just in the new-products activities.

Individuals with several strains of experience in their background are likely to uncover more creative solutions to nontechnical problems than people who have always been in, say, production. The accountant who has sold is more likely to translate the call for "market driveness" with credit innovations than one who has only passed through the accounting chairs. Catching hell about bugs directly from a disappointed customer can be a humbling— but broadening—experience for even the most died-in-the-wool computer scientist. And where broadening (growth) happens, that is where the better people stay (or go) to work.

Research for this book indicates that . . .

• Resourceful people join smaller and emerging companies to grow. They find the prospect of having to be good at more than one thing appealing.

Certainly the same opportunity to grow is readily available in established companies. In fact, as most people with experience in both larger and smaller companies will probably attest, the breath of functional experience potentially accessible to the comer in an established company is usually far greater than in the upstart rival which typically subcontracts many activities. The problem in the established company is that in this regard—and many others— *management consistently underplays its hand*. Out of habit based on an antiquated allegiance to orderliness, there is a fear of mixing things—people, functions, and responsibilities. This fear must be overcome. Functional specialization should be an option based on exposure, not an obligation based on simplifying the administration of the talent bank.

Arch Patton, a retired McKinsey & Co. director, published a short, provocative article entitled, "Industry's Misguided Shift to Staff Jobs." In it he quoted the chairman of one of Japan's most successful electronic manufacturers: "The United States puts its best young minds to work in staff jobs and has for years. Bright people have gotten

95

the message. They avoid line jobs. Japan, on the other hand, wants its brightest men in line jobs. After all, that is what manufacturing is all about. Our people understand that while we may rotate them from line to staff, and vice versa, line jobs are critical for what you in America call fast-track executives."[3]

Entrepreneurial companies, by nature, emphasize "designing it," "making it," and "selling it," regardless of a person's primary assignment at the moment. And that assignment is likely to change. In this general regard, one major European company has given all its departments letter names, A, B, C and so on. They have done away with functional designations altogether!

ONE-WAY CAREER PATHS

How do talented people get ahead in corporate America? The answer in most companies is by moving up into management. Typically, that is the only game in town. If you perform well *doing* something, you are rewarded with a promotion into a position in which you may do less well, namely, managing others. Some years ago the book, *The Peter Principle*, highlighted the negative characteristics of this sequence: People get promoted because they excel to the organizational level where their performance is less than excellent; then they are left there.

This nitty-gritty observation on American managing practices bears revision. It suggests that moving excellent performers "up" into management may not always be the smart thing from the company's standpoint. Findings presented earlier in the book suggest that "getting into management" has lost its luster for many talented people (Chapter Two). And by being organizationally finessed to look only upward (in the chosen functional area), an ambitious person has little incentive to look around . . . to consider the broader company environment, including the competitive health of the organization. And the latter is what most business leaders say they want, people interested in the total enterprise, people who identify with the company.

Corporate Career Path

What can be done? Dual career ladders have been around for years in a few industries. In some insurance companies, for example, members can decide at some point in their careers whether they want to be "personal producers" or managers. Each route can lead to fame (Million Dollar Round Table or a vice presidency) and, perhaps, fortune. The point is that an individual gets a choice, and typically it is even reversible. The times ahead require more human engineering of this kind. Multiple career paths is one idea, and the paths themselves should go in all directions—not just up (into management).

Many established companies are experimenting with organizational designs to cope better with the elastic environment. There are independent business units, and other variations aimed, generally, at entrepreneurial ends. These designs do give a few people a new lease on life, another career so to speak. And often such moves are lateral, not up. Such forks in the road need to be built into the mainstream of corporate life.

A final point on this member-building matter. Historically, corporate reward systems have paid their best and brightest in proportion to the amount of turf they controlled. Turf has usually been measured, roughly, by body count (sometimes by budget size). As discussed briefly in a previous chapter, this formula is breaking down. It is now better to be lean than fat, organizationally speaking. It may soon also be equally as rewarding (in the organizational tender) to be an individual contributor as to be a manager, i.e., to be turfless as to be well turfed. Managing and doing are two different kinds of work. Both are needed. Managing is not coming down in value; the power and endowment of individual staff members are coming up. And managers who can manage in such an eclectic environment are the ones with a practical feel for managing by consent which was the subject of Chapter Six.

The field research indicates . . .

- Doing your own thing is not dead. Only more complicated. In smaller companies people keep learning because they have to.

UNINSPIRED ORIENTATION OF NEW MEMBERS

Entrepreneurial companies tend to be heterogeneous in their composition. They are often little melting pots. But what happens, over time, as they are successful and grow up? At some point along the way, *because they are successful,* a tendency to set standards for the people joining the company starts to creep in. "After all, we can't have *just anybody* working here, now can we . . . ?" And by the time the company is well established, there is a fairly fine mesh through which all neophytes must pass. This fine mesh accomplishes several things. It simplifies administrative matters. It makes hiring delegatable . . . so senior people can spend their time on "larger" matters.

And it reduces the likelihood of misfits and malcontents getting on board and stirring things up.

The field research indicates . . .

• Overall, as companies grow, the degree of heterogeneity in the workforce decreases.

It does not take a blinding insight to suggest that homogeneity and new ideas/innovation are enemies. As discussed earlier, good new ideas come from having lots of ideas. This happens when there is a flood of different thoughts swirling about from which unique connections are made. When hiring practices tame all the wild rivers, the probability of finding fresh approaches to the rapids in the life of the business goes down.

In the published studies of successful companies . . .

• The hiring and development of the young was a continuing, high priority task of line management.

What is the proper thrust of such a boss-led development effort? More often than not in an established company it is in vogue today to espouse teamwork. The term has come to mean in practice something less valuable than the general concept, however. Too often today, teamwork means . . .

Let us work together in peace.
Let us have harmony, unity.
Let us have agreement.
Don't rock the boat.

Such a philosophy is inconsistent with the business times. What is called for today is *conflict* within reason; *dissonance* that generates new highs, even if the cost is some lows, some bruises; *disagreement* that encourages advocates to dig deeper; *boat rocking,* if that's the only way to get it to move. Such effervescence is more likely when there is an eclectic membership—in the company, in the department, in the taskforce. An eclectic membership, a mix of talents, personalities, and outlooks come, over the longer run, primarily via the hiring and development practices of the line managers. It comes from putting someone on the team who doesn't fit so well. On purpose.

1 2 ③ 4 5 6 7 8 9 10

Orientation (New People)

Suppose the staffing gates are opened a bit. What happens next? One huge but largely untouched opportunity in American business in the orientation program. Regardless of organizational level, a person's mind is never wider open to influence than during the early days after arriving on the job. Yet typically what is imprinted on the *tabula rasa* is the benefits package (security); some performance guidelines (how to avoid making mistakes here); and how to get ahead at good old XYZ (keep your nose clean, head down). What is typically *not* covered? Here's a short list:

Why this is a great place.
What we do (products, services) in some detail.
Who we do it for (markets served).
Why we do it (mission, goals).
How long have we been doing it.
Our plans for the future.
How you can contribute.
Our competitors.
Our current problems.
What you can do to help solve the problems.
How we operate (quality, customers, and so forth).
How you can contribute.

This is the kind of information most business leaders would like to have imprinted indelibly on the open minds of new recruits—Ph.D.s or high school grads. And it is doable. The pacesetters in the company must develop a fairly well-defined vision of what the company is about. (More on this in the chapters ahead.) Time and money must be invested in the orientation process. Supervisors and managers must both communicate and reinforce the messages and behavior extolled. All this can happen if there is an underlying belief that the enterprise is extremely dependent upon the initiative and judgment of individual members, and that a climate for continued personal development is critical and needs to be instilled . . . as well as displayed in the early days aboard.

CONCLUSION

Companies moving toward more entrepreneurial behavior must staff for innovation, not merely wish for it. This means the entire chain of personnel events—hiring, orienting, placement, special assignments, career paths, and training—must become a hotbed of experimentation and change. This will be a big change for many established companies where sparks are encouraged, at best, only in product and perhaps process matters. But there can be no other way. The staffs of established companies need to be thoroughly mixed and stirred as 2000 approaches. Or those companies can sit out the 21st century.

Rx: *Take a longer view, too*

In the Olympics of high technology, there is an insightful, if not scary, book entitled, *The Fifth Generation: Artificial*

Intelligence and Japan's Computer Challenge to the World.
It contains this observation and admonition:

"On the floor of the Honda factory in Saitama outside
Tokyo, there are signs in both English and Japanese.
Here is what they say:

1. Proceed always with ambition and youthfulness.
2. Respect sound theory, develop fresh ideas, and make
   the most effective use of time.
3. Enjoy your work and always brighten your working
   atmosphere.
4. Strive constantly for a harmonious flow of work.
5. Be ever mindful of the value of research and endeavor.

"We shall leave as an exercise for the reader the
construction of a set of comparable rules for an American factory floor. Advanced students may try them for a
British factory floor. Only professionals had better attempt them for a Soviet factory floor."[4]

Staffing for innovation is not optional in a hardball
world where knowledge *is* power.

Chapter Nine

Decoupling Systems from Structure

Four years after taking over the top job at GM, Mr. Smith is cruising in high gear for new ideas. Driven by the notion that GM has become too rigid in a fluid environment, the chairman is reorganizing the company's elephantine bureaucracy and encouraging entrepreneurial methods and thinking in nearly every aspect of GM's business.

THE WALL STREET JOURNAL, MARCH 14, 1985

Professional managing has traditionally meant "let's be organized." The basic thrust of professionalizing in a business setting has normally been to orchestrate the human element so that everyone will run along predictable tracks into the future. The means to this end has been the installation of systems and procedures. In an established company, there are usually prescribed ways to do just about everything:

Get money to spend
Go on vacation

Hire a new person
Fire a person
Spend money
Change the structure
Evaluate a new idea
. . . and so on

The evidence is mounting that the end product of so much love and attention is the gradual suffocation of the core of the enterprise. It is probably fair to say that most effective internal entrepreneurs today are able to succeed in spite of the system, not because of it.

The positive impacts of getting organized are obvious. Human effort is channeled; large-scale undertakings become manageable; fairness and equity are built in, but depersonalized. The negative impacts—the costs—have begun to show. The issue isn't that innovation is dead in American companies. It isn't. The issue is that American companies are not moving sufficiently fast vis-à-vis their competition in a world turned upside down (Chapters One through Four). So it is a relative game. American companies have to be big *and* innovative now, just like the National Football League teams have to pass *and* run the ball if they are to win future Super Bowls.

The costs of too much professional management show up in a number of ways that directly impact the latent entrepreneurial quotient present in every firm of any size. One cost is that sharp minds get insulated from the reality of the times. Another is that incentives become generalized and, therefore, neutralized. And, finally, power becomes diluted to the point where no one member has enough to make an impact.

INSULATION

One distinguishing characteristic of successful, emerging companies is that everyone seems to know what is going on. This means that the head accountant knows who the major competitors are; researchers understand why the last big order was lost; manufacturing clerks can tell you the net income of the company last quarter (positive or negative); and company officers know who is running the night shift. In short, the membership understands how the club is doing and has at least a rough feel for why. Such is often not the case in larger companies, only partially due to their size.

Insulation

In the established enterprise, there are normally four major channels of communication through which the members find out about reality. Channel one is direct contact and observation. Marketing people presumably know about the competitors; accounting people may know about the overdue accounts; and production folks hopefully have a fix on quality matters. But the overlap between these various people is small—the result, once again, of compartmentalization and functional specialization. A second channel, channel two, is the boss. He or she, by words and

105

actions, conveys downward a version of what's going on in the life of the enterprise. The limitations of that version are obvious: the boss most likely wears the same functional goggles as the recipient. The only real difference in terms of exposure to the realities of the enterprise is a slightly higher vantage point.

Channel three includes the house organ and various official pronouncements that are periodically made to the troops. As a rule, however, channel three is G-rated. This means that house organs are usually plain vanilla up until the point in time when a true crisis is boiling and the chance for creative responsiveness is passed. For example, recently a large West Coast retail chain went bankrupt. Store managers arrived at their stores on a Saturday morning to find the doors chained. It was the managers' first official news of the deep troubles confronting their company.

And finally, channel four contains news from fellow workers, public newspapers, and the rumor mills of the world. Four is the PBS of corporate life.

So what is the problem? The problem is that in the established company these four channels are inadequate to these fast-changing times. Key people are unfamiliar with competitors, costs, quality issues, foreign exchange rates, changing technology—things that affect their working life very directly. People do not commit their best when "it's only a job." It is only a job when one is not in the mainstream. Mainstream status goes to those who know. Today the web of systems and procedures that serve as the nerve system for hierarchical, compartmentalized structures do a great job of making sure no one makes any big mistakes in hiring, spending money, reviewing performance, and so forth. But the web also inhibits information flow and, therefore, prohibits the spontaneous generation of ideas that could come if people knew what was going on—the business challenges—and had the freedom to do something responsive about them in real time.

As a related aside, one symptom of the overinsulation is unionization. Stephen J. Cabot, a Philadelphia lawyer specializing in labor relations, at a recent speech in San Francisco, rattled off a list of five employer errors that have resulted in successful union organization of employees. He said that in most cases management . . .

1. Gave employees only a minimum of information about the status of the company's health, its financial position, its goals, sales and productive achievement.
2. Introduced changes in plant equipment, tooling, or policy without advance notice or subsequent explanations to the workforce.
3. Made key decisions in a vacuum of ignorance about what their employees really wanted.
4. Used pressure tactics rather than leadership to secure high productivity.
5. Played down or ignored employee dissatisfaction in their plants.[1]

Incidentally, a large percentage of those attending the speech were from sizable service companies.

There is an old saying that the best bilge pump in the world is a sailor with a bucket standing in rising water. Many American companies are standing in rising water. The last 10 years shook those in the Fortune 500 and their friends. The work force gets smarter every year. *But each individual must feel the water about his or her knees.* As that happens, all manner of ways to get the boats back in the race again will be forthcoming.

In entrepreneurial companies . . .

- A majority of the people have their noses pressed up against the glass of reality. Everyone understands what's happening.

Keeping people "informed" is not quite the right answer to this challenge. While more honest house organs and videotape messages from the president will be helpful, the important lane on the longer term road to corporate rejuvenation is the one that uses systems and procedures to *liberate* people rather than to *control* them. What if one procedure in an enterprise required everyone to visit a customer once a year or work in the plant a week or draft a paper on competition? Not doable!! Nonsense. The modern corporation isn't composed of uneducated, work-or-die, indentured servants. The lines between managers and members are increasingly indistinct. These are new times. Researcher after researcher finds time after time that when people have the power and the information to do something creative or innovative, they often do. People don't leave the corporate womb primarily for wealth. They flee for freedom—even the freedom to make mistakes. Harold Geneen has it wrong: They leave for cash. Rosabeth Kanter has it right: They seek power to try things, smart things.

When looking at a cross section of companies . . .

- The striking characteristic of those slamming their way into the top 1,000 is the absence of endless, suffocating rules and regs. The officers of such companies take great pride in policy manuals that are truly slim. They are willing to bet on the people. . . .

Many systems exist today in order to keep track of things (people, money) in the organizational structure. The systems are structure-driven and structure-dependent. Technology is increasingly making it possible to separate the two. Systems *can* serve a need (e.g., budgeting) independent of the current structure. This frontier must be pushed back by entrepreneurially oriented managers with a new view on controlling practices.

Rx: *Decouple systems from the structure*

INCENTIVES

The most visible system hamstringing the average company is the incentive system. The business idea behind incentive systems, and they are usually costly, is that they will encourage incremental productive behavior in the cause of the enterprise. The idea was once sound enough, but in practice, most such systems have become so homogenized that they end up all cost and no incentive. In the name of administrative simplicity, equity, and fairness, money is spent in ways that are, at best, neutral in impact. And the expenditures may even produce counterproductive behavior when people with experience see that there is often little correlation between contribution and payoff . . . a finding that is showing up in social trend research.

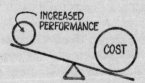

Incentives

First off, going back to the small company/big company model for comparison, in fast-rising outfits, a *variety* of incentives are typically found. Different people can pursue different stars. If state-of-the-art research is the thing, do a

109

good job now and the reward is more research to do. If capital gains is the target, ISOs (incentive stock options) are available to all hands. Perhaps fame is the turn on; working long hours on a hot idea is bound to make the member a centerpiece at cocktail parties.

Larger companies tend to have less variety and less flexibility on their incentive menu. But is it because they are big, or because their managing practices in this arena are long of tooth? From frontier research to capital gains to fame, larger companies actually have potentially more variety in their incentive arsenals than most smaller ones. But it doesn't get used because it is messy to administer. A system that tailors rewards to individuals is considerably more complex than one that generalizes across departments and levels. A system that rewards individuals in the fuzzy tomorrows is more complicated than one that merely pays off once a year for measurable results of yesterday. The cry and clamor in America is for *autonomy* within the context of a going concern. *It is not for anonymity*. The ultimate control system, lifetime employment, is not what makes the people of this country go. Some freedom to maneuver, even to fail, is part of the pioneering heritage. Aggressive, multifaceted incentive systems can be a managing practice that helps bring out the best of that heritage in individuals.

After variety, a second characteristic of successful incentives is *fast feedback*. There is the case, made earlier, that one of the greatest attractions of traditional entrepreneurial companies is that the players always know how they are doing—individually and collectively. Feedback is nearly instantaneous on a continuing basis. In fact, speed of feedback may be a very useful way to discriminate between innovation-centered companies and more bureaucratic ones. Bureaucracies, indeed, tend to protect themselves from feedback with systems and procedures and a complicated, often incomprehensible, hierarchy.

Feedback

How short is the feedback loop in the average established enterprise? At the top, it is probably too short. For the rest of the organization, it probably tends to be too long. Enough has been written about top management's overemphasis on short-term results and the tendency today to operate with one eye on Wall Street rather than on the horizon. (See Reading Three in the Appendix, for example.) But there may be a lesson here. *It is human nature to want feedback.* Our brains do operate somewhat like servomechanisms, i.e., they take in information and make midcourse corrections in real time. Corporate officers must find the Wall Street reaction to their moves (new product introductions, plant closures, acquisitions, divestitures) satisfying. A bad reaction even may be better than none at all. Perhaps this is one of the key attractions of corporate life at the top of the pyramid: the winners get both to know what's going on (finally) and quick feedback on decisions made.

But what about the rest of the organization? There is, of course, the whole catalog of strokes that bosses can disseminate—in one minute or more—throughout the year. Then there is the annual review, a perfunctory feedback event in most parts of most companies. Even if the review is done well (rare), look at the weak points. It is typically

111

done by the immediate superior, a person who enjoys less awe (respect?) and authority (to judge) than 20 years ago. It is typically done long after many key events in the member's work life have transpired, for better or worse. And it is typically done with a high degree of abstraction (professional coolness, objectivity) in order to factor out any tentacles of emotion that might taint the evaluation. All this happens today, of course, at the end of some 12-month period during which corporate officers are making speeches imploring people to get excited!, get committed!, be innovative! productive!

What is to be done? The feedback cycle must be compressed. Along with more information about corporate reality in general, individual members need direct input on their contributions. The input doesn't have to be in the form of rewards or sanctions necessarily; nor must it always come from the boss. The ideal is probably direct reactions from the environment—customers, other departments, and project results. Here again, managing practices that put members one-on-one with the challenges of the times, rather than practices that buffer the challenges from the people and vice versa, are the wave of the future. Here's Harold Geneen again on the past: "In sizable corporations, an executive on his way up has to make at least five brilliant moves before he is considered on the fast track; one mistake will plant a seed of distrust that may destroy his career."[2] The day is at hand when the guys and gals who make sizable mistakes are the ones who will get the medals! For they are the only ones who will make the big breakthroughs, too. There is no way to bat 100 percent at innovating.

POWER DILUTION

The fangs that systems have are subtle. By definition, systems require due process and approvals. Responsibility is spread out and around. People with new ideas, innovation champions, are required to gather support—often from peers and from people up the line. This is not all bad. Even in smart, smaller companies, important decisions are frequently not unilateral. It is the underlying purpose of the procedures in many established companies that is suspect.

In larger companies, the aim of systems people is to minimize risks; in smaller ones, the management uses systems to insure concentration of resources on the most attractive opportunities. This is the difference: *risk minimizing vs. resource optimizing*. It may be true that the large, established company often has more to lose from big mistakes; but that is merely an argument for working to limit downside risks, not dampening the search for opportunity.

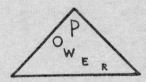

Dilution

The systems that permeate the modern corporation essentially disburse the power to do things. The intention is to ensure that no one individual, acting alone, can garner enough resources to do something big, to obtain a critical mass. Essentially the systems inherited by the managements of today's established companies reflect the design philosophy of the linear 1960s. *The systems are defensive in nature*. When success was pretty much of a sure thing (keep on doing better what you have been doing), it made sense to control employees with plenty of checks and balances in order to stay in the game. As Jack Steele, the dean of the business school at the University of Southern California (USC) remarked with reference to a well-known enterprise that seems to have lost its zest, "One good thing about being in a rut is that it's hard to get lost." Systems have traditionally provided the walls for the rut.

CONCLUSION

Decoupling the systems from the structure needs to be a high-priority agenda item for managers intent on doing something more than merely "rearranging the deck chairs on the *Titanic*" in search of more entrepreneurial behavior. The key is systems oriented to individuals and perhaps teams; systems with time cycles tied to events rather than to the calendar; systems aimed at encouraging radical ideas rather than simplifying administration.

Under the heading of professionalism, torrents of managerial energy have been channeled into designing ways to minimize mistakes in going concerns. Each individual policy, system, or procedure alone makes (made) eminent sense; collectively, in many companies, they have become a tight web that ensnarls desired, innovative behavior. The web was constructed one strand at a time; it will probably have to be loosened the same way.

Chapter Ten

Funding Ideas

Money is like manure. You have to spread it around to do any good.

The lead quote about money was popularized in the musical *Hello, Dolly!* It is a useful guideline to one of the easiest changes that established companies can address, namely, loosening the purse strings. There is no faster indicator that management is serious about getting entrepreneurial than to see them putting some bucks on the line.

It is conventional wisdom today that the senior officials of many of America's larger enterprises act more like trustees or stewards than like business builders. The critics label the executives and directors disparagingly as administrators, mere resource shufflers. The recent continuing wave of megabuck mergers is giving the commentators plenty of additional ammunition. Attacking management from the other side have been the social-responsibility interests intent on reshaping the corporation to be cooperative (with their causes) rather than competitive. Of course, over the longer haul, both sides may well meet as management practitioners grapple with the reality that jobs and business increasingly have "political, cultural, and moral significance as well as economic meaning."[1] In the meantime, there is a long row to hoe to cultivate aggressive entrepreneurship in the nation's established companies. Money—once again—is the fertilizer for the job.

There are two specific questions that corporate leaders need to consider: *Who* should have access to pots of dollars to spend? And *how*, by what process, are ideas/applications to be funded? The issue of *how much* in a given circumstance pretty well takes care of itself. A new inventory control scheme can't be created for $100. At the same time, companies that have experimented with funding programs for ideas usually do set pot and project limits.

ACCESS

Historically, the who question has been answerable outside the R&D lab with a single word: managers. Only managers could officially get money to spend. In the future, all members of the enterprise should ideally have access to funds. All. If management wants everyone to open up to change, then management must be willing to give everyone some change. The drop-your-ideas-in-the-suggestion-box days of yesteryear are inadequate. Random ahas from the membership are wonderful, but the target is a turned-on workforce that is aggressively innovative by intent.

Experience indicates that only a relatively small percentage of the total membership will actually get and spend hard cash. But here is what is important. When people believe they have access to funds, the whole climate for and receptivity to change can improve. There is a self-selection process associated with internal—as well as external—entrepreneuring. A lot of the management job is to create conditions under which latent innovators can come out of the closet. Venture capitalists have done just this on the outside. Over 2,500 new corporations were backed by professional investors in 1984 alone. Many were staffed by managers and doers who left the corporate fold for expressive reasons, not to get rich, or even because the outside opportunity was so red hot. It was a quality of working life decision, not an economic one. And a high quality of working life includes access to the resources needed to try some things.

People with ideas in companies need support. The most important support, by far, is that provided by senior management. In a study of 20 Fortune 500 companies attempting to foster venturing, I. C. MacMillan and Robin George found: "The fact is that without an intense and personal commitment on the part of the general management, particularly the CEO, significant new business development just will not occur."[2]

In a company setting, a second and very tangible form of support are resources to use—dollars or time, or both. Individuals often need a push towards the relatively new notion that *they* are supposed to think up and act on innovations in every phase of the life of the enterprise. MacMillan and George went on in the study referenced above to identify six increasingly difficult levels of corporate venturing opportunities:

1. New processes to improve the method of production, the packaging, the handling, distribution, and marketing of current products; new sources of raw materials or new processes to produce raw materials; new enhancements to current products and services.

2. New products and services to be sold to current customers/markets within one to two years.

3. Existing products and services for new markets within one to two years.

4. New product/service concepts that can be sold to current customers/markets but will take more than two years to reach the commercialization stage.

5. Products/services that are unfamiliar to the company but are already being produced and sold by other companies.

6. Products/services that do not exist today but could be developed and that, if successful, will replace current products/services (known markets) or serve entirely new functions (unknown markets) or both.

The authors assert that their research indicates that it is "virtually impossible to go beyond level 3 without creating a separate organization to develop its new business." The authors further suggest that it is up to the CEO to select "appropriate levels of opportunities, by which the organization can *learn* . . . and acquire the requisite skills." Members require access to resources to learn. Companies must pay the dues.

PROCESS

How is a discrete (and finite) amount of money to be smartly distributed among the members who respond to the innovation climate with a nonstandard request for resources? There is no one best way known so far. Various companies around the country are experimenting. And the key in a given organization is probably to try more than one approach. There are President's Funds and Wild Hare funds and XYZ Fellows, and so on. Creating *budget detours* is the philosophy and, once again, experimentation is the key. The use of peer or near-peer councils of some kind to decide who gets how much seems to be common practice where working budget detours have been established. In terms of corporate sociology, the use of nonupper management in this way appears consistent with the direction in which things need to go as discussed elsewhere in this book. Peer reviews entail less stratification, less rank consciousness, less "we" and "themness," i.e., compartmentalization. Idea funding organized in this way may be the harbinger of systems of the future.

Another way funds are being used to spur frontier thinking is as rewards for jobs well done. Instead of a merit bonus to take home and decorate the bank account, successful innovators and change agents are given a grubstake to use on their next bright idea. What a difference! A person does well and recognition comes in the form of getting to "play" some more. If one pitches well on Tuesday, he or she gets to pitch again on Saturday. That is what an entrepreneurial breeze feels like. Richard Pascale in "The Paradox of Corporate Culture" referenced in Chapter Eight sums up the picture this way: "An inordinate amount of energy in American companies is invested in fighting the system. (We often find ourselves playing games to work around it.) When an organization instills a strong, consistent set of implicit understandings, it is effectively establishing a common law to supplement its statutory laws. This enables us to interpret formal systems in the context for which they were designed, to use them as tools rather than straightjackets." Budgets are such statutory laws; detours are a form of understandings.

CONCLUSION

Enough attention has been heaped on how large, established companies missed out when they turned down a bright person with a new product idea (Hewlett-Packard turned down Steve Wozniak, Atari turned down Steve Jobs, and so forth). New product ideas are important and so are new product idea people. But there is a whole universe of business activities that cry out for fresh ways of thinking and doing. Manufacturing, warehousing, inbound freight, energy costs, invoicing, advertising, stockholder relations, complaint handling, bad debts, inventory control, transportation costs, sales call effectiveness . . . the list is essentially endless. That is what makes business a terrific place to be. There is so much to be done as technology and social change once again intersect with ambition. The management task is to get those who inhabit the large, complex companies charged up about what each individual can *and must* do to succeed under the new rules. By putting some money behind the entrepreneurial rhetoric, corporate leaders can spread some power to make desired things happen all around.

Rx: *Replace dividing up with resource sharing*

Chapter Eleven

Leading from Behind

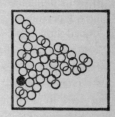

The advice of a wise man refreshes like water from a mountain spring. Those accepting it become aware of the pitfalls on ahead.

PROVERBS 13:14

Given an exciting professional challenge and a set of graying management practices, what are responsible bosses to do? How should they personally conduct themselves to improve the chances of being the coach of a winning team? This is perhaps the toughest of the action questions. Everyone is a product of past experience; managers tend to boss as they were bossed, particularly when they are under pressure. And to the extent that the past is less useful as a guide to the future than before, some fresh thinking is appropriate.

Most of the classic work on leadership revolves around examining the mix of task and people orientation in a manager's makeup. The most recent refinements suggest

121

that a contingency or situational approach is the most valid. This is to say that the optimum leadership style varies with the circumstances. A style effective in an office of experienced salespeople may be less than effective if those managed are young computer programmers. A style that is good on steady-state matters may be counterproductive in emergencies. And, of course, the classic illustration is the one about the traditional, start-in-a-garage entrepreneur who successfully launches a new enterprise but fails to keep it in the air because of an ineffective adjustment to the changed circumstances of success.

CORPORATE CULTURE

Given all the theory and the baggage of past experience, thoughtful managers need an updated platform of understanding from which to consider their individual leadership styles. The relatively new concept of corporate culture provides such a platform. Culture in a business context has come of age very quickly. It is a fuzzy subject spawned because corporate times are indeed fuzzy and the time-tested set of tools long employed by the rational manager no longer produce answers to the pressing questions surrounding corporate vitality. Actually, corporate culture is not really an answer either; it is more of a question. What is required to bring the attitudes and behavior of those in the organization into sync with the times? Whatever collage of actions make up the total answer, the behavior of the corporate leaders will be a prime ingredient. Hence, a thoughtful position on the *desired* culture for an enterprise should provide a clue or two on what smart leadership probably should be doing in that organization at this time in its life. As every trained observer of how companies work well knows, it is the combination of little things that bosses *do* or do not do over time that add up to what the members do. Leaders, by definition, need followers.

What is a culture? Thinkers on the subject say it is an amorphous collection of fairly deep-seated concepts that influence how those in the culture behave. So, in a corporate setting, if a decision is made that the enterprise needs to become, in total, more "market-driven" (Touche Ross), more smaller project oriented (Bechtel), more "value conscious" (Saga), more "aggressive" (Bank of America), or whatever, it is clear that something more than wall posters is needed.

How is a desired culture obtained? To start with, all companies have a culture—for better or worse. *The issue is whether that enterprise has the culture—values, behavior—it needs downstream.* The culture of a company can be defined—or at least profiled—by looking critically at six factors borrowed from the field of anthropology.

Vocabulary

One can learn a lot about the culture of a company by identifying the special words that are used within the organization by its members. Words (and phrases) are the tracks that ideas and values run on. Without a word for it, an idea or concept cannot exist in a company setting. Without the words, "quality" or "entrepreneurship," it is difficult to get more of either, for example. Try this little exercise: Get a group of people together and give each of them a 3- × 5-inch card. Ask each person to write down three to six common words that are unique to the company, words that convey a special meaning to insiders. See what turns up.

Chances are good, first off, that when everyone's words are compared there will be a fairly high level of agreement. As the various words are listed on a flipchart, for example, there is likely to be a good assortment of "tee

123

hees'' and ''oh, yeahs'' as certain words are mentioned. Many present will identify with the organization-unique character of certain terms. Second, by examining the most special words in a little depth, you will find out something about the culture of the organization. Here are a couple of examples to illustrate the point.

The above exercise was used with a group of relatively young partners in a Big Eight, national accounting firm. A short list of the special words that brought laughs of recognition to the group included ''billable hours,'' ''Boca Raton'' (a city in Florida), ''A.E.,'' ''Gible.'' Every person present instantly recognized the extra layer of meaning conveyed by the vocabulary: Billable hours were *the* measuring stick in the firm; Boca Raton was the source of all truth—the place where the partners met annually to decide on the big issues; A.E. translated to Assignment Expansion (ha-ha), the heart of increasing billings to a given client; and Gible was the green bible of professional conduct that was used to guide just about every move of every person in the firm.

Now consider the words above and their organization-unique meanings. Don't they provide the start of a profile of the firm's culture? Don't they give a hint of the objectives of the enterprise, the organization structure, the way things tend to work around the place? And if, as was the case in this example, the senior people in the firm are concurrently calling for increased ''customer centeredness,'' more ''creativeness in the field,'' and an ''expansion of the customer base,'' one gets a glimpse of what a culture-change *problem* looks like. A.E. for example, may be quite incompatible with adding new clients to the customer base. (A new term, N.C. needs to be woven into the vocabulary of the firm!)

Here is an even more revealing example. A group of middle managers and one officer from a very large consumer goods company tried the vocabulary exercise. The company was a particularly aggressive TV advertiser. The people at the meeting were responsible for identifying new products and for selling more of all the company's products to the consuming public via TV. Among the words that showed up on the short list of the vocabulary of this influential group were "couch potato," "vidiot," and "Joe 6-pack." The listing of the words from the 3- by 5-inch cards brought a lot of laughs; it also brought home a surprising insight into the culture of at least that part of the company, namely, that the people paying the bills, i.e., TV-watching customers, were looked upon with derision, if not contempt. (The insight was not particularly welcomed . . . because the behavioral implications to alter this element of the culture were obvious.)

The special vocabulary that every established organization has provides a clue to the culture of that organization.

Methodology

The word "methodology" used here means how things get done. Every going concern has some set ways in which work is accomplished. Usually it is a combination of individual effort, committee meetings, one-on-one discussions, Joe or Jane (the boss) said, and paperwork. There are a growing number of cases where technology plays an important part in the methodology. When the dominant mode in use is identified, once again, something more about the culture of the organization is known. Methodology is a descriptor and, therefore, a potential lever that managers can use to affect the culture, and, therefore, the behavior of their people. Another example can help make this point clear.

The senior 25 people of a major, nationwide service company met in March of 1981 to review and agree upon a strategic plan for the decade ahead. The plan was the product of many, many months of work. After three days of deep deliberation, one officer commented almost offhandedly in connection with a discussion of mainframe computer requirements that maybe the company was missing the boat by not looking into microcomputers. Further discussion revealed that not a soul in the assembly knew what a microcomputer was! This was particularly significant in that the company was in the financial services industry (a big player, even), and top management prided itself on having a company that was "state of the art." At that point in time, however, the dominant methodology throughout the company was individual professional effort, meetings, and memos . . . just like everyone else in the industry.

Following the March meeting, one thing led to another. Then at a mammoth April meeting at which the strategic plan was described to over 100 key office managers, the president closed the four-day meeting with an unusual twist. In addition to her normal admonition to go forth and make profits, the president gave each of the 100 managers a brand new microcomputer ($2,500 each) to take home. Her parting words were: "I'm not quite sure just how we should put these to work here, but I believe we must. And to help the process along, I'll give $25,000 to the one of you who finds the best applications for the company between today and our meeting a year from now!" Needless to say, the methodology of that company started changing that very day. Four years later, the officers of the company credit the president's bold move with sparking a powerful cultural change that has enabled the company to prosper vis-à-vis its competitors during the recent years when the financial services industry has been in turmoil. The company has become "electronic," "with it," "modern," and a "what if . . . " kind of an enterprise clearly different from its more traditional rivals. A change in methodology was the catalyst in this case.

Rx: *Augment controllers with catalysts*

Rules of Conduct

Another way to sharpen the profile of the culture of an enterprise is to isolate the typically *unwritten* dos and don'ts that guide the day-to-day actions of the people therein. When the rules about everything from dress and office protocol to decision making and etiquette are understood, one has more insight into the culture. For example, if the unspoken law is that all meetings are conducted with a published agenda and a reverent, hushful tone, creative group activities such as brainstorming are going to be hard to put into place no matter how many speeches the executives make about "a new era of entrepreneuring here." If the enterprise is mired in procedural pomp and circumstance that has been passed down from generation to generation, increased customer responsiveness may be hard to come by. If the way to the top has historically been via the finance/control side of the house, achieving a companywide, product quality orientation based on manufacturing finesse may encounter some extra, unseen hurdles.

Professor Dave Jemison at the Stanford Graduate School of Business has a neat little exercise to explore this element of a company's culture. He suggests that a group of managers picture themselves stranded unexpectedly on a verdant South Seas island. They are the total officer corps of their company. They know that rescue is on the way, but it will be 90 days before the pickup. In the meantime, there are several minutes of battery power left for the radio, and the group is asked by those at home to quickly relay any guidelines it has for the conduct of the company during the absence of its leaders. Jemison then asks those present to write down the rules they would relay. Here is a sample of what various groups have produced:

Stay within budget. (This is a big favorite.)
Watch the (inventory) turns.
Listen.
Keep the place clean.
Don't hire MBAs.
Look professional (dark suits, pearls, and so forth).
Remember the customer is boss.
Don't do anything until I get back!
Be there Saturday mornings.
Check things out with somebody before you proceed.
Get it in writing.

When you can identify the subterranean code that guides the conduct of the people in an enterprise, you know something more about its culture. Alter the code and you alter the culture; alter the culture and you change the behavior of the members. And rules of conduct are most evident in the ways in which the leaders of the enterprise conduct themselves, day in and day out.

Values

The notion of values, particularly shared values, is an important by-product of the crescendo of interest in Japanese management techniques. Going back to the stages of company-growth typology used in Chapter One of this book, there is a lot to be said for consciously building a sense of primacy into the membership of a company as it grows up. This is typically easier than trying to instill one on the working population from outside, i.e., from on high, after the company is large and complex. A great deal of the corporate overhead found in many established companies is a reflection of attempts—often successful, but costly—to impose a sense of purpose and order, values, across the organization.

As a practical matter, what is meant by values? Do multifaceted, operating entities really have such things, and particularly, do they revolve around some primary value or superordinate goal as several writers have termed it? The answer is yes . . . at least the more successful ones do. In fact, all enterprises with any history have a theme, perhaps faint, running through them. The members know what counts, what is really important *when the chips are down*. Most companies want everything, of course: growth, profitability, market share, quality, happy customers, staff development, responsiveness, reputation, and so forth. But the way to crystallize the true system of beliefs that drive (or retard) the enterprise is to look at what factor or concept prevails when the pressure is on and a hard choice has to be made. For example, if a choice has to be made on the very last day of the quarter between 1) shipping a finished unit (that may have a slight, noncritical defect) in order to make the budgeted sales figure, or 2) delaying the shipment a week for further inspection—which choice will prevail?

Or try this one: A report from the internal, customer audit staff indicates that a product the company has had in the marketplace for over a year really does not do what it claims to do. While the product does no harm, its efficacy is almost (not quite) zero. The report goes on to say that there is no significant evidence of customer dissatisfaction. How would the report be handled? What value would take precedence? When what counts when push comes to shove and a hard choice has to be made are identified, then something important is known about the culture of the organization. Changing the values—if necessary—then becomes something else the leaders of the enterprise can do to alter the culture, and subsequently behavior.

In *In Search of Excellence*, Peters and Waterman list the "specific content of the dominant belief of the excellent companies" they studied:

1. A belief in being the "best."
2. A belief in the importance of the details of execution, the nuts and bolts of doing the job well.
3. A belief in the importance of people as individuals.
4. A belief in superior quality and service.
5. A belief that most members of the organization should be innovators, and its corollary, the willingness to support failure.
6. A belief in the importance of informality to enhance communication.
7. Explicit belief in and recognition of the importance of economic growth and profits.[1]

Values or beliefs, i.e., what a company stands for, are becoming more important as a factor to smart people entering the workforce. Corporate answers to the stock questions about location, salary, benefits, and opportunities are no longer enough. Many people are discovering that work can satisfy their hunger for self-expression and creative challenge, and the word is getting around. An explicit value system can be a major determinant to the meaning associated with work in a given company. A heavy emphasis on financial measures is not obsolete; it just is not enough. ROI alone, for example, doesn't create much excitement in the minds of most people in an organization!

Peter Drucker made the pithy observation that we may now be nearing the end of our 100-year belief in a free lunch. The question is, what is to replace the resulting belief vacuum? Companies with a thoughtful answer coupled with managing practices that ennoble human initiative and effort are going to be the growth companies of tomorrow.

Rituals

A critical look at the prominent rituals practiced in a company reveals other information on the culture. Rituals? Why we don't have rituals here is often the response. But all companies have rituals, and both their presence and content help define that web that connects the members together at some level of purposeful effort.

Dictionary definitions of ritual include "a prescribed or established rite, proceeding, ceremony, or service" and "the observance of set forms of behavior in social conduct." Look at any established company and you will find an endless collection of rituals covering all phases of organization life. A short list would include rituals for:

Hiring and introducing new people
Firing or laying off people
Announcing new products
Promotions
Acknowledging a major failure
Holiday parties
Management meetings offsite
Quarterly results announcements
Retirements
Plant closings

Everyone in a company is touched by such rituals. The management question is, of course, what does their content, or absence even, convey to the membership? Consider the messages transmitted by these variations on the list above.

Hiring: New employees are greeted on a group

131

basis during their first week by a company officer and given a 60-minute talk/slide show on the mission of the company. This event is one part of a 20-hour program each new person receives during the first six weeks.

vs.

New employees are welcomed by a junior person on the personnel staff and talked through the benefits program and safety procedures. The new person is then turned over to his or her supervisor with a smile and admonished to "call if any questions arise."

Firing: Discharged members (with over a year of service) are given optional, extensive out-placement counseling service and, in most cases, a going-away luncheon.

vs.

Discharged members are asked on Friday afternoon to simply not appear on the upcoming Monday morning.

New Products: The addition to the product family is ballyhooed throughout the organization. Supporting materials are distributed to all hands—even to people in accounting!

vs.

Nothing happens internally when a new product is introduced.

Promotions: When someone is moved into a position with increased organizational responsibility, that person is pictured and written about in the quarterly, company house organ.

vs.

Newly promoted people receive a signed note of congratulations from the president.

vs.

News of a given promotion is disseminated via word of mouth outside of the directly affected unit. People in the unit itself usually receive a memo from personnel.

vs.

A party is held and everybody shakes the promotee's hand before departing.

And so on. This issue is not one of good or bad, right or wrong. The issue is simply that different rituals give off different signals, and signals influence behavior. And influencing behavior is ultimately what leadership in a business enterprise is about.

Myths and Stories

Perhaps the shortest route to a handle on the culture of an organization is to hear what the field force (sales, service, audit team, or others) talks about after a few drinks and dinner together on the road.

What kinds of people emerge in the conversations as heroes and heroines?
Are the stars acknowledged to be making positive contributions or are they the people beating the system?
What is the nature of the tales that are swapped? Is it good or foolish to work long and hard for the outfit?
Are people proud of responding well to customer re-

quirements or critical of the jerks in engineering or quality control?

What is the folklore of the company . . . the inside scoop on how things are really decided upstairs?

Do those gathered in the booth talk about how to make the enterprise stronger or about résumé writing?

In short, the myths and stories that permeate any company carry a flavor of what the company was and is. And they taint—for better or worse—what the enterprise is to become. What leaders at different levels do over time is the genesis of most such material.

So, in summary to this point, there are some discrete levers that managers and executives can use to transform the culture of an organization *if it is in need of transformation*. Managers in recently deregulated industries are keenly aware of such needs; many managers directly involved with fast-changing technologies know from experience that their cultures must be adaptive; increasingly, managers in all companies with traditional managing practices must at least ask the culture transformation question. It's the crux of the business leadership challenge. In America at least, there is a new set of values afoot in the population at large. These new values are permeating the workforce, and they can be shaped, molded, and encouraged into productive effort . . . or they can be ignored. But they can not be bullied or wished away. Appropriate leadership for the times will be that which draws out talents and energies spawned by the times and inhibited frequently by practices grown old.

CONCLUSION

Given perspective, levers, and desire, what does effective leadership boil down to? The Aspen Study mentioned earlier provides a data point that vividly outlines at least one corner of the necessary action plan:

> Military officers recognize that one way to win the commitment necessary to ensure extremely high levels of effort and risk in situations that demand virtually total discretion is for the leaders to share the hardships of their troops. The standard advice to young officers goes something like this: "If you never eat, drink, or rest before all of your men do, they will follow you into the gates of Hell." To put it aphoristically, soldiers respond to leadership (follow my lead), not management (do as I say).[2]

In other words, lead from behind. Or as Peters and Austin put it in *A Passion for Excellence*, "Leadership must be present at all levels of the organization. It depends upon a million little things done with obsession, consistency, and care. . . ."[3]

Chapter Twelve

Cheerleading for the Professional

The organization man is dead.

BUSINESS WEEK

It is easy to get enthusiastic about corporate culture, too easy, perhaps. In being intellectually stimulating, culture runs some risk of being sidelined as a legitimate, full-time management issue. Such has generally been the fate of earlier, soft-side subjects like motivation and communication. Culture, in the broad sense of the word, should not have such a fate. Too much is at stake.

In the *Business Week* cover story, "The New Corporate Elite," some of the characteristics of the prototypical environment espoused by those who are deemed to be setting the pace for businesses managed for these times were mentioned. Paraphrased, they include . . .

The little guy in the organization is the center of focus
Populism, both left and right views of it, is good

Corporate status/position/trappings are held in contempt
Bigness, per se, is bad
Dispersed stock ownership is necessary within an enterprise
Merit should be the only measure of personal worth
Hierarchy is an enemy
Charisma is important
Vision is noteworthy
Self-enrichment comes through self-enhancement
Corporations need internal social values
Line driveness (not staff) is right
First-name usage helps communication
Everyone should be internationally minded
Success should be shared.[1]

These are the new values that are at least getting the press. Assume that they are only half accurate . . . that the rumblings in established companies that render them less than fleet-of-foot only reflect discontent or concerns with part of the list above. The message is still clear: the culture of American business is changing . . . for better or for worse. Much has already been said about the need for an updated managerial attitude that gets translated into changed practices in organizing, planning, leading, and controlling the activities in the life of an enterprise. *But there is a danger in overorganizing the effort to change.* In a sense, the internal business problems of now are the direct result of too much managing. What is needed is more cheerleading!

Think about it. What is it that cheerleaders do? They stir up people's emotions. They get people involved. They energize. They lead with no real authority to direct; people follow along voluntarily. Cheerleading connotes a slew of wholesome attributes: enthusiasm, spirit, belief, togetherness, and, perhaps, even dedication to the cause at hand. Most business managers espouse such attributes; few, however, step up to the line and demonstrate them. To do so would be unprofessional, uncool, awkward. Such psychic echoes of the past bear scrutiny, but for the purposes of this chapter, cheerleading should simply be considered as a daily antidote to being too serious, too managerial. As the younger generation keeps saying, work and enjoyment do not have to be mutually exclusive.

PERSONAL CULTURE

Busy managers have at least five regular opportunities to consciously cheerlead with different degrees of subtlety, depending upon their bravado and experience. The opportunities include the choice of words used (vocabulary); the way time is spent (rules of conduct); how meetings are conducted (methodology); the decision rules followed in public (values); and the habits displayed day in, day out (rituals). In short, the personal culture of the manager is what can be used to cheerlead during the competitive contests ahead.

Why should these opportunities be exercised? Very simple. They should be exercised because without some enthusiasm and excitement, established companies are not going to attract or hold onto enough good people to generate all the changes required to remain viable competitors. Some laughter is needed to make the medicine go down.

For decades American business had been conducted within an accepted set of rules. The government regulated many industries. A few giant companies dominated many markets. Smokestack industries reigned supreme. Foreign trade was quite small, and foreign competitors were puny. The domestic borders defined the players in the game. . . . Much of that world has been blasted away in the last decade, leaving a radically different business environment.[2]

It is the "blasted away" element that justifies some cheerleading . . . because there are still a lot of unbelievers suffering shellshock of sorts. They think the 60s will reappear. They await the return of "business as usual." They need to be stirred up to the realities of the times—for the country's sake if not their own. As indicated in the Introduction, all the nation's software, computer, telecommunications, real estate, and chocolate chip cookie companies— existing and coming—are not enough to make a difference in the world business league. America's established companies must join the renaissance! The management movers and shakers of the land must get on with it—they must start moving and shaking. That's what cheerleaders do! It is not taught in business schools, one more reason why it may be an idea whose time has come.

Words

Every manager picks up and hones a vocabulary for use in business life. Remember when "discounted cash flow" came down the pike? Or, "OD," or "MBO," or "market driven"? The point is that words do make a difference, and the perceptive manager wishing to have an impact will make the choice of words a conscious act. Here is a small example.

This author has taught a course called New Enterprise Management for some time now. Almost inadvertently, a few years ago I introduced the term "WOO" into class one day. A WOO was a window of opportunity—and I originally used the term in connection with the importance of timing in starting a new venture. Since that day, WOOs have become embedded in the fabric of the course. (Today, there are occasionally NO-WOOs, SUPER-WOOs,

139

and WOO-WOOs.) Most important, however, the notion of timing seems to have a firm foothold in the minds of those who pass through the course and go on out into the real world. WOO has helped it happen. There have already been alumni occasions when the opening conversation with a graduate somehow or another gets quickly around to the fact that he or she has or has not found a WOO yet. Their new enterprise instincts include a factor and respect for the critical factor of timing. A word has influenced behavior in a desired direction.

One more short example of the impact a term or phrase can have. This author also teaches a general management course in the summer, Stanford Executive Program. Some time back (1978, I believe), I decided that it was important to make the point more strongly that in considering business policy and strategic planning matters, the challenge is to achieve *internal consistency* . . . not to find truth or *the* strategic answer. I settled on the notion of "keeping your TOES straight," i.e., making sure that at any given point in *T*ime, the *O*bjectives, the *E*nvironment, and the *S*trategy of the enterprise were in alignment. Visually, the idea was quite memorable.

And the phraseology caught on. Not a year passes that I don't get several Christmas cards from executives somewhere in the world who mention TOES. The phrase has hopefully been of value to the bearers as they wrestle with the business challenges of the times. Incidentally, the "S" in the TOES I now use is an $\underline{S}$ to the eighth power, S^8: strategy, structure, style, systems, staff, skills, superordinate goals, and science (McKinsey 7 S's plus 1). There is more to get into alignment today!

One picture is worth a thousand words. True. One word can be a useful hook into a thousand minds. Also true. Managers interested in doing some cheerleading will do well to introduce some select terms into the mainstream of what is going on. Brainstorming with those in the mainstream might be a creative way of taking advantage of a WOO! One last possibility: Reading Four in the Appendix is a classic business school case on Marks and Spencer, one of the top retailers in the world for many years. Consider reading the case and exploring the significance of the words ''probing'' and ''simplicity.''

Time

People tend to do what management *in*spects—more so than what it *ex*pects. This old adage packs a lot of insight. It is what the boss does that counts. How the boss spends time reveals a lot about priorities. It is one thing to advocate customer-centeredness; it is another thing to actually go out on sales calls, for example. To quote an allegory picked up somewhere this last year: ''I,'' said the chicken, ''am committed to a healthy breakfast for all Americans.'' ''I,'' said the pig, ''am involved.'' There is a difference.

Readers can check themselves in this matter. In an average working week, say a representative cross section of the last four weeks, what percentage of working time was spent on each of the following activities:

_(%)_ Budgets, planning or reviews

_____ Handling complaints

_____ Talking with people who are organizationally senior

_____ Talking with peers

_____ Talking with people who are organizationally junior

_____ Inventing

_____ Singing

_____ Working with customers

_____ Working with quality matters

_____ Just thinking

_____ Performance reviews, formal or informal

_____ Walking around

_____ Writing

_____ Speaking/presenting

_____ Solving problems

_____ Drawing/doodling

_____ Attending meetings . . . to observe

_____ Reviewing/generating new ideas

_____ Staying physically fit

_____ Lunching

_____ Making lists

_____ Reading

_____ Traveling

Other:_____

_____

100%

Now review the distribution. What does it say about what is deemed important? What signals does the above use of time give off to others? What is the lead cheerleader for some group of people saying with his or her time language?

Meetings

Interesting research work has been done to correlate the content of agendas with the actual output of those involved in the meeting event. The indications are that, over time, there is a significant correlation. To illustrate the point, consider these two hypothetical agendas that were used weekly by two plant managers operating identical facilities for company X:

Plant A	Plant B
Schedule	Quality Report
Maintenance	Schedule
Cost Report	Maintenance
Quality Report	New Process Designs
Overtime/Productivity	Cost Report
Scrap	Productivity/Overtime
Customer Complaint Report	Scrap
New Process Designs	Customer Complaint Report

Assume that the agendas were indeed used by the respective managers for an extended series of regular Monday morning meetings that typically ran from 7:30 to 8:30 A.M. Please speculate on the answers to these questions:

At the end of the year . . .

• Which plant made the most progress on new processes?
• Which plant had the best quality record?
• How popular is each plant with its customers?
• Which plant had the lowest, total cost performance?

Of course, meetings aren't the whole story, but the agendas do give some clues, almost subliminal clues, as to what counts in the operations *to the particular manager* By altering an agenda, a boss can signal a new direction. Put singing the company song on the agenda and see what happens! Or how about New Ideas and Competitors as items to be covered on alternate weeks?

An analysis of the Board of Directors minutes over an extended period was done at two mining companies. At the start of the period, the two companies were much alike. At the end of the period, one company had vastly outdone the other in terms of successful exploration efforts. The Board's minutes provided some insight into why the one company did so well in exploration. The directors of the successful exploration company spent a lot of time discussing deposits and finding them. In the less successful company, exploration received far less attention.[3]

Professionally done, cheerleading can be quite subtle.

Decision Rules

By definition, those in leadership positions must make decisions. At least some version of the basis for the various decisions generally becomes public knowledge. In an established company, the fundamental driving forces at work become open secrets over time. When Mesa Petroleum Chairman T. Boone Pickens tells the press and packed houses that "top executives are only concerned with their perks, hunting lodges, and fishing camps," people either agree or disagree that such are the driving forces at work in corporate America. When Apple Chairman Steve Jobs tells his membership that they are together on a mission to revitalize the world, the listeners either agree (believe) or not. People in a working environment do develop some view on the underlying value structure in a company, and much of it stems from choices—decisions—made by the visible managers and executives.

Harold Geneen drove his organization on a continuing search for the "unshakable fact" in making each decision of consequence in the life of ITT. IBM is noted for making decisions that revolve first around the issue of what impact the choice made will have on the customer. One of the major paper companies in the Northwest will decide nothing until the projected effect on ROI is calculated to several decimal places. Whatever the rules are at the top of the organization, they will tend to percolate down to all levels.

Here's a short exercise related to making an elephant tap dance a bit. Picture a big, established company. A decision between alternative A and alternative B must be made. Either A or B will require a significant commitment. A is chosen. Is A chosen because . . .

A is in the budget—B would take special approval.

A is favored by a customer.

A has been proposed by someone and it is her first new idea ever.

A is the higher quality choice.

B was tried some time ago and didn't work well.

A is easier to implement.

A is fresh.

A is easier to sell to the membership.

A is more dramatic. It makes a statement.

A is simple.

The basis for decisions reflect values (ease, simplicity, quality, cost, and so on). People key off their bosses. What moderns do in their work—their behavior—depends a lot on their (cheer)leaders.

Habits

Everyone has habits. Habits communicate. They too bear scrutiny in pursuit of ways to keep on winning in the face of changing times.

There is a Silicon Valley company president who, after three years in the West, still wears a three-piece suit to the office every day of the year. He arrives precisely at 8:15 A.M. rain or shine, and, no matter what, he will be the last to leave at night. It is a matter of habit, or pride, or both. What he does is neither good nor bad, right or

145

wrong. It just is. But it does influence the conduct of the business. The point is that the perceptive leader is the one who at least considers the effects of his or her habits.

There are any number of other stories about habits and the behavior they may induce.

> One famous semiconductor CEO drives a battered pickup truck to work.
> A beer company executive is known for napping mid-morning.
> Rand Araskog, ITT chairman, abhors banter and joking at meetings.
> R. Gordon McGovern, Campbell Soup president, roams supermarket aisles.
> John G. McCoy, Bank One's legendary leader, nags people about turning off lights and forbids food and drink—even coffee—on the premises.[4]

And so on. From dress and dining to phone habits and party attendance, the personal habits of managers add up to a message that is received. Change the habits and change the message.

"One of the key problems facing organizations in American society is that they are underled and overmanaged," said USC professor Warren Bennis in a *Wall Street Journal* series on executive style. One article in the series went on to say that ". . . all require lean, flexible organizations able to catch trends, develop new ideas, and make decisions with lightning speed." Another article in the series suggests that effective leaders "excite, stimulate, and drive other people to work hard and create reality out of fantasy." Pure cheerleading!

CONCLUSION

Under the triple flags of business professionalism, academic distance, and managerial objectivity, it has become unfashionable in established American companies to bubble (with excitement), cheer (for competitive victories), compete (to win), and sign on (for the duration). The business professionalism has been carried to the point of diminishing returns; as a class, many established companies of the country are no longer winning in their worldwide leagues. Academic distance and pseudosophistication are distorting both business education and hiring practices. There are more and more business school graduates every year of late (65,000 MBA degrees granted in 1984), yet the composite competitive position of the employers of all this talent appears to be deteriorating. Perhaps the students are studying too many models of the nonworld. And finally, managerial objectivity has been sanctified to the point where emotion has become a no-no; adrenalin and business don't mix, so the story goes. Together, these flags do not add up to a formula for success in a competitive world where a lot of people are today saluting more aggressive colors.

Chapter Thirteen

Adding Value

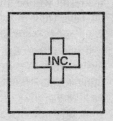

The quest: To do well while doing good.

Value added has long been an idea from the economics side of the house. Manufacturers convert (add value to) raw materials; distributors buy in big lots, break them down, carry inventory and service smaller, scattered buyers—and hence add economic value; and retailers provide a roof and display space for a wide variety of goods as well as sales, service, and credit to individual end users. Each level of business effort gets a piece of the ultimate sales dollar spent. The size of the piece has historically been presumed to be somewhat proportional to the amount of "value added."

While this mathematical approach has its place, the notion of adding value is one that must be brought out of the economics corner into the mainstream of corporate thinking in the days ahead. Ask 100 supervisors and department heads what it is that their company or division contributes to the larger scheme of things and one is likely to get a listing of products and/or services. Ask them what it is that their products and/or services do for end-users and the result will be a wide range of answers including a few, "I never thought much about it." And finally, ask them who *out there* would hurt if the operation ceased being, and one might well encounter silence. The absence of an answer may be symptomatic of a deeper problem contributing to the corporate malaise of the times, namely, the lack of purpose in work. Swiss psychotherapist, Carl G. Jung said in a BBC interview two years before his death in 1961 that "Man cannot stand a meaningless life."[1] Viktor E. Frankl in his increasingly famous little book, *Man's Search for Meaning,* quotes Nietzsche on several occasions: "He who has a *why* to live can bear almost any *how*."[2] While work is not the only source of purpose or meaning in life for the individual, a void in one's vocation can certainly be stress-inducing, particularly for the educated worker—the kind upon which companies are increasingly dependent.

BUSINESS BASICS

Theoretically, in a capitalistic, competitive environment, any enterprise must truly add value of consequence to the products or services it sells or it will not be successful as a business entity. There is at least some evidence that this theoretical model was not fully functional over all of the past 40 years. The argument has already been made that the existence of a huge domestic market, government policy, weak international competitors, and so on—the now familiar litany—distorted the model, and that it is now snapping back into place (with a vengeance). The need for an enterprise indeed to have a crisp sense of legitimacy plus some evidence that there is perhaps a growing need for people to feel some grander purpose as they earn a livelihood fit nicely together. When the key players in an enterprise understand and identify with a unique something provided to the customers served, the critical mass of dedicated support needed to compete smartly may well exist. And when it exists, members care about the company: service departments are quick to respond; phones get answered at 5:05 P.M.; costs get squeezed automatically; people do experiment on their own time, if necessary; sales people use self-serve when filling up their cars; quality gets built, rather than inspected, in; and so on. Stress may even go down.

The notion of adding value is a powerful one. In the context of entrepreneuring in established companies, it may be one of the most important levers that managers have to *tap directly into the psychology of the times*. Without exception, the acknowledged, leading companies of the mid-80s have an identifiable, distinctive competence of one sort or another. The older ones have had it for years. (See, for example, Reading IV in the Appendix, the Marks and Spencer case.) The younger ones are fighting to keep it. Having a distinctive competence is another way of saying, have a discrete, and hopefully unique, value added.

Cliff Morton, a Boise Cascade vice president, defines adding value as "providing services, functions, or facilities that distinguish you from competitors, at a competitive price." This definition carries with it some weighty implications about efficiency. It also focuses on providing something to the customer. Finally, it implies a state of mind that shouts: "Hey world, we've got something special here!"—whether it's delivery, ease of order entry, broader selection, or gee-whiz performance. Getting the established company to that state of mind is the central concern of this chapter.

As a practical matter, a state of mind favorable to the notion of adding value can be cultivated by managers along three dimensions: By having an *explicit mission;* by promoting *quality* in all matters; and by making *technology* in appropriate forms a part of everyone's repertoire. When the membership of a company can articulate a mission that seems worthwhile and maybe even important in the served world, meaning is added to the work to be done. Entrepreneurial companies *do* have a noticeable missionary zeal about them. When quality is the open sesame in an enterprise, pride becomes its own reward. Everyone can add quality; everyone can identify with good, better, BEST! from their own life experience. And when an enterprise makes a continuing effort to upgrade its members in a technological sense to the state of the art (in pursuit of the mission), *the enterprise is adding tangible value to its people*. All benefit. Many people understand this. Some will appreciate it; an important few will reciprocate and lead the way toward adding value in the enterprise. As John Gardner said: "If we are to renew, it's because we have a vision of something worth saving or worth doing."

Mission

Statements of mission, purpose, and more recently, superordinate goals, have been advocated for many years. Traditionally, when they have been used, they have been slanted towards answering "what business are we in?" kinds of questions—e.g., transportation vs. railroading. Statements about what it is the enterprise will specially do for those buying are rare. One reason is that they are difficult to write. And the difficulty is on the rise.

Visualize, for example, the challenge a big bank like the Bank of America would have—or will have—in creating a meaningful mission statement as the management, using the traditional tool kit of practices, "reorganizes," "consolidates," "streamlines," and "tightens" in order to get into a more competitive position.[3] The troubles being experienced by one of the country's major banks are not at all trivial: big surprises ($95 million escrow agent loss); large margin pressures; industry turmoil; powerful new competitors; and so on. But the message of this chapter is that unleashing the latent innovative talent buried in the membership of the bank requires more than survival pressure which, at best, is useful for only a limited time. If such pressure is the solitary driving force, some of the best people are going to depart for better opportunities. The extra, and to some extent, new, ingredient needed is a sense of destiny, a calling, a believable mission that points up *why* the bank must come right at this time and place in history. One can imagine similar needs at Caterpillar, International Harvester, and other famous, established companies in which the heartbeat of success has grown faint.

Can companies get along without lofty statements of intention? Yes: most have, many can, and a good number will. When—in what circumstances—does a mission take on importance? The answer is straightforward: *When future successful performance along a variety of measuring sticks is dependent upon entrepreneurial/innovative behavior from a large number of people dispersed throughout the enterprise, then the presence of an indigenous mission becomes important.* It opens up the possibility of individuals responding in unity to singular challenges in the absence of written policies or experienced managers, neither of which are going to be available for all events (*singular* challenges). When the members buy in on the mission of an enterprise, it becomes the magnetic north of behavior. And the backside of the metaphor is that a company without a magnetic north may find itself adrift in the stormy times.

Bradford and Cohen in *Managing for Excellence* suggest some characteristics of a sound mission or goal. It should:

Reflect the core purpose of the unit
Be feasible
Be challenging
Have larger significance[4]

The last point has special value to managers intent on creating a climate for entrepreneuring. Bradford and Cohen go on to discuss how the presence of mission can "alter the nature of the relationships" between managers and their subordinates and can serve as a "vehicle of change." Anyone familiar with traditional entrepreneurial companies would have to support their observation: it is not unusual for people on a mission in smaller companies to perform exceptionally well *in spite of the management*, not because of it.

An acknowledged mission can be the starting point for justifying the mental commitment required to add value.

Quality

The second dimension for cultivation by aggressive managers is quality. Quality has risen on the horizon as a competitive necessity. Today, for many manufacturing companies, quality is the *only* unique value added. Successful product differentiation via features has become too tough. The auto companies, in particular, learned their lesson the hard way when the Japanese manufacturers took great bites of market share with a simple formula: make and sell a higher quality car. The cars were not faster, prettier, bigger, or, in many cases, more fuel efficient. They simply ran better, longer. Now quality is oozing out beyond cars and TV sets into all facets of business activity. Adding value via quality may become a national way of life. The driving forces behind the rise of quality consciousness are several.

First, there seems to be a psychological force at work. "Nothing corrodes the work ethic more than the perception that employers and managers are indifferent to quality."[5] The study goes on to say that a strict, "even harsh," emphasis on quality reinforces the conviction that the work has intrinsic *worth* and *meaning*. This is strong medicine. Work ethic and quality are relatives.

Second, quality can be counted. Over the past 10 years, the direct cost of low quality is something the controllers of the world have now figured out. In many corners of the business world, it turns out to be a big number. In fact, it is often less expensive to build quality in than to make repairs later in the field. For many, this is news. And customers, the ultimate users, are on the flip-side of the same cost coin. In America, many things are actually thrown away because it is cheaper to buy a new one than get the old one fixed. It is easy to understand why buying trends favor the company that provides products that run better, longer. Americans vote with their checkbooks.

Third, education, communications, and affluence are resulting in a steady upgrading of tastes. People want higher quality because they know it is available and others are getting it. *People do not want the hassle that often accompanies low quality*. The demand for good goods is bound to escalate. And an individual oriented toward having quality goods and services in private life can only respond warmly to working in a quality-oriented atmosphere.

Setting and actually maintaining high standards of quality in the established company involves a great deal more than wishful thinking, of course. Managers must be willing to lead and, for example, to sacrifice to make the idea stick. When the membership sees a complete shipment actually scrapped or a line actually shut down or an inferior report rejected out of hand, it becomes easier for individual members to become serious about the matter of quality.

There is a fourth and final point to consider about quality. A bone-deep concern about quality may be a product of evolution. As such, perceptive managers have no choice but to get on board in an advocacy role. Over the years many authors have analyzed and labeled the elements they see in the changing times. There is a common theme running through much of the work. It is not unusual at all to find psychological history divided into three epochs (waves, societies, value-eras). The common theme is that individually and collectively people are driven by needs for . . .

Physiological Survival. Then . . .
Material Success. And then . . .
Self-Expression.

Now what drives people in a given corporate setting in the mid-1980s depends upon a lot of factors including the country, the industry, characteristics of the job to be done, and so on. But what is important for the purposes of this chapter is that the evidence in survey after survey indicates a *continuing march towards self-expression*. And when that march is impeded by aging management practices, conflict is inevitable. Qualify-of-life issues are here to stay for they are at the heart of self-expression—or self-fulfillment as it is often called. When quality of life is respected, it can become a potent force for molding behavioral change in the established company.

What is extraordinary about the search for self-fulfillment in America is that it is not confined to a few bold spirits or a privileged class. Cross-sectional studies of Americans show unmistakably that the search for self-fulfillment is instead an outpouring of popular sentiment and experimentation, an authentic grass-roots phenomenon involving, in one way or another, perhaps as many as 80 percent of all adult Americans.[6]

Quality of life and self-fulfillment are intertwined. Quality of life on the job flows from what you do there. Quality comes, in part, from adding value.

Technology

Today, the assembly line is still synonymous with American business in many minds. An assembly line mind-set permeates many industries, even health care and financial services which are a long way from manufacturing. The fundamental law of the assembly line was and is that the discretion of individual workers be absolutely minimized. The human factor was designed out to the extent possible. Robots, of course, represent the ultimate in assemblyline staffing. The price in human terms for assemblyline industrialization has been high; the benefits have also been high. Henry Ford's low-priced car put the country on wheels and the standard of living in gear. Eighty years later, the tide is turning. *Technology is giving those who work increased discretion on the job.* The Aspen Institute study covering six countries referenced earlier says, ". . . we find that there is an increased number of jobs involving greater freedom to plan and to execute job-related tasks. This conclusion is clearly indicated by our findings on the impact of technology. Most of those who have experienced technological changes say that it has made their work more interesting, rather than downgrading and deskilling their work."[7] The report goes on to say that the high levels of discretion on the job does not mean that the legacy of

Taylorism (scientific management) is gone but that "the trend is moving in the other direction."[8]

What does this mean to business leaders adamant about adding value? It means that given an overarching mission and a bone-deep commitment to quality, *technology is the means* for facilitating a value-adding disposition in the enterprise. As mentioned earlier, until recent times, technology favored large-scale operations, centralization, and standardization. The efficiencies gained outweighed the problems created including alienation, low personal productivity, and so forth. But the new technology, particularly in the form of accessible computers, favors smaller-scale operations and autonomy—values entirely consistent with the trends in individual preferences as outlined above. So technology can be the can opener for the human spirit! But it needs to be applied proactively. Traditional human resource development (HRD) methods may require reorchestration to bring them up to speed, to let the membership taste what is happening. Most HRD today is designed to perpetuate the past.

One of the real strengths of an established company can be its capacity for upgrading people. Too often, however, the HRD people are the least informed in the organization on technology matters. That increases the demand for the "manager-as-developer" as called for in *Managing for Excellence* where the need for a post-heroic leader is developed by the authors.[9] But if the role of technological upgrader is going to be adequately discharged by the operating manager, he or she must be comfortable with the subjects. This need bubbles organizationally upward and illuminates, once again, the importance of fresh thinking on all facets of corporate existence—sizing, systems, and technology. For years, participation has been "something the top orders the middle to do for the bottom."[10] It is important, critical even, that technology not be something the top orders the middle to do for itself and others.

CONCLUSION

American business has been on the defensive for too long now and it is time to face up to the question of legitimacy hurled at it from many quarters starting in the 1960s. The answer is coming in many shades, but it boils down to the production of very tangible products like jobs and, of course, goods and services that are competitive. To be competitive in the world marketplace requires managing practices that tap deeper into, rather than screen out, the human factor in corporate life. Innovations come only from people. And it is clear that many established companies do need to innovate in serious ways to survive, let alone prosper. Adding value is a concept that business can use on the offensive. When any entity adds value in the society of which it is a part, there is no question of legitimacy. Further, the concept of adding value in one's vocation can be a compelling one for individual members of the workforce in this period when there exists a widespread quest for meaning, expression, and fulfillment. Business management can amplify the importance of adding value with explicit statements of mission to raise sights; a demonstrable commitment to quality in all things; and actions that fearlessly feed technology to the enterprise as a whole. Consciously adding discernible value is a business imperative.

Chapter Fourteen

Managing with Surprises

The first law of management: no surprises.

The unwritten, first law of management has been around a long time. That is why it can be unwritten. It is embedded in the mind.

Planning, whatever the range, has always been a management art form aimed at minimizing surprises. There is hardly anything more comforting than a solid budget and/or plan for the year or so ahead. It makes everything so, well, predictable. And predictability is the antithesis of surprise. So planning continues to be a favored activity. One problem in most established companies is that as environmental turbulence increases, the actual validity of plans made decreases. In fact, the very presence of adopted plans may indeed create a false sense of security. Then, when the unpredictable, unexpected actually happens, it precipitates a crisis rather than a smooth response.

A related problem in many larger companies is "complexity creep." Inexorably, the intersections of products, services, markets, technologies, social change, and competitors become more numerous and more enigmatic. Complexity, too, confounds the efficacy of planning. First, it increases the difficulty and, therefore, the cost of identifying and mapping the inputs for the planning process. Second, it increases the likelihood of "multifront wars," i.e., of having to respond smartly in several places at once with limited resources. And third, complexity mates with itself and breeds more complexity—a geometric progression. If the truth were known, one of the reasons so many strategic plans have died "drawer deaths" is that they were too intricate for practical execution by ordinary mortals, however dedicated and innovative.

A variety of updated planning practices are already in the mill in progressive companies with managements determined to land on their feet as 1990 rolls around. Experimentation is the order of the day. In Chapter Four, the drift of formal planning practices was plotted as being toward deep member participation in the organization, toward more focus on responsiveness, and toward a longer view. In this chapter, managing with surprises, it is timely to review a broader alternative open to managers and executives. *An organized planning process will continue to be a necessary and high order managing practice*. The larger question is just what all it should include given the challenges of technology, social change, and competitors. Planning can and will be used to try to increase predictability and, thereby, reduce surprises. Proper planning will confront turbulence and complexity head on. But, business leaders can also try to *reduce the turbulence* by altering the routing of the enterprise. It can opt to intentionally *reduce the complexity* of the enterprise. It can decide to manage in a more direct, hands-on manner by *walking around* and, thereby, lessen its dependence on formal systems—planning and otherwise—altogether. And finally, business leaders can institute some form of *surprise planning* as the modus operandi for the organization. These four possibilities are examined in the balance of this chapter.

TURBULENCE

In a fairly typical statement these days, Donald Brooks, the new president and CEO of troubled Fairchild Camera and Instrument Corporation, said on his second day as CEO, "My job is to bring focus to Fairchild." Focus is a new best seller on the buzzword hit parade. Brooks went on to say that the company would shed several product lines in order to concentrate "where there is less competition."[1] In short, Brooks wants to move the once high-flying semiconductor company to a new, hopefully less bumpy altitude after unsuccessful forays into computers, watches, and video games. He wants to reduce the turbulence. He, of course, is not alone. Many executives are consciously trying to "change the game" for their companies. There are at least four major avenues of exploration toward this end.

One way to reduce the turbulence is to alter, over time, the primary basis upon which the enterprise competes. The most obvious illustration of this point would be to shift from competing via R&D and the resulting new products to competing on the basis of delivery, service, or price. This would require a metamorphosis to a new mode of operation. The enterprise would become a technology follower rather than a technology leader. Of course, this is no small task for an established company. It certainly would not be in vogue with all the brouhaha surrounding technology these days. But it might be smart. There is hardly anything more turbulent than technology. It is expensive;

results from R&D are always uncertain; surprises can come from many outside sources; life cycles tend to be short so returns are problematical; and so on. So turbulence and technology go hand in hand. Reduce technology *dependence,* reduce turbulence. It may be worth considering.

There are other possibilities, potentially smoother altitudes. Competing aggressively in international markets is probably second in turbulence only to depending on technology for a competitive edge. Here the environmental uncontrollables reach their peak. Distance, cultural differences, and other factors reduce the predictability of business done away from home base. Take the matter of time as one small example. *Psychology Today* carried a cover story on how time perspectives govern lives.[2] One article in the issue on the subject reported, "Brazilians said they would wait 23 minutes before considering someone late. North Americans drew the line at 19 minutes." And in the same vein, Brazilians allow an average of 54 minutes before they consider someone early; Americans draw the line at 24. In another part of the same article on time perception, the following table was presented. The number-one ranking indicates the most accurate or the fastest; six is the least accurate or slowest.

The Pace of Life In Six Countries

	Accuracy of Bank Clocks	Walking Speed	Post Office Speed*
Japan	1	1	1
United States	2	3	2
England	4	2	3
Italy	5	4	6
Taiwan	3	5	4
Indonesia	6	6	5

*Average time for postal clerk to sell one stamp.

The point is, of course, that there are significant differences between countries. If business people wish to avoid the turbulence that comes from misreading issues that involve time perceptions, they need to understand the cultural biases—their own and others. There is a price to be paid to obtain such understanding. Part of the price is a broader band of matters for management to address in the course of conducting the business of the enterprise. Like going for technology, going international is in fashion— both for good, proper, rational reasons. But international may not be the best ticket for each and every established company in the country. In this author's travels, managements in every foreign country visited, east, west, and south, are eyeballing the U.S. market. They see plenty of opportunity here. Perhaps U.S. managements are suffering unduly from a turbulence-inducing, "grass is greener" syndrome. The question is at least worth visiting—perhaps prior to the traditional market attractiveness issues addressed in the regular planning process.

There are other valid ways to try to mitigate the surprise factor prior to planning. *Forming useful alliances is on the increase.* They are often labeled "strategic marriages" in that they do usually facilitate access to important resources, markets, distribution channels, or something. Some of the hidden (unnecessarily) rationale for the deals is often, however, the fact that they subtract a sector of uncertainty from the management horizon. In some sense, turbulence reduction needs to be brought out of the closet and into the executive suite and boardroom as a proper and timely management issue. Smart pilots bypass weather fronts if they can.

H. Igor Ansoff does a creative job of diagnosing environmental turbulence in terms of three characteristics:

Familiarity of events:
1.0 Familiar
| Events are extrapolations of experience

| They are discontinuous but related to experience
5.0 They are discontinuous and novel, i.e., brand new

Rapidity of change:
1.0 Events occur slower than firms' responses to them
| Firms' response is comparable to pace of events
5.0 Events outrun firms' capability to respond

Visibility of future:
1.0 Events are recurring
2.0 Events are forecastable
3.0 Predictable threats and opportunities
4.0 Partially predictable
5.0 Unpredictable[3]

Ansoff surveyed senior managers (more than 1,000) around the world in terms of their expectations about turbulence using the 1.0 to 5.0 scales suggested above. He found ". . . surprising agreement among managers of developed countries that the turbulence of the 1980s will be on the level from 3.5 to 4.5," Ansoff concludes ". . . this means frequent discontinuities, changes which will be faster than the firm's response, events will be only partially predictable before they impact on the firm."[4]

President Harry Truman once said something to the effect that in the political arena, "If you can't stand the heat, stay out of the kitchen." Perhaps the analogue in the management arena is if turbulence is a headache, stay out of the stormy weather. Move over, up, down, or around to a heading where you have favorable winds . . . even if you have to pick out a new destination.

COMPLEXITY

Traditional entrepreneurial companies, i.e., startups, are almost by definition, simple. They sell *a* product or service to *a* market niche of some kind. With success, more products will be found to be sold to the same customer base—a *product development* approach to building the business. At some point, new niches will be found in which to sell the existing product line(s) and the company will add a *market development* angle to building the business. Up to this point, the internal complexity of the once-simple business is increasing along reasonably predictable lines. (The external turbulence may also be increasing, depending on the markets served and products sold.) Size, too, adds to complexity; both the total number of employees and the rate at which they are added are contributing factors. Hierarchies of managing practices for dealing with this kind of linear complexity were covered in Chapters Two through Five.

Finally, as certainly as the sunrise, at some point on the standard success curve most companies diversify: management makes decisions that carry it into product/market combinations where it has a very shallow, if any, experience base. When this happens, the probability of surprises goes way up. Effective planning can, of course, make a dent in the problem. But the idea of consciously *controlling complexity as an end in itself* will be one meriting attention as the 1980s roll on. Innovation and entrepreneurial behavior become increasingly difficult to muster in critical masses when the leadership energy of an enterprise is diluted with too many kinds of challenges.

A few years ago (1982) this author wrote a book entitled, *Entrepreneuring, The Ten Commandments for Building a Growth Company*. The third commandment reads:

Concentrate all available resources on accomplishing two or three specific, operational objectives within a given time period.

Enterprises have finite resources. A smaller company achieves competitive advantage when playing for limited, explicit gains in a marketplace of its own choosing. Specialization breeds an organization sensitive to opportunities and quick to act. But any advantage withers if follow-through is weak. It will be weak if resources are dissipated. Resource dilution is a sure formula for mediocrity, a state of being that aspiring growth businesses cannot afford.[5]

The principles suggested above would seem to be equally applicable to established companies. (Note: All ten commandments are included in the Appendix as Reading Five. The reader is invited to explore them for other notions applicable to his or her established business.)

In summary to this point, complexity increases the probability of surprises.

There are four obvious ways to decrease complexity. One is to reduce the number of services, products, or product lines being sold. Another is to consciously reduce the number of discrete markets served. A third is to shrink the size of the enterprise. For example, there seems to be some movement toward more subcontracting and alliance building across the nation. A very successful Texas CEO put it succinctly: "I don't invest in parking lots anymore." And a fourth possibility is to de-diversify. "Sticking to your knitting" may not be prudent across the board, but building a business off a solid, value-adding experience base has a nice ring to it.

There are also less obvious ways to decrease complexity in pursuit of creating more entrepreneurial companies. Business leaders can alter the *budget cycle*. There is nothing particularly magic about a fiscal year for most of the people in a company. Yet virtually every established company has an operating rhythm fitted to the auditors and

SEC requirements. If it is a force fit, it adds to the complexity of managing the business.

Business leaders can reduce the amount of *secrecy* in the business. "Confidentiality is the enemy of trust" says the author of "Of Boxes and Bubbles."[6] (See Reading Two in the Appendix.) Lack of trust begets complexity because untrusting smart people generate their own versions of truth. This action simplifies their individual lives, but multiple versions of truth afloat in a business do not simplify the managing task. Secrecy creates other problems. In the absence of a clear, complete picture of what is actually going on, members will assume that things are going either poorly or better than they really are. Given the track record of the last 10 years, there is probably some bias toward thinking things are worse than they are since a lot of business problems *have* been covered up—or at least not mentioned—in recent times. Overly insulated members were mentioned in an earlier chapter. When people in an enterprise are negative or pessimistic or cynical, intrigue, CYA (cover your ass), and NIH (not invented here) flourish. So, once again, complexity increases.

Secrecy, to some extent, is a carryover from the days when one's position in the hierarchy was defined by the totality of information one possessed. So information was hoarded at each level; it symbolized power. It was power. It still is power. But in innovative companies, there is a conscious attempt to spread power—information—around, to make it a "commodity" as Kanter calls it. This is important for positive reasons: with some power members can do things like experiment. Information is also important for eliminating the complexities bred when intelligent people work too long in the dark.

Finally, business leaders can come out in favor of *Why Not!* over *Why?* as a guiding philosophy for an intentionally, less-complex enterprise. By nature, smaller companies are gung-ho—often out of ignorance. A damn-the-torpedoes attitude prevails. *Why not!* is the password; no boundaries are acknowledged to the art of the possible. And, of course, a percentage fail. At the other extreme, however, is the stagnant, larger company where inertia regularly rolls over initiative and *Why?* is the formidable barrier to anything new: channels of distribution, packaging, computers, suppliers, procedures, forms, or whatever.

There is a tendency, as a company grows, for the management to become increasingly asset driven, rather than *opportunity driven*. Such a tendency is natural, perhaps, for as a company increases in size, a higher and higher percentage of it—careers, buildings, systems, and customers—is invested in the past. Unlike a smaller company on the move, the larger firm has a lot to lose—a big asset base. The net result is sometimes inertia. A body in motion tends to stay in motion—along the same track. "It's much easier and safer for companies to stay with the familiar than to explore the unknown. Staying with the familiar may have its dangers, however, in today's fast-changing world."[7]

What does it take to come out in favor of why not!? Lee Iacocca in his autobiography suggests a couple of tried and proven approaches. "A good manager can't wait for all the facts." Iacocca, in effect, is speaking against paralysis by analysis. The point is that 90 percent of the facts and a timely decision is better than 100 percent and a stale decision, i.e., one too late to do any good. "Despite what the textbooks say, most important decisions in corporate life are made by individuals, not by committees. My policy has always been to be democratic all the way to the point of decision. Then I become a ruthless commander."[8] Here the Chrysler CEO suggests that managers have to be willing to personally accept the responsibility for deciding. In the final analysis, *Why not!* comes back to having a perspective on what it takes to keep on winning under the new rules of the times.

In summary to this point, there are at least four obvious and three, not-so-obvious ways to try to reduce complexity and, therefore, the chances of surprises. Easing the complexity of an established company is a worthy objective for consideration.

WALKING AROUND

Another way for senior people to avoid surprises is for them to short circuit the established information flow system and go directly to the source(s). This hands-on approach to managing is very much in vogue at the moment. A recent *Wall Street Journal* article described how J. Willard Marriott, CEO of Marriott Corporation, wanders around hotel basements inspecting washed dishes; how Jim Treybig, CEO of Tandem Computers, scans listings of customer complaints; and how Dick Rodgers, president of Syntex Corporation, eats breakfast each morning in the employee cafeteria in order to stay in touch with employee concerns.[9] These examples suggest several points for thoughtful pondering. One, it may well be that the formal information systems in existence today do not—and cannot—provide all of the important information needed to successfully pilot an enterprise. More "soft" information is needed . . . because of the times. Two, senior people can behave in entrepreneurial ways—e.g., mixing with the troops—without loss of standing. And three, getting (or staying) in touch via walking around is likely to be a time-consuming activity.

Is the cost in time and opportunity loss (from other activities not done) lower than the value of the information received in terms of surprise reduction? There is no general answer to this question. American management has probably become too abstract, too hands-off, too distant and professional in many respects. This means that senior people will often get filtered information, a risky state of affairs in turbulent, complex times. It also means that the membership may well have a filtered (diluted) view of the leadership, a condition not particularly conducive to thoughtful risk-taking which often requires some reasonably high confidence level in the top brass to get it going. So the notion of walking around represents an appropriate swing of the pendulum. Properly done it provides *some* information of value to the senior leadership; properly done, it does show the colors and to some degree humanize the company, an eloquent result in this high-tech, high-touch age. What makes it "properly done"? Sincerity and consistency. Walking around should reflect a real interest in learning; walking around can't be a once-a-quarter routine.

There are, of course, some potential negatives to walking around as a primary methodology for managing with surprises. Walking around can be . . .

Hard on the middle managers. "Walking around" can mean *or be interpreted as* end-running the intermediate levels of management. This can be counterproductive. The influence of the people in the middle is emasculated. And when the person who is walking around, walks away, the entity bogs down . . . waiting, perhaps, for the next visit.

Confusing to the membership. In a sense, walking around gives individual members two or more bosses, depending on how many people are on the trail. With multiple bosses, the potential for mixed signals, good or bad, goes way up as anyone with experience in matrix structures will attest.

Transparent tokenism. As a practical matter, not everyone is cut out to mix well with the membership in the informal mode suggested by the term ''walking around.'' There are senior people who in fact do not feel a bone-deep commitment to the mission of the enterprise. Others feel it but cannot express it. Either way, the impact on the membership over time from exposure will be the same: cynicism.

So there are *potential* negatives to walking around; the act could generate more surprises than it negates. At the same time, there are some underlying principles to walking around that do need airing if an entrepreneurial renaissance is to be nourished. The principles a walker should have include . . .

Curiosity . . . about what is *really* going on?

Mental vigor . . . for taking on whatever the future holds.

Interest. . . in those who must make things happen.

Community . . . we're all in this effort together.

Results . . . we're playing to win.

A casual look at this list could result in an ''apple pie and flag'' assessment by the practicing manager, particularly one who has been in the saddle a long time or one educated to be a rational manager. For it is just such people who often operate under the assumption that what counts in business success is figuring out the right product/ market strategy, verifying the numbers, allocating the resources in a balanced fashion, and following through on the plans made in a firm but fair manner with the human resources. Strategy, numbers, and so on are important.

171

They are necessary but not sufficient . . . because in these stormy times, such factors are precisely the ones that are surpriseful. *The only practical antidote to the inevitable surprises is a company where thousands of eyes and ears are intelligently tuned to the environment, ready to respond, empowered to respond, and COMMITTED . . . to winning.*

Curiosity, vigor, interest, community, results—additional factors in the emerging formula for managing with surprises. Walking around, or creative variations on it, is one way to plant the word by example . . . a form of cheerleading.

SURPRISE PLANNING

A final way for key people to mitigate the impact of the inevitable unforeseen is to actually plan for surprises. This means that in addition to the evolving planning practices described in Chapter Four, established companies should consider the formation of broadly constituted teams to role play and formulate corporate responses to both identifiable and unknown possibilities.

What are such possibilities? Here is a round dozen to tickle the imagination.

A major accident attributable to your company results in numerous public deaths and copious publicity.

A huge, foreign company announces an unexpected and immediate entry into the market from which 86 percent of your company's profits flow.

A large union announces in a press conference that it is initiating an all-out drive for your white-collar work force.

Your largest competitor (you two battle for second place in market share) makes a big mistake and is likely to receive bad press for some months to come.

The nation's armed forces are put on Red Alert due to coordinated attacks on American embassies in three parts of the world and the downing of another civilian 747 near Japan by the Soviets.

Your top seven R&D people are killed in a hotel fire.

Radioactive wastes are detected beneath your largest production facility.

Brazil announces it will no longer make loan repayments to foreign banks and government agencies. Mexico follows suit.

Your largest customer (18 percent of sales; 23 percent of profits) advises you that it will backward integrate next year.

Your part of the country is into what is predicted to be a six months' brown-out due to an extended hot spell and a meltdown at a nuclear power plant that resulted in all such plants being closed indefinitely.

The Sierra Club and other major environmental groups announce a well-organized national boycott of all the services you sell across the country.

Your technical people report to you in hushed tones at a requested emergency meeting that they have discovered a nonpatentable way to cut your very substantial raw material cost per unit in half with zero capital investment if you move quickly in the acquisition of a medium-sized vendor located in France.

Is the imagination tickled? There are not many laughing

matters on the list above, and, of course, the standard issues like the prime rate, inflation/deflation, international exchange rates, government policies (tax reform, and so forth) and competitor moves are not shown. The point of the above is to illustrate the types of things that do not typically show up in planners' thinking, nor most executives' thinking for that matter . . . until they become realities. These are precisely the types of events for which surprise planning needs to be done, however, to facilitate managing with surprises.

How can such planning be done? First, there needs to be the philosophical base that a lot of members eventually need to be involved so "thousands of eyes and ears are intelligently tuned to the environment" as proposed earlier. Second, an ad hoc group of senior members needs to brainstorm on the classes of surprises—postive and negative—that could conceivably occur. This sort of thing is perhaps best done offsite so the imagination can run more wildly than normal. The same group should also then identify specific, ad hoc, heterogeneous teams from across the enterprise to address the different classes of possible surprises. The charters of the teams would be to better define those events that could happen and role play a range of responses the organization could make.

Third, then, the teams should meet periodically to execute their charters. Some "war-gaming" might be encouraged to elicit realistic reactions to the challenges. Finally, as a result of the process, at least some tentative approaches to the various classes of surprises might be agreed upon by the teams and the senior people in the company. More important, everyone involved will have had some drill and practice in handling bolts from the blue. Forewarned is forearmed.

Most established companies do have what-to-do plans for act-of-God emergencies. Many officer groups also have procedures in place (phone numbers to call, places to report, and so on) for responding to things like hostile takeover attempts and kidnappings. Surprise planning simply expands (1) the diameter of the circle of interests to which smart responses would be desirable, and (2) the percentage of the organization involved in formulating and, perhaps, executing the smartness. Surprise planning is a young cousin of strategic planning.

CONCLUSION

Entrepreneuring in established companies has to do with creating an organizational climate where new ideas on every aspect of the business bubble up from an informed membership. As the world turns the corner on the 20th century, the ingredients seem to be in place for an increasing flow of such ideas in places where the management practices are in tune with the times. On top of the induced changes, there is also a burst of unpredictables originating in the environment—surprises. In general, business people would prefer to avoid surprises, and rightly so. Much of planning is aimed precisely at such avoidance. But, in addition to effective planning, managers and executives can take some steps to accept and better manage with surprises. Specifically, business leaders can proactively seek to reduce the turbulence and complexity of the existing business; encourage, by example, more hands-on managing practices in the company; and experiment with ways of doing surprise planning in the days ahead.

Chapter Fifteen

TNS: The
Next Step

> When the way of reason has become a cul-de-sac, which is
> its inevitable and constant tendency, then, from the side where
> one least expects it, the solution comes.
>
> CARL G. JUNG

Here is a way to conceptualize the total task of keeping
a company flying high, regardless of the elements—the
turbulent environment.

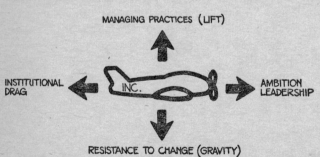

MANAGING PRACTICES (LIFT)

INSTITUTIONAL
DRAG

INC.

AMBITION
LEADERSHIP

RESISTANCE TO CHANGE (GRAVITY)

Forces at Work

Starting on the right of the figure, the corporation is pulled forward by the ambitions of individual members and the foresight and effectiveness of the leadership of the business—managers at all levels. Tugging the company downward is resistance to change, a human phenomenon as natural as gravity. Retarding the forward motion of the enterprise is institutional drag, an aggregation of frictions that consumes energy and makes maneuvering more difficult even in the best of times. And on top are managing practices designed by men and women (as are airplane wings) to provide the lift needed for sustained flight. It is the net combination of these forces at work in the operating environment that determines how high, how far, and how fast a company will fly.

The illustration lends itself to many useful questions. Do successful growth companies fly high and fast primarily because of ambition and leadership power, or because they have a small amount of institutional drag? Is the performance of some larger companies sagging today due to poor lift characteristics vis-à-vis the weight of the organization? Are the headwinds of the times revealing weaknesses in the traditional ways of overcoming resistance? The general answer, once again, that it is the net of the forces that produces a given performance level. In the final analysis, all four must be taken into account, along with the conditions.

AMBITION/LEADERSHIP

Cold war, the ongoing threat of nuclear annihilation, and daily human cruelties notwithstanding, mankind is getting better. It is evolving. The current generation is an improvement on many fronts over the generation before. "Each of us has his or her own urge to grow, and each of us, in exercising that urge, must single-handedly fight against his or her own resistance. As we evolve as individuals, so do we cause our society to evolve. The culture that nurtures us in childhood is nurtured by our leadership in adulthood. Those who achieve growth not only enjoy the fruits of growth but give the same fruits to the world. Evolving as individuals, we carry humanity on our backs. And so humanity evolves."[1] This evolution is pulled along by the "urge to grow," by ambition. Regardless of whether one feels that the root of the restlessness is sex (Freud), power (Adler), or archetypes in the collective unconscious (Jung), the end result is the same: a driveness that appropriate leadership can channel into productive behavior, entrepreneuring in the broad, adaptive sense of the word.

In this book, the reader has been asked to reconsider the tremendous power potentially available in every organization, the power available in the members. The word "members" has purposely been used without explanation beginning since Chapter Four. How does the word feel? How does it go down? Does it say something useful that employees or personnel or workers or staff do not say, given the changing times? Entrepreneurial companies tend to have a membership flavor about them—a certain clublike tone; they are still managed, of course, but, within limits, they are managed by consent. In such companies men and women have the power to use their power . . . and it becomes the motive force that moves the enterprise ahead.

RESISTANCE TO CHANGE

Like gravity, resistance is always present—at *all* organizational levels. It is mostly human nature at work rather than a malicious or even conscious effort to hamper corporate progress and competitiveness. Much of what managers are prone to label as resistance in the workplace is a reflection of a psychic law that corresponds to Newton's law of inertia. Newton's law pertains to physical bodies. It says that any body will remain in a state of motion or rest unless compelled to change from that state by an external force acting on it. E. C. Whitmont suggests that the same law applies to any entity existing in time and space *including the psyche*. He writes, "In the psyche, inertia is seen as a tendency towards habit formation and ritualization . . . essential for the sense of stability and permanence which is the basis of consciousness. . . . Every pattern of adaptation, outer and inner, is maintained in essentially the same unaltered form and anxiously defended against change until an equally strong or stronger impulse is able to displace it."[2]

In short, "psychic inertia manifests itself as resistance to change, however desirable such change may be."[3] In a business context, this means that managers are dealing with a force like gravity—in themselves as well as in their people. Airplane designers don't fight gravity, they *accept it* for what it is, *respect it,* and *find creative ways to overcome it*. The task is the same for managers as a phase shift in the world of business stirs and exposes a corre-

179

sponding amount of psychic inertia. When the inevitable, truly human resistance is taken as a personal affront by managers or seen as a failure of hiring policies, that is when the cursing begins—at the expense of creativeness. Everyone, including members of the managerial corps, has their own gravity to overcome. Everyone puts their shoes on, one at a time!

"Much of our fear is a fear of a change in the status quo, a fear that we might lose what we have if we venture forth from where we are now . . . people find new information distinctly threatening, because if they incorporate it they will have to do a good deal of work to revise their maps of reality, and they *instinctively* seek to avoid that work. Consequently, more often than not, they will fight against the new information rather than for its assimilation."[4] (Emphasis added.)

Recognizing resistance as part of the natural order of things rather than human spitefulness does not make it go away. But the recognition can help usher in a more healthy and creative climate for mitigating the obvious impediments to corporate flight, company wide.

INSTITUTIONAL DRAG

It is concern about this subject that has brought many readers to this book. Drag on a company can come from a variety of sources:

Too much weight. Many corporations are into leanness of late.

Surface friction caused by ill-fitting parts. A fair amount of top-level energy is aimed, today, at streamlining operations. *Business Week* recently featured a cover story on ''Splitting Up: The Other Side of Merger Mania,'' with numerous examples.[5]

Poor aerodynamic design, given new factors in the environment. Chapter Seven was about resizing.

Improper use of various control systems (pilot error), e.g., trying for speed and efficiency simultaneously. Decoupling systems was discussed in Chapter Nine; staffing in Chapter Eight.

And so on. Unlike resistance to change, institutional drag is made by people. That being the case, it can be unmade. Drag tends to be a function of size and complexity and lack of attention. The attention seems to be forthcoming, of necessity. As institutional drag is consciously reduced, there will be more time and energy for those still aboard to work out new ways to do things, to be the entrepreneurs. Extracting and guiding the use of that time and energy *with* the members of the crew is what managing practices, the fourth force, is all about.

MANAGING PRACTICES

Like institutional drag, managing practices also come from people. And it has been the message of this book that many practices in wide use today are obsolete. They no longer provide the necessary lift to keep the nation's established companies competitively airborne, given the turbulent conditions. The practices of planning, organizing, leading, and controlling need to be redesigned, updated, freshened. Ten guidelines to doing just that have been recommended for the reader's consideration and use:

1. Shrink the number of organizational levels.
2. Nurture guerrilla profit centers, porous departments.
3. Decouple systems from the structure.
4. Replace dividing up with resource sharing.
5. Press planning deep into the organization.
6. Focus on responsiveness.
7. Take a longer view, too.
8. Share information.
9. Allow for more specials.
10. Augment controllers with catalysts.

Most established companies remain exciting networks of *potential* opportunity with which a charged-up membership can excel against international competitive forces on the flight into the 21st century. A key force is a set of management practices that provides the necessary lift to the enterprise. For managers, The Next Step is to take a step, a bold one.

Notes

CHAPTER ONE

1. Edward C. Bursk, Donald T. Clark, and Ralph W. Hidy, *The World of Business* (New York: Simon and Schuster, 1962), p. 51. Copyright © 1962 by Simon & Schuster.
2. Peter F. Drucker, *Managing in Turbulent Times* (London; Pan Books, 1980), p. 5l. Copyright © 1980 by Peter F. Drucker.
3. Carl Sandburg, "Chicago" in *Chicago Poems* (New York: Holt, Rinehart & Winston, 1916), pp. 3–4.
4. Theodore Levitt, "Marketing Myopia," *Harvard Business Review* 38 (July–August 1960), p. 45. Copyright © 1960 by the President and Fellows of Harvard College.
5. Aspen Institute, *Work and Human Values: An International Report on Jobs in the 1980s and 1990s* (New York: Aspen Institute for Humanistic Studies, 1983), pp. 9–58. Copyright © 1983 Aspen Institute for Humanistic Studies.

6. Saying attributed to John Wooden, retired UCLA basketball coach.

CHAPTER TWO

1. Mutation as defined in *Webster's Unabridged Dictionary*.
2. Michael Porter, *Competitive Strategy* (New York: The Free Press, 1980), p. 4. Copyright © 1980 by The Free Press.
3. Steven C. Brandt, *Strategic Planning in Emerging Companies* (Reading, Mass.: Addison-Wesley Publishing, 1981), p. 53. Copyright © 1981 by Steven C. Brandt.
4. H. Igor Ansoff, *Implanting Strategic Management* (Englewood Cliffs, N.J.: Prentice-Hall, 1984), p. 377. Copyright © 1984 by H. Igor Ansoff.
5. Donald E. Peterson as quoted in "Top-Down Managing Won't Work Anymore," *USA Today*, February 5, 1985, p. 2.
6. Daniel Yankelovich, *New Rules: Searching for Self-Fulfillment in a World Turned Upside Down* (New York: Random House, 1981), p. 262. Copyright © 1981 by Daniel Yankelovich.
7. Edward Gibbon, *Decline and Fall of the Roman Empire.*

CHAPTER THREE

1. Daniel Yankelovich, *New Rules: Searching for Self-Fulfillment in a World Turned Upside Down* (New York: Random House, 1981), p. 146. Copyright © 1981 by Daniel Yankelovich.
2. Aspen Institute, *Work and Human Values: An International Report on Jobs in the 1980s and 1990s* (New

York: Aspen Institute for Humanistic Studies, 1983), p. 43–44.

3. H. Igor Ansoff, *Implanting Strategic Management* (Englewood Cliffs, N.J.: Prentice-Hall, 1984), p. 108. Copyright © 1984 by H. Igor Ansoff.

4. Alvin Toffler, *The Third Wave* (New York: William Morrow, 1980), p. 263. Copyright © 1980 by Alvin Toffler.

CHAPTER FOUR

1. David K. Hurst, "Of Boxes, Bubbles, and Effective Management," *Harvard Business Review* 62 (May–June 1984), p. 78. Copyright © 1984 by the President and Fellows of Harvard College.

2. H. Igor Ansoff, *Implanting Strategic Management* (Englewood Cliffs, N.J.: Prentice-Hall, 1984), p. 24. Copyright © 1984 by H. Igor Ansoff.

3. "The Brain Drain: U.S. Basic Industries Are Hindered by Loss of Scientific Talent," *The Wall Street Journal*, July 27, 1984, p. 1.

4. "Allied Unit, Free of Red tape, Seeks to Develop Orphan Technologies," *The Wall Street Journal*, September 13, 1984, p. 29.

CHAPTER FIVE

1. Henri Fayol, *General and Industrial Management* (London and Dunod, Paris: Sir Issac Pitman & Sons, 1916). Published in *The World of Business* (New York: Simon & Schuster, 1962), pp. 1685–1704. The fourteen partial quotes are from a 1949 translation by Constance Storrs.

CHAPTER SIX

1. Daniel Yankelovich, *New Rules: Searching for Self-Fulfillment in a World Turned Upside Down* (New York: Random House, 1981), p. 3. Copyright © 1981 by Daniel Yankelovich.
2. Michael Rodgers, "Boom or Bust on the New Frontier," *Science Digest*, March 1985, p. 33.
3. Karl H. Vesper, *Entrepreneurship and National Policy* (Chicago: Heller Institute for Small Business, 1983), p. 21.
4. *Inc.*, March, 1985.
5. Kenneth Blanchard and Spencer Johnson, *One Minute Manager* (New York: Berkley Books, 1983), p. 67. Copyright © 1982 by Blanchard Family Partnership and Candle Communications Corporation.
6. Douglas McGregor, *The Human Side of Enterprise* (New York: McGraw-Hill, 1960), pp. 33–48.
7. "Baby Boomers," *Business Week*, July 2, 1984, p. 68.
8. Blanchard and Johnson, *One Minute Manager*, p. 98.

CHAPTER SEVEN

1. "The New Corporate Elite," *Business Week*, January 21, 1985, p. 62.
2. Robert Hayes and William J. Abernathy, "Managing Our Way to Economic Decline," *Harvard Business Review* 51 (July–August 1980), p. 67. Copyright © 1980 by the President and Fellows of Harvard College.
3. "Fran Tarkenton, Corporate Quarterback," *Fortune*, January 21, 1985, p. 118.

CHAPTER EIGHT

1. Richard Pascale, "The Paradox of Corporate Culture: Reconciling Ourselves to Socialization," Research Paper No. 738, Stanford Graduate School of Business, April 1984, p. 18.
2. Harold S. Geneen, *Managing* (New York: Doubleday, 1984), Chapter 11. Copyright © 1984 by Harold S. Geneen and Alvin Moscow, as published in *Venture*, January 1985, p. 46.
3. Arch Patton, "Industry's Misguided Shift to Staff Jobs," *Business Week*, April 5, 1983, p. 12.
4. Edward A. Feigenbaum and Pamela McCorduck, *The Fifth Generation* (Reading, Mass.: Addison-Wesley, 1983), p. 193. Copyright © 1983 by Edward A. Feigenbaum and Pamela McCorduck.

CHAPTER NINE

1. "Union Buster Shows How Companies Can Do It," *San Francisco Chronicle*, March 22, 1985, p. 38.
2. Harold S. Geneen, *Managing* (New York: Doubleday, 1984), Chapter 11. Copyright © 1984 by Harold S. Geneen and Alvin Moscow, as published in *Venture*, January 1985, p. 46.

CHAPTER TEN

1. Aspen Institute, *Work and Human Values: An International Report on Jobs in the 1980s and 1990s* (New York: Aspen Institute for Humanistic Studies, 1983), p. 6.

2. I. C. MacMillan and Robin George, "Corporate Venturing: Challenges for Senior Managers," *The Journal of Business Strategy* 5 (Winter 1985), p. 34.

CHAPTER ELEVEN

1. Thomas J. Peters and Robert H. Waterman, Jr., *In Search of Excellence* (New York: Harper & Row, 1982), p. 285. Copyright © 1982 by Thomas J. Peters and Robert H. Waterman, Jr.
2. Aspen Institute, *Work and Human Values: An International Report on Jobs in the 1980s and 1990s* (New York: Aspen Institute for Humanistic Studies, 1983), p. 89.
3. Thomas J. Peters and Nancy Austin, *A Passion for Excellence* (New York: Random House, 1985), p. 6. Copyright © 1985 by Thomas J. Peters and Nancy Austin.

CHAPTER TWELVE

1. "The New Corporate Elite," *Business Week*, January 21, 1985, p. 62.
2. Ibid.
3. Jeffrey Pfeffer, "Making Sense with Symbolism," *Stanford GSB*, Winter 1981–82, p. 82.
4. Examples are primarily from various stories published in *The Wall Street Journal* in 1984–85.

CHAPTER THIRTEEN

1. Wallace B. Clift, *Jung and Christianity* (New York: Crossroad, 1983), p. *ix*. Copyright © 1982 by Wallace B. Clift.

2. Viktor E. Frankl, *Man's Search for Meaning* (New York: Simon & Schuster, 1984), p. 9. Copyright © 1984 by Viktor Frankl.

3. Statement in news story on Bank of America published in *San Francisco Chronicle*, February 27, 1985.

4. David L. Bradford and Allan R. Cohen, *Managing for Excellence* (New York: John Wiley & Sons, 1984), p. 108. Copyright © 1984 by John Wiley & Sons.

5. Aspen Institute, *Work and Human Values: An International Report on Jobs in the 1980s and 1990s* (New York: Aspen Institute for Humanistic Studies, 1983), p. 85.

6. Daniel Yankelovich, *New Rules: Searching for Self-Fulfillment in a World Turned Upside Down* (New York: Random House, 1981), p. 3. Copyright © 1981 by Daniel Yankelovich.

7. Aspen Institute, *Work and Human Values*, p. 43.

8. Ibid., p. 44.

9. Bradford and Cohen, *Managing for Excellence*, p. 60.

10. Rosabeth Moss Kanter, *The Change Masters* (New York: Simon & Schuster, 1983), p. 244. Copyright © 1983 by Rosabeth Moss Kanter.

CHAPTER FOURTEEN

1. Interview published in the *San Francisco Chronicle*, January 4, 1985, p. 31.

2. Robert Levine, "Social Time: The Heartbeat of Culture," *Psychology Today*, March 1985, p. 35.

3. H. Igor Ansoff, *Implanting Strategic Management* (Englewood Cliffs, N.J.: Prentice-Hall, 1984), p. 12. Copyright © 1984 by H. Igor Ansoff.

4. Ibid., p. 13.

5. Steven C. Brandt, *Entrepreneuring* (Reading, Mass.: Addison-Wesley, 1982), p. 14. Copyright © 1982 by Steven C. Brandt.

6. David K. Hurst, "Of Boxes, Bubbles, and Effective Management," *Harvard Business Review* 62 (May–June 1984), p. 80. Copyright © 1984 by the President and Fellows of Harvard College.

7. Howard A. Stevenson and David E. Gumpert, "The Heart of Entrepreneurship," *Harvard Business Review* 63 (March–April 1985), p. 85.

8. Lee Iacocca, *Iacocca: An Autobiography* (New York: Bantam Books, 1984), various pages as excerpted in United Airlines inflight magazine, December, 1984.

9. News story published in *The Wall Street Journal*, February 27, 1985, p. 1.

CHAPTER FIFTEEN

1. M. Scott Peck, *The Road Less Traveled* (New York: Simon & Schuster, 1978), pp. 266–67. Copyright © 1978 by M. Scott Peck, M.D.

2. E. C. Whitmont, *The Symbolic Quest* (London: Barrie & Rockliff, 1969), p. 123 as quoted in reference 3 below on p. 147.

3. Anthony Stevens, *Archetypes: A Natural History of the Self* (New York: Quill, 1983), p. 147. Copyright © 1982 by Anthony Stevens.

4. Peck, *The Road Less Traveled*, p. 274.

5. "Splitting Up: The Other Side of Merger Mania," *Business Week*, July 1, 1985, p. 50.

Appendix

Readings

One

The New Breed of Strategic Planner
Number-Crunching Professionals Are Giving Way to Line Managers

After more than a decade of near-dictatorial sway over the future of U.S. corporations, the reign of the strategic planner may be at an end. In a fundamental shift of corporate power, line managers in one company after another are successfully challenging the hordes of professional planners and are forcing them from positions of influence.

Two examples out of many make the point: At Sonat Inc., planners from headquarters were accustomed to write a blueprint for each subsidiary and "present" it to the management of the operating unit. Now members of a greatly reduced planning staff report directly to the operating units—not to corporate headquarters. And what they do is considered a "support" function. "We've gone 180 degrees," says Ronald L. Kuehn, Jr., chief executive officer of the Birmingham-based energy company.

Reprinted from the September 17, 1984 issue of *Business Week* by special permission, © 1984 by McGraw-Hill, Inc.

At General Motors Corp., the change is even more striking. Chairman Roger B. Smith is known throughout GM as the man who introduced strategic planning to the company in 1971. But he is also known as the man who, after three "unsuccessful tries" at establishing a strategic planning system at headquarters, decentralized the process and decreed that operating-division managers, not planners, should carry the ball. Now, says Michael E. Naylor, GM's general director of corporate strategic planning, "planning is the responsibility of every line manager. The role of the planner is to be a catalyst for change—not to do the planning for each business unit."

Key Formula

Perhaps the most telling sign of change is at the famed Boston Consulting Group, which is widely considered the parent of strategic planning. Even BCG is abandoning some of the planners' buzzwords in favor of a new emphasis on "implementation."

The revolution against the planners is especially impressive considering the enormous impact that the strategic-planning discipline made on business operations in the late 1960s. Planning offered—for the first time—a systematic means of analyzing the economic and competitive prospects for corporate operations and charting a long-term course of action. Among the leading theorists was BCG, which developed a couple of key formulas that helped plot strategies for gaining market share and for determining how to deploy assets.

Another important force was General Electric Co., which, along with consultant McKinsey & Co., added other seminal concepts. These enabled diversified companies to focus more intensely on the market outlooks and competitive factors for each of their operations.

From these ideas emerged a profession of strategic planners that, by the mid-1970s, emerged as a separate function. Its practitioners became dominant figures in their companies. But as their power grew, the influence of operating managers waned, and hostility between the two escalated. The result: Few of the supposedly brilliant strategies concocted by planners were successfully implemented. Says GM Chairman Smith: "We got these great plans together, put them on the shelf, and marched off to do what we would be doing anyway. It took us a little while to realize that wasn't getting us anywhere."

The disenchantment runs deep. In a refrain that is echoed in dozens of companies, Roger W. Schipke, the senior vice-president in charge of General Electric's Major Appliance Business Group, talks of "gaining ownership of the business, grabbing hold of it" from "an isolated bureaucracy" of planners.

Depicting the upheaval as a bloody battle between planners and managers may sound extreme. But judging from the way line managers tell their stories, it has been nothing less. There have been plenty of casualties, too. In a bid to return strategic planning to its original intent—forcing managers to take "a massive, massive look outside ourselves"— GE Chairman John F. Welch Jr. has slashed the corporate planning group from 58 to 33, and scores of planners have been purged in GE's operating sectors, groups, and divisions.

Planocrats

Cleveland-based Eaton Corp. finally reacted to a rebellion of operations people against planners by cutting its staff of corporate "planocrats" from 35 to 16. And in the wake of cutbacks at U.S. Steel Corp., Rockwell International Corp., and many other companies, the two trade associations for planners—the Planning Executives Institute and the North American Society for Corporate Planning—are negotiating a merger.

If operating managers display new confidence in challenging the mystique of strategic planning, one reason may be that they themselves are thoroughly at home with the concepts by this time—educated by the business schools and tutored by the consultants. And—despite all the drawbacks—they have had to participate in "the process" or "the ritual" of putting together what was supposedly their business' strategic plan, but in too many instances was only the planner's plan.

The CEOs of the generation now coming to power feel they are the "strategic thinkers"—and believe that their key operating lieutenants should be as well. "Those who succeed in thinking strategically and executing strategically are the people who are going to move ahead at this company," says Hicks B. Waldron, chairman of Avon Products Inc. The same is true at Norton Co., the Worcester (Mass.) abrasives maker. Says CEO Donald R. Melville: "You can't get ahead just thinking in terms of operations. You won't become a top manager unless you think strategically."

Strategic planning's fall has another explanation as well. Managers not only know how the magic trick works; they question whether the magic is there at all. To put it bluntly, it has become obvious that very few strategies seem to succeed. Indeed, a reassessment of 33 strategies described in BUSINESS WEEK in 1979 and 1980 found that 19 failed, ran into trouble, or were abandoned, while only 14 could be deemed successful (see Exhibit 1).

The companies in the survey were drawn from a random sample of hundreds of stories on corporate strategies that appeared in the magazine in those years. These reviews are snapshots of how the strategies are currently faring, not reports on their ultimate outcome. But even taken as a rough measure, the survey's findings are not good news.

Exhibit 1
A Sampling of Strategic Planning's Track Record

Companies were selected from those whose strategies were described by BUSINESS WEEK in 1979 and 1980 and reassessed since by BUSINESS WEEK.

PLANS THAT DIDN'T WORK . . .

Company	Strategy	BW Assessment
Adolph Coors	Regain lost market share and become a national force in the beer industry	Largely unsuccessful because of weak marketing clout
American Natural Resources	Offset sagging natural gas sales by diversifying into trucking, coal mining, oil/gas exploration, and coal gasification	Ran into trouble because anticipated gas shortages and higher prices failed to materialize
Ashland Oil	Sell off energy exploration/production business and diversify into insurance and other nonoil areas	Largely unsuccessful, partly because of industry problems in refining and insurance
Campbell Soup	Diversify away from food	Abandoned by new CEO who successfully expanded into new food products
Church's Fried Chicken	Build modular, efficient fast-food outlets aimed at the lower end of the market	Failed because upscale chicken restaurants are capturing most of the market growth
Exxon	Diversify into electrical equipment and office automation, offset shrinking U.S. oil reserves by investing in shale oil and synfuels	Failed because of poor acquisitions, management problems in office automation, and falling oil prices

Exhibit 1 *(continued)*

PLANS THAT DIDN'T WORK . . .

Company	Strategy	BW Assessment
Foothill Group	Diversify from commercial financing into leasing—especially oil-field drilling equipment	Failed because the equipment market slumped and the company failed to obtain adequate collateral from borrowers
General Motors	Gain market share by out-spending U.S. competitors in the race to offer more fuel-efficient, downsized cars	Failed as import market share grew. Modified strategy to pursue diversification
International Multifoods	Diversify away from flour milling by developing niche products in consumer foods and expanding restaurant business	Largely unsuccessful because of management timidity, problems overseas, and the recession
Lone Star Industries	Focus entirely on cement-related businesses and sell off other operations	Ran into trouble because cement shortages and higher prices did not materialize
Napco Industries	Become the dominant distributor of non-food items to grocery stores	Ran into trouble through bad acquisitions, logistical and management problems, and the recession

Exhibit 1 *(continued)*

PLANS THAT DIDN'T WORK . . .

Company	Strategy	BW Assessment
Oak Industries	Diversify into subscription TV and cable TV equipment	Failed because cable TV competition was underestimated; it also did not keep abreast of TV equipment technology
Shaklee	Streamline product lines and become the leading nutritional products company	Ran into trouble because of the recession and sales-force turnover
Standard Oil (Ohio)	Use the cash flow from giant Prudhoe Bay oilfield to expand energy base and diversify into nonoil businesses	Largely unsuccessful so far. Kennecott acquisition is still a big loser, and efforts to find new oil have met with mixed success
Toro	Capitalize on brand recognition and reputation for quality in mowers and snowblowers by expanding into other home-care products	Failed because of snowless winters and distribution mistakes; new management changed strategies

Exhibit 1 *(continued)*

PLANS THAT DIDN'T WORK . . .

Company	Strategy	BW Assessment
Trailways	Survive in the bus business by striking alliances with independent carriers and persuading regulators to hold Greyhound to 67% of intercity bus traffic	Failed because of deregulation and Greyhound's market-share war
Union Carbide	Reduce dependence on commodity chemicals and plastics and build up six faster-growing, higher-margin lines	Deep economic slump hit all chemical markets and delayed sale of undesired businesses
U.S. Home	Use economies of scale in land development and financial clout to take a commanding position in home-building	Ran into trouble when interest rates rose and its home sales sank
Wang Laboratories	Become the leader in the office-of-the-future market by introducing new products to combine data and word processing	Largely unsuccessful because of rise of personal computers

Exhibit 1 (continued)
. . . AND PLANS THAT DID

Company	Strategy	BW Assessment
Abbott Laboratories	Become less vulnerable to cost-containment pressures in traditional hospital products	Won a leading share of the diagnostic-products market through acquisitions and internal development and built a highly profitable dietary supplements business
American Motors	Capitalize on a consumer shift to small cars by building autos designed by Renault to broaden its product line	New Renault cars perked up AMC, breaking 14 quarters of consecutive losses. Product timing still a threat
Bausch & Lomb	Regain dominance in soft contact lenses through intensive marketing and aggressive pricing. Become a major force in lens solutions	Boosted share of daily-wear lens market to 60%
Bekins	Return to profitability by selling real estate, building market share in basic moving business, and remedying poor diversification moves	Increased moving's market share through improved marketing. Divested bad businesses
Borg-Warner	Offset the cyclicality of manufacturing-related businesses	Expanded into financial and protective services through acquisitions and internal development; services now account for a third of earnings

201

Exhibit 1 *(continued)*

. . . AND PLANS THAT DID

Company	Strategy	BW Assessment
Dayton Hudson	Maintain impressive sales and earnings growth by diversifying retail operations	Jumped to No. 5 in retailing by dramatically expanding Target, Mervyn's promotional apparel, and B. Dalton Booksellers chains
Gould	Move from an industrial and electrical manufacturer into an electronics company via divestitures and acquisitions	Built electronics to 100% of earnings by buying nine high-tech companies and divesting old-line operations
Hershey Foods	Diversify into non-candy foods, nonchocolate candy, and food services	Reduced dependence on chocolate via new candies and snack foods. Expanded pasta and restaurant divisions
National Intergroup	Improve efficiency of and reduce dependence on steel operations	Became an efficient steel-maker by modernizing. Diversified into financial services, sold a steel plant to workers, and sold a 50% share of steel operations to Nippon Kokan

Exhibit 1 *(continued)*

. . . AND PLANS THAT DID

Company	Strategy	BW Assessment
New England Electric System	Reduce dependence on oil by switching to coal, developing other fuel sources, and promoting conservation	Switch to coal saved over $200 million, cut oil consumption 58%
Ralston Purina	Refocus on basic grocery-products and feed business	Shed mushroom and European pet food divisions, revitalized core business through product development and improved marketing
Southern California Edison	Reduce dependence on oil and gas	Developed alternate energy sources and is well on the way to generating 2,200 megawatts from new sources by 1992
Triangle Pacific	Become less vulnerable to swings in housing market	Sold off wholesale lumber business and expanded kitchen cabinet fabrication operations
Uniroyal	Revive ailing tire business and abandon lackluster businesses	Shut two U.S. tire plants, shed many foreign and U.S. operations, and is expanding in specialty chemicals

Clearly, the quantitative, formula-matrix approaches to strategic planning developed by BCG in the 1960s are out of favor. One reason is that these concepts grew out of the boom decade of the 1960s, when growth seemed eternal and market structures were relatively stable.

These overly quantitative techniques caused companies to place a great deal of emphasis on market-share growth. As a result, companies were devoting too much time to corporate portfolio planning and too little to hammering out strategies to turn sick operations into healthy ones or ensure that a strong business remained strong. In too many instances, strategic planning degenerated into acquiring growth businesses that the buyers did not know how to manage and selling or milking to death mature ones. Notes Stephen R. Hardis, the executive vice-president who oversees strategic planning at Eaton: "It's great to say, 'Why don't we all go into growth businesses?' But those are not all highly profitable. If there's a hell for planners, over the portal will be carved the term 'cash cow.' "

Many companies painfully learned about the shortcomings of the formulas and matrixes. Monsanto Co.'s President Richard J. Mahoney notes that his company recently had "to terminate" a unit in the "enchanted land" of high share and high growth "because we were losing our shirts."

Thanks to the BCG-type formulas, Monsanto also made an acquisition in a bid to become No. 2 in polyester—on the assumption that leisure suits would stay in style forever. "Using conventional analysis, we thought it might be possible that we could be a strong No. 2 and [enjoy] a lot of good things that would accrue to a strong No. 2," says Mahoney. A few years later, leisure suits went out of style, and Monsanto sold the entire business. Sighs Mahoney: "Our assumption that there was growth enough disappeared in a hurry."

Formula planning, warns GM's Naylor, also tends to make a company's strategy "dangerously transparent" to its competitors. "It was a search for shortcuts," says Frederick W. Gluck, a director of McKinsey & Co. "It took the thinking out of what you had to do to be competitively successful in the future." This is why Mead Corp. has dumped analytical formula planning—along with a slew of businesses ranging from ink-jet printing to a foundry. Now the company is focusing on forest products and data services. In establishing strategy, each of its business units now compares itself with its intra-industry competition.

Second-Class Citizens

"The belief that you didn't have to look at the specific industry just didn't work," says Michael Raoul-Duval, Mead's former chief strategic officer. "The old process was just too mechanized. The real world is just too complicated for that." Adds Donald J. Povejsil, vice-president for corporate planning at Westinghouse Electric Corp.: "The notion that an effective strategy can be constructed by someone in an ivory tower is totally bankrupt."

The big problem is that strategic planning grew further and further away from the external world of customers and competitors. Companies hired consultants and MBAs schooled in the latest techniques, making operating people feel like second-class citizens. As more elaborate formulas and theories sprang up, bigger staffs were needed to collect more data from operations. Pretty soon the size of the planning bureaucracies and their demands on operating managers grew out of control.

At Mead, Raoul-Duval recalls, "plans became much too voluminous. We had the feeling that people prepared their business plans as a matter of routine, trying to add more papers and numbers than [were in] the previous year's plan."

Robert M. Lockerd, vice-president for corporate staff at Texas Instruments Inc., says his company let its management system, which can "track the fall of every sparrow, creep into the planning process so we were making more and more detailed plans. It [became] a morale problem because managers knew they couldn't project numbers out five years to two decimal points."

'Us vs. Them'

The end result is that strategic planners disrupt a company's ability to assess the outside world and to create strategies for a sustainable competitive advantage. The experiences of GE's Major Appliance Business Group serve as an excel¹ent case study of how disruptive strategic planning can be.

The relationship between the Appliance Group's operating managers and strategic planners was "us vs. them" from the start. Many of the planners, whose numbers grew to more than 50 by the late 1970s, were recruited from consulting firms. "A lot of operating people—and I was one of them—[interpreted the buildup to mean that] we were not smart enough to think our way through these things," says Roger Schipke, who ran the dishwasher business before assuming the Appliance Group's top job in 1982.

A "natural resistance" that escalated into out-and-out hostility meant that even when the planners were right, operating managers often would not listen to them. In the 1970s, planners correctly recognized the internationalization of markets, including appliances. But operating managers, who then saw Sears, Roebuck & Co. as the competition, paid them little heed. Only recently—now that the planners are gone—has the Appliance Group awakened to the threat that is being posed by the Japanese.

If the planners were sometimes right, they were frequently wrong—usually because they relied on data, not market instincts, to make their judgments. Says Schipke: "An awful lot of conclusions were drawn by that group somewhat in isolation. We had a lot of bad assumptions leading to some bad strategies."

Waste from Haste

When data indicated that houses and families were shrinking, for instance, planners concluded that smaller appliances were the wave of the future. Because the planners had little contact with homebuilders and retailers, they did not realize that kitchens and bathrooms were the two rooms that were not shrinking and that working women wanted big refrigerators to cut down on trips to the supermarket. Moreover, top management, which also lacked contact with the market, did not see that the planners' data failed to tell the true story. The result: GE wasted a lot of time designing smaller appliances.

Even more harmful to the Appliance Group was the planners' obsession with predicting the unpredictable—such as oil prices—and then hastily reacting when events did not turn out as expected. When the energy crunch hit, planners predicted that the government would set energy-efficiency standards for appliances. "They thought the refrigeration business was going to come to an end because of the energy crunch," says Schipke. The reaction: a crash program to improve refrigerator insulation. As it turned out, efficiency standards never came to pass. And Schipke notes that improving the refrigerator's compressor—not the insulation—is the best way to increase energy efficiency.

But by the time these facts were realized, the damage

had long been done. The comprehensive program for building state-of-the-art refrigerators in state-of-the-art facilities now under way—and which Schipke calls "our No. 1 priority"—was side-tracked for four years. Instead, says Schipke, Appliance Park's automated dishwasher plant was built "because the program looked like a nifty program." Though the dishwasher plant is successful, Schipke insists the returns would "definitely have been better if we put the same effort into refrigeration."

Schipke also blames planners for hurting the relationship between GE's top management and the Appliance Group's management. When planners rushed into headquarters "raising red flags" such as energy, says Schipke, "top management would say, 'Gee, didn't this dumb [operating] guy know about this energy issue?' " Schipke says the energy *cause célèbre* in refrigeration cost at least four general managers their jobs.

As strategic planning became less of a creative thinking exercise and more of a bureaucratic process, its original purpose was lost to GE and other enthusiastic corporate disciples. Managers began to confuse strategy with planning and implementation. To GE Chairman Welch, that is the difference between being externally or internally focused. Making sure that his managers understand the difference is an obvious obsession.

'Here to There'

Strategy, says Welch, "is trying to understand where you sit today in today's world. Not where you wish you were and where you hoped you would be, but where you are. And [it's trying to understand] where you want to be in 1990. [It's] assessing with everything in your head the competitive changes, the market changes that you can capitalize on or ward off to go from here to there. It's assessing the realistic chances of getting from here to there.''

A strategy, says Welch, can be summarized in a page or two. "It is different from plan appropriation requests, building a plant, developing a product," he explains. "That's implementation of a strategy of where you want to be."

This distinction has been lost and has hurt plenty of companies. Of the 19 companies in BUSINESS WEEK's survey whose strategies failed, ran into trouble, or were abandoned, 14 appear to have made the wrong assumptions about the business environment—ranging from interest rates to competitors' strategies.

By focusing on its plant's capacity and not on the market, Hydril Co., a Los Angeles manufacturer of oilfield equipment, chose not to build the new capacity that might have prevented new competitors from entering its market. An inward focus caused some of TRW Inc.'s industrial and automotive businesses to suffer from changes in distribution patterns because they had seen distributors— rather than end users—as their customer. "We did not try to anticipate what our competitors might do to the extent that we should have," says Richard L. Erickson, vice-president for planning and development at TRW Automotive Worldwide.

To correct the mistakes of the past, GE, Westinghouse, and scores of other companies are tearing down their rigid strategic-planning structures. Westinghouse's Povejsil has cut the strategic planning instructions for operating units "that looked like an auto repair manual" to five or six pages. To make sure that strategies are not presented at the annual meeting and then forgotten, both GE and Westinghouse have abandoned the practice of holding "a strategic planning month" each year. For each unit at GE, says Schipke, "the meeting would last 10 to 20 minutes. It was 'Pass Appliance through, bring in Television.' " The Appliance Group's most recent strategic review with Jack Welch lasted from 8:00 A.M. to 3:30 P.M.

One Job Into Two

GE and other companies are also taking pains to separate operational and budget issues from strategy. Avery International, a Pasadena (Calif.) maker of labels, tape, and office products, has split its planning vice-president's job into two. One focuses on such long-term strategic issues as competition, technology, and acquisition. The other concentrates on operational issues. GE and, reportedly, Shell Chemical and Fluor discuss budget and strategy issues with operating managers at separate sessions to make sure ideas—and not numbers—dominate strategies.

The very way strategic planning—or "strategic thinking"—is done is dramatically changing. At Millipore Corp., a maker of high-tech filtration systems, the planners are noticeably absent: Chairman Dimitri V. d'Arbeloff fired the company's six. Instead, "environmental" task forces of operating managers meet every 18 months to two years to brainstorm on what is happening in their markets and where those markets are likely to go in the next 5 to 10 years. This approach has enabled Millipore to keep apace of the increasingly demanding filtration needs of the semiconductor industry by introducing new technology. "One reason we're a leader today in contamination control in microelectronics is because we took this approach," says Anthony J. Lucas, director of microelectronics marketing. "We just had to be there at an operational level rather than at a top-down corporate level."

Some companies are also incorporating their contingency or "what-if" planning into overall strategy. This contrasts with the old approach of creating a separate, rigid contingency plan that was often proved to be worthless. The new approach enables such companies as Monsanto to take the initiative to shape events—such as the public acceptance of biotechnology—rather than simply to react to them.

The role of strategic planners is also changing in a big way. Borg-Warner Corp.'s three corporate planners—down from 10 three years ago—now serve as consultants to business units. The heads of its seven groups act as their "chief strategists," says Donald C. Trauscht, vice-president for corporate planning.

At GE, David W. Keller, manager of strategic planning for the Aerospace Business Group, says that the time he spends pestering divisions and departments for information ordered by the corporate and sector offices has dropped about 90%. "People mired in their markets are asking us how we can bring a broader perspective to them in assessing their new opportunities," he says.

For example, Keller is helping managers of GE's simulation and training business assess a possible move into the graphics market. "In the past," he says, "they wouldn't dare to call us and ask for our help or another point of view, fearing it would more likely generate more requests of them rather than be more help to them."

At GM, planners are "facilitators" to help operating managers do the planning themselves. Raymond K. Fears, the planner in GM's Buick City complex, says, he is "working my way out of a job." Fears figures Buick City's plant manager will be ready to handle strategic planning without his help in a year.

Some companies, though, may find it a lot harder to turn operating managers into strategic thinkers. Many operating managers at a Midwestern manufacturer continue to fill out strategic-planning forms that headquarters no longer requires. "You almost had to rip them out of their hands," says an executive.

Pressing the Flesh

Still, management gurus believe the biggest challenge in strategic planning will be turning CEOs into true strategic thinkers. A McKinsey study found that corporate executives now spend only 10% to 15% of their time thinking. That the rest of their time is devoted to meetings, crunching numbers, and pressing the flesh is not an encouraging sign.

Perhaps this explains why so few companies appear to have a bona fide corporate strategy. Harvard Business School's Michael E. Porter says this should be more than a compilation of individual business units' plans—it should be a device to integrate business units and enable the parent company to capitalize on synergies so that the whole of the corporation is more than just the sum of its units. Some examples of companies trying to do just this: American Express, Citicorp, and GE. Declares Porter: "Companies that are on top of forging integrated strategies are the companies that are going to succeed in the future."

HOW GM TAKES PLANNING INTO THE TRENCHES

Only eight years ago, General Motors Corp. had no strategic planners in its divisions, let alone in a lowly car plant. But as Raymond K. Fears, the strategic planner for GM's Buick City complex in Flint, Mich., amply demonstrates, times have changed. Fears, who turns 30 in mid-September, moved from GM's corporate strategic planning group in 1983 to Buick City—the trio of 60-year-old plants that GM aspires to turn into the world's most efficient auto factory. His assignment: "To get [operating managers], who are used to thinking in terms of nuts and bolts, to think in strategic terms." That, he concedes, "is a major educational job."

Fears's transfer is part of GM Chairman Roger B. Smith's master plan to integrate strategic planning "into our daily lives.'' In Smith's book, that means ''true integration with the operating organization.''

Marching in Step

Fears served as a product planner for three years in GM's Chevrolet Motor Div. before moving in 1982 to corporate, where he worked as a business-plan consultant to nine GM divisions. At Buick City, which will begin cranking out full-size 1986 cars a year from now, Fears's job is to aid in devising and implementing its piece of Buick Motor Div.'s strategy.

Chairman Smith insists that ''the guy in charge of strategic planning is the general manager.'' Indeed, Fears's job will probably be phased out next year when the plant manager assumes all strategic-planning duties. One of Fears's tasks is to coordinate the strategic committee charged with insuring that all corporate groups involved in pilot production are marching in step. He also has helped to scout the competition to make sure Buick City will not be made obsolete—even by newer GM plants that adopt the facility's manufacturing practices.

Does he have regrets about moving from headquarters to the down-in-the-trenches atmosphere of a car plant? Absolutely none, says Fears, who aspires to an operating job. ''I see the move as getting closer to the action.''

HOW GE TURNS MANAGERS INTO STRATEGISTS

No senior executive in General Electric Co. can boast of a strategic planning staff leaner than Roger W. Schipke's. The senior vice-president, who heads GE's Major Appliance Business Group, has none.

Soon after assuming the top job at Appliance Park in Louisville in early 1982, Schipke finished the job that

213

Vice-Chairman John F. Welch Jr. began before becoming GE's chairman. Welch had slashed the planning staff from more than 50 to 25. As far as Schipke was concerned, that was still 25 too many. He now takes his "visions" for the group to his top operating managers, who "hash out a consensus" and then "drive it" through the organization. Insists Schipke: "For any strategy to succeed, you need [operating] people to understand it, embrace it, and make it happen."

Schipke is just as adamant in his belief that being a strategist means being externally focused. That explains his obsession with Whirlpool Corp., GE's major competitor in appliances. One of Schipke's pastimes is trying to understand how Jack D. Sparks, his counterpart at Whirlpool, thinks—and he expects his lieutenants to do the same.

'We Woke Up'

Upon assuming his current job, Schipke ordered an analysis of Whirlpool. One lesson: the danger of an internal focus. For instance, by introducing new features, Whirlpool had almost eliminated GE's share lead in side-by-side refrigerator-freezers. GE's model had remained virtually unchanged since 1970. Says Schipke: "We were sitting here and saying, 'Gee, our figures look good. We're holding our share. Nothing must be happening.' We woke up."

He is now paying just as much attention to the Japanese. That explains why GE improved the evaporators on some single-door-refrigerator models—to make sure the Japanese could not use the niche to expand in the U.S.

Schipke, who replaced three of his top four appliance executives, says being good operationally is no longer enough at GE. "Now it's a question of, 'Can they develop a strategy for their business?' ", he says. "Some will make that cut. Some won't."

Two

Of Boxes, Bubbles, and Effective Management
David K. Hurst

Harvard Business Review
Soldiers Field Road
Boston, Massachusetts 02163

Dear Editors:

We are writing to tell you how events from 1979 on have forced us, a team of four general managers indistinguishable from thousands of others, to change our view of what managers should do. In 1979 we were working for Hugh Russel Inc., the fiftieth largest public company in Canada. Hugh Russel was an industrial distributor with some $535 million in sales and a net income of $14 million. The organization structure was conventional: 16 divisions in four groups, each with a group president reporting to the corporate office. Three volumes of corporate policy manuals spelled out detailed aspects of corporate life, including our corporate philosophy. In short, in

1979 our corporation was like thousands of other businesses in North America.

During 1980, however, through a series of unlikely turns, that situation changed drastically. Hugh Russel found itself acquired in a 100 percent leveraged buyout and then merged with a large, unprofitable (that's being kind!) steel fabricator, York Steel Construction, Ltd. The resulting entity was York Russel Inc., a privately held company except for the existence of some publicly owned preferred stock which obliged us to report to the public.

As members of the acquired company's corporate office, we waited nervously for the ax to fall. Nothing happened. Finally, after about six weeks, Wayne (now our president) asked the new owner if we could do anything to help the deal along. The new chairman was delighted and gave us complete access to information about the acquirer.

It soon became apparent that the acquiring organization had little management strength. The business had been run in an entrepreneurial style with hundreds of people reporting to a single autocrat. The business had, therefore, no comprehensive plan and, worse still, no money. The deal had been desperately conceived to shelter our profits from taxes and use the resulting cash flow to fund the excessive debt of the steel fabrication business.

Our first job was to hastily assemble a task force to put together a $300 million bank loan application and a credible turnaround plan. Our four-member management team (plus six others who formed a task force) did it in only six weeks. The merged business, York Russel, ended up with $10 million of equity and $275 million of debt on the eve of a recession that turned out to be the worst Canada had experienced since the Great Depression. It was our job then to save the new company, somehow.

Conceptual frameworks are important aids to managers' perceptions, and every team should have a member who can build them. Before the acquisition, the framework implicit in our organization was a "hard," rational model rather like those Thomas Peters and Robert Waterman describe.[1] Jay Galbraith's elaborate model is one of the purest examples of the structure-follows-strategy school.[2] The model clearly defines all elements and their relationships to each other, presumably so that they can be measured (see Exhibit 1).

Because circumstances changed after the acquisition, our framework fell apart almost immediately. Overnight we went from working for a growth company to working for one whose only objective was survival. Our old decentralized organization was cumbersome and expensive; our new organization needed cash, not profits. Bankers and suppliers swarmed all over us, and the quiet life of a management-controlled public company was gone.

Compounding our difficulties, the recession quickly revealed all sorts of problems in businesses that up to that time had given us no trouble. Even the core nuggets offered up only meager profits, while interest rates of up to 25 percent quickly destroyed what was left of the balance sheet.

In the heat of the crisis, the management team jelled quickly. At first each member muddled in his own way, but as time went by, we started to gain a new understanding of how to be effective. Even now we do not completely understand the conceptual framework that has evolved, and maybe we never will. What follows is our best attempt to describe to you and your readers what guides us today,

Yours truly,
The management team

[1] Thomas J. Peters and Robert H. Waterman, *In Search of Excellence* (New York: Harper & Row, 1982), p. 29.
[2] For the best of the hard box models we have come across, see Jay R. Galbraith, *Organization Design* (Reading, Mass.: Addison-Wesley, 1977).

Exhibit 1
The Hard and Soft Model and How They Work Together

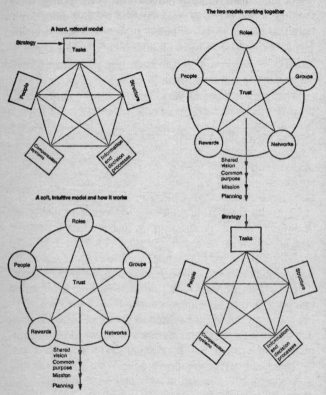

Source: The hard, rational model is from J.R. Galbraith, *Organization Design* (Reading, Mass.: Addison-Wesley, 1977).

TWO MODELS ARE BETTER THAN ONE

The hard, rational model isn't wrong; it just isn't enough. There is something more. As it turns out, there is a great deal more.

At York Russel we have had to develop a "soft," intuitive framework that offers a counterpart to every element in the hard, rational framework. As the exhibit shows and the following sections discuss, in the soft model, roles are the counterparts of tasks, groups replace structure, networks operate instead of information systems, the rewards are soft as opposed to hard, and people are viewed as social animals rather than as rational beings.

That may not sound very new. But we found that the key to effective management of not only our crisis but also the routine is to know whether we are in a hard "box" or a soft "bubble" context. By recognizing the dichotomy between the two, we can choose the appropriate framework.

☐ **Tasks . . . & . . .**	○ **Roles**
☐ *Static*	○ *Fluid*
☐ *Clarity*	○ *Ambiguity*
☐ *Content*	○ *Process*
☐ *Fact*	○ *Perception*
☐ *Science*	○ *Art*

These are some of our favorite words for contrasting these two aspects of management. Here's how we discovered them.

The merger changed our agenda completely. We had new shareholders, a new bank, a new business (the steel fabrication operations consisted of nine divisions), and a new relationship with the managers of our subsidiaries, who were used to being left alone to grow. The recession and high interest rates rendered the corporation insolvent. Bankruptcy loomed large. Further, our previously static way of operating became very fluid.

In general, few of us had clear tasks, and for the most part we saw the future as ambiguous and fearful. We found ourselves describing what we had to do as roles rather than as tasks. At first our descriptions were crude. We talked of having an "inside man" who deals with administration, lawyers, and bankers versus an "outside man" who deals with operations, customers, and suppliers. Some of us were "readers," others "writers," some "talkers," and others "listeners." As the readers studied the work of behavioral science researchers and talked to the listeners, we found some more useful classifications. Henry Mintzberg's description of managers' work in terms of three roles—interpersonal (figurehead, leader, liaison), informational (monitor, disseminator, spokesperson), and decisional—helped us see the variety of the job.[3] Edgar Schein's analysis of group roles helped us concentrate on the process of communication as well as on what was communicated.[4]

The most useful framework we used was the one Ichak Adize developed for decision-making roles.[5] In his view, a successful management team needs to play four distinct parts. The first is that of producer of results. A *producer* is action oriented and knowledgeable in his or her field; he or she helps compile plans with an eye to their implementability. The *administrator* supervises the system and manages the detail. The *entrepreneur* is a creative risk taker who initiates action, comes up with new ideas, and challenges existing policies. And the *integrator* brings people together socially and their ideas intellectually, and interprets the significance of events. The integrator gives the team a sense of direction and shared experience.

[3]Henry Mintzberg, "The Manager's Job: Folklore and Fact," HBR July-August 1975, p. 49.

[4]Edgar H. Schein, *Process Consultation: Its Role in Organization Development* (Reading, Mass.: Addison-Wesley, 1969).

[5]Ichak Adize, *How to Solve the Mismanagement Crisis* (Los Angeles: MDOR Institute, 1979).

According to Adize, each member must have some appreciation of the others' roles (by having some facility in those areas), and it is essential that they get along socially. At York Russel the producers (who typically come out of operations) and administrators (usually accountants) tend to be hard box players, while the entrepreneurs tend to live in the soft bubble. Integrators (friendly, unusually humble MBAs) move between the hard and the soft, and we've found a sense of humor is essential to being able to do that well.

The key to a functioning harmonious group, however, has been for members to understand that they might disagree with each other because they are in two different contexts. Different conceptual frameworks may lead people to different conclusions based on the same facts. Of the words describing tasks and roles, our favorite pair is "fact" versus "perception." People in different boxes will argue with each other over facts, for facts in boxes are compelling—they seem so tangible. Only from the bubble can one see them for what they are: abstractions based on the logical frameworks, or boxes, being used.

☐ **Structure** . . . & . . .	○ **Groups**
☐ *Cool*	○ *Warm*
☐ *Formal*	○ *Informal*
☐ *Closed*	○ *Open*
☐ *Obedience*	○ *Trust*
☐ *Independence*	○ *Autonomy*

Our premerger corporation was a pretty cold place to work. Senior management kept control in a tight inner circle and then played hardball (in a hard box, of course) with the group presidents. Managers negotiated budgets and plans on a win-lose basis; action plans almost exclusively controlled what was done in the organization. Top managers kept a lot of information to themselves. People didn't trust each other very much.

The crises that struck the corporation in 1980 were so serious that we could not have concealed them even if we had wanted to. We were forced to put together a multitude of task forces consisting of people from all parts of the organization to address these urgent issues, and in the process, we had to reveal everything we knew, whether it was confidential or not.

We were amazed at the task forces' responses: instead of resigning en masse (the hard box players had said that people would leave the company when they found out that it was insolvent), the teams tackled their projects with passion. Warmth, a sense of belonging, and trust characterized the groups; the more we let them know what was going on, the more we received from them. Confidentiality is the enemy of trust. In the old days strategic plans were stamped "confidential." Now we know that paper plans mean nothing if they are not in the minds of the managers.

Division managers at first resented our intrusion into their formal, closed world. "What happened to independence?" they demanded. We described the soft counterpart—autonomy—to them. Unlike independence, autonomy cannot be granted once and for all. In our earlier life, division personnel told the corporate office what they thought it wanted to hear. "You've got to keep those guys at arm's length" was a typical division belief. An autonomous relationship depends on trust for its nourishment. "The more you level with us," we said, "the more we'll leave you alone." That took some getting used to.

But in the end autonomy worked. We gave division managers confidential information, shared our hopes and fears, and incorporated their views in our bubble. They needed to be helped out of their boxes, not to abandon them altogether but to gain a deeper appreciation of and insight into how they were running their businesses. Few could resist when we walked around showing a genuine interest in their views. Because easy access to each other and opportunities for communication determine how groups form and work together, we encouraged managers to keep their doors open. We called this creation of opportunities for communication by making senior management accessible "management by walking around." Chance encounters should not be left to chance.

Although the primary objective of all this communication is to produce trust among group members, an important by-product is that the integrators among us have started to "see" the communication process.[6] In other words, they are beginning to understand why people say what they say. This ability to "see" communication is elusive at times, but when it is present, it enables us to "jump out of the box"—that is, to talk about the frameworks' supporting conclusions rather than the conclusions themselves. We have defused many potential confrontations and struck many deals by changing the context of the debate rather than the debate itself.[7]

Perhaps the best example of this process was our changing relationship with our lead banker. As the corporation's financial position deteriorated, our relationship with the bank became increasingly adversarial. The responsibility for our account rose steadily up the bank's hierarchy (we had eight different account managers in 18 months), and we received tougher and tougher "banker's speeches" from successively more senior executives. Although we

---

[6] Edgar H. Schein's *Process Consultation*, p. 10, was very helpful in showing us how the process differs from the content.

[7] Getting consensus among a group of managers poses the same challenge as negotiating a deal. *Getting to Yes* by Roger Fisher and William Ury (Boston: Houghton Mifflin, 1981) is a most helpful book for understanding the process.

worried a great deal that the bank might call the loan, the real risk was that our good businesses would be choked by overzealous efforts on the part of individual bankers to "hold the line."

Key to our ability to change the relationship was to understand why individuals were taking the positions they were. To achieve that understanding, we had to rely on a network of contacts both inside and outside the bank. We found that the bank had as many views as there were people we talked to. Fortunately, the severity of the recession and the proliferation of corporate loan problems had already blown everyone out of the old policy "boxes." It remained for us to gain the confidence of our contacts, exchange candid views of our positions, and present options that addressed the corporation's problems in the bank's context and dealt with the bank's interests.

The "hard" vehicle for this was the renegotiation of our main financing agreement. During the more than six month negotiating process, our relationship with the bank swung 180 degrees from confrontation to collaboration. The corporation's problem became a joint bank-corporation problem. We had used the bubble to find a new box in which both the corporation and the bank could live.

☐ **Information processes . . . & . . .**	○ **Networks**
☐ *Hard*	○ *Soft*
☐ *Written*	○ *Oral*
☐ *Know*	○ *Feel*
☐ *Control*	○ *Influence*
☐ *Decision*	○ *Implementation*

Over the years our corporation has developed some excellent information systems. Our EDP facility is second to none in our industry. Before the acquisition and merger, when people talked about or requested information, they meant hard, quantitative data and written reports that would be used for control and decision making. The crisis required that we make significant changes to these systems. Because, for example, we became more interested in cash flow than earnings per share, data had to be aggregated and presented in a new way.

The pivotal change, however, was our need to communicate with a slew of new audiences over which we had little control. For instance, although we still have preferred stock quoted in the public market, our principal new shareholders were family members with little experience in professional management of public companies. Our new bankers were in organizational turmoil themselves and took 18 months to realize the horror of what they had financed. Our suppliers, hitherto benign, faced a stream of bad financial news about us and other members of the industry. The rumor mill had us in receivership on a weekly basis.

Our plant closures and cutbacks across North America brought us into a new relationship with government, unions, and the press. And we had a new internal audience: our employees, who were understandably nervous about the ''imminent'' bankruptcy.

We had always had some relationship with these audiences, but now we saw what important sources of information they were and expanded these networks vastly.[8] Just as we had informed the division managers at the outset, we decided not to conceal from these other groups the fact that the corporation was insolvent but worthy of support. We made oral presentations supported by formal written material to cover the most important bases.

To our surprise, this candid approach totally disarmed

---

[8]For discussion of the importance of networks, see John P. Kotter, ''What Effective General Managers Really Do,'' HBR November-December 1982, p. 156.

potential antagonists. For instance, major suppliers could not understand why we had told them we were in trouble before the numbers revealed the fact. By the time the entire war story was news, there was no doubt that our suppliers' top managers, who tended not to live in the hard accounting box, were on our side. When their financial specialists concluded that we were insolvent, top management blithely responded, "We've known that for six months."

Sharing our view of the world with constituencies external to the corporation led to other unexpected benefits, such as working in each other's interests. Our reassurance to customers that we would be around to deliver on contracts strengthened the relationship. Adversity truly is opportunity!

Management by walking around was the key to communicating with employees in all parts of the company. As a result of the continual open communication, all employees appreciated the corporation's position. Their support has been most gratifying. One of our best talker-listeners (our president) tells of a meeting with a very nervous group of employees at one facility. After he had spent several hours explaining the company's situation, one blue-collar worker who had been with the company for years took him aside and told him that a group of employees would be prepared to take heavy pay cuts if it would save the business. It turns out that when others hear this story it reinforces *their* belief in the organization.

We have found that sharing our views and incorporating the views of others as appropriate has a curious effect on the making and the implementing of decisions. As we've said, in our previous existence the decisions we made were always backed up by hard information; management was decisive, and that was good. Unfortunately, too few of these "good" decisions ever got implemented. The simple process of making the decision the way we did often set up resistance down the line. As the decision was handed down to consecutive organizational levels, it lost impetus until eventually it was unclear whether the decision was right in the first place.

Now we worry a good deal less about making decisions; they arise as fairly obvious conclusions drawn from a mass of shared assumptions. It's the assumptions that we spend our time working on. One of our "producers" (an executive vice president) calls it "conditioning," and indeed it is. Of course, making decisions this way requires that senior management build networks with people many layers down in the organization. This kind of communication is directly at odds with the communication policy laid down in the premerger corporation, which emphasized direct-line reporting.

A consequence of this network information process is that we often have to wait for the right time to make a decision. We call the wait a "creative stall." In the old organization, it would have been called procrastination, but what we're doing is waiting for some important players to come "on-side" before making an announcement.[9] In our terms, you "prepare in the box and wait in the bubble."

Once the time is right, however, implementation is rapid. Everyone is totally involved and has given thought to what has to be done. Not only is the time it takes for the decision to be made and implemented shorter than in the past but also the whole process strengthens the organization rather than weakening it through bitterness about how the decision was made.

[9]For discussion of a "creative stall" being applied in practice, see Stratford P. Sherman, "Muddling to Victory at Geico," *Fortune*, September 5, 1983, p. 66.

☐ **People . . . & . . .**　　　　○ **People**
☐ *Rational*　　　　　　　　　○ *Social*
☐ *Produce*　　　　　　　　　○ *Create*
☐ *Think*　　　　　　　　　　○ *Imagine*
☐ *Tell*　　　　　　　　　　　○ *Inspire*
☐ *Work*　　　　　　　　　　○ *Play*

In the old, premerger days, it was convenient to regard employees as rational, welfare-maximizing beings; it made motivating them so much easier and planning less messy.

But because the crisis made it necessary to close many operations and terminate thousands of employees, we had to deal with people's social nature. We could prepare people intellectually by sharing our opinions and, to some extent, protect them physically with severance packages, but we struggled with how to handle the emotional aspects. Especially for long-service employees, severing the bond with the company was the emotional equivalent of death.

Humor is what rescued us. Laughter allows people to jump out of their emotional boxes, or rigid belief structures. None of us can remember having laughed as much as we have over the past three years. Although much of the humor has inevitably been of the gallows variety, it has been an important ingredient in releasing tension and building trust.

Now everyone knows that people are social as well as rational animals. Indeed, we knew it back in the premerger days, but somehow back then we never came to grips with the social aspect, maybe because the rational view of people has an appealing simplicity and clarity. Lombard's Law applied to us—routine, structured tasks drove out nonroutine, unstructured activities.[10]

---

[10] Louis B. Barnes, "Managing the Paradox of Organizational Trust," HBR March-April 1981, p. 107.

☐ **Compensation systems . . . & . . . ○ Rewards**
☐ *Direct*	○ *Indirect*
☐ *Objective*	○ *Subjective*
☐ *Profit*	○ *Fun*
☐ *Failure*	○ *Mistake*
☐ *Hygiene*	○ *Motivator*
☐ *Managing*	○ *Caring*

In our premerger organization, the "total compensation policy" meant you could take your money any way you liked—salary, loans, fringes, and so forth. Management thought this policy catered to individual needs and was, therefore, motivating. Similarly, the "Personnel Development Program" required managers to make formal annual reviews of their employees' performances. For some reason, management thought that this also had something to do with motivation. The annual reviews, however, had become a meaningless routine, with managers constrained to be nice to the review subject because they had to work with him or her the next day.

The 1981 recession put a stop to all this by spurring us to freeze all direct compensation. Profit-based compensation disappeared; morale went up.

The management team discussed this decision for hours. As the savings from the freeze would pay for a few weeks' interest only, the numbers made no sense at all. Some of us prophesied doom. "We will lose the best people," we argued. Instead, the symbolic freeze brought the crisis home to everyone. We had all made a sacrifice, a contribution that senior management could recognize at a future time.

Even though the academics say they aren't scientifically valid, we still like Frederick Herzberg's definition of motivators (our interpretations of them are in parentheses):[11]

---

[11]In "One More Time: How Do You Motivate Employees?" HBR January-February 1968, p. 53.

Achievement (what you believe you did).

Recognition (what others think you did).

Work itself (what you really do).

Responsibility (what you help others do).

Advancement (what you think you can do).

Growth (what you believe you might do).

THE NEW FRAMEWORK AT WORK

The diagram of the soft model in Exhibit 1 shows our view of how our management process seems to work. When the motivating rewards are applied to people playing the necessary roles and working together in groups that are characterized by open communication and are linked to networks throughout the organization, the immediate product is a high degree of mutual trust. This trust allows groups to develop a shared vision that in turn enhances a sense of common purpose. From this process people develop a feeling of having a mission of their own. The mission is spiritual in the sense of being an important effort much larger than oneself. This kind of involvement is highly motivating. Mission is the soft counterpart of strategy.

☐ **Strategy . . . & . . .**   ◯ **Mission**
☐ *Objectives*   ◯ *Values*
☐ *Policies*   ◯ *Norms*
☐ *Forecast*   ◯ *Vision*
☐ *Clockworks*   ◯ *Frameworks*
☐ *Right*   ◯ *Useful*
☐ *Target*   ◯ *Direction*
☐ *Precise*   ◯ *Vague*
☐ *Necessary*   ◯ *Sufficient*

Listed are some of our favorite words for contrasting these two polarities. We find them useful for understanding why clear definition of objectives is not essential for motivating people. Hard box planners advocate the hard box elements and tend to be overinvested in using their various models, or "clockworks" as we call them. Whether it's a Boston Consulting Group matrix or an Arthur D. Little life-cycle curve, too often planners wind them up and managers act according to what they dictate without looking at the assumptions, many of which may be invalid, implicit in the frameworks.

We use the models only as take-off points for discussion. They do not have to be right, only useful. If they don't yield genuine insights we put them aside. The hard box cannot be dispensed with. On the contrary, it is essential—but not sufficient.

The key element in developing a shared purpose is mutual trust. Without trust, people will engage in all kinds of self-centered behavior to assert their own identities and influence coworkers to their own ends. Under these circumstances, they just won't hear others, and efforts to develop a shared vision are doomed. Nothing destroys trust faster than hard box attitudes toward problems that don't require such treatment.

Trust is self-reproductive. When trust is present in a situation, chain reactions occur as people share frameworks and exchange unshielded views. The closer and more tightly knit the group is, the more likely it is that these reactions will spread, generating a shared vision and common purpose.

Once the sense of common purpose and mission is established, the managing group is ready to enter the hard box of strategy (see the righthand side of the exhibit). Now the specifics of task, structure, information, and decision processes are no longer likely to be controversial or threatening. Implementation becomes astonishingly simple. Action plans are necessary to control hard box implementation, but once the participants in the soft bubble share the picture, things seem to happen by themselves as team members play their roles and fill the gaps as they see them. Since efforts to seize control of bubble activity are likely to prove disastrous, it is most fortunate that people act spontaneously without being "organized." Paradoxically, one can achieve control in the bubble only by letting go—which gets right back to trust.

In the hard box, the leadership model is that of the general who gives crisp, precise instructions as to who is to do what and when. In the soft bubble, the leadership model is that of the shepherd, who follows his flock watchfully as it meanders along the natural contours of the land. He carries the weak and collects the strays, for they all have a contribution to make. This style may be inefficient, but it is effective. The whole flock reaches its destination at more or less the same time.[12]

☐ **Boxes . . . & . . .**	○ **Bubbles**
☐ *Solve*	○ *Dissolve*
☐ *Sequential*	○ *Lateral*
☐ *Left brain*	○ *Right brain*
☐ *Serious*	○ *Humorous*
☐ *Explain*	○ *Explore*
☐ *Rational*	○ *Intuitive*
☐ *Conscious*	○ *Unconscious*
☐ *Learn*	○ *Remember*
☐ *Knowledge*	○ *Wisdom*
☐ *Lens*	○ *Mirror*
☐ *Full*	○ *Empty*
☐ *Words*	○ *Pictures*
☐ *Objects*	○ *Symbols*
☐ *Description*	○ *Parable*

[12]For another view of the shepherd role, see the poem by Nancy Esposito, "The Good Shepherd," HBR July-August 1983, p. 121.

Thought and language are keys to changing perceptions. Boxes and bubbles describe the hard and soft thought structures, respectively. Boxes have rigid, opaque sides; walls have to be broken down to join boxes, although if the lid is off one can jump out. Bubbles have flexible, transparent sides that can easily expand and join with other bubbles. Bubbles float but can easily burst. In boxes problems are to be solved; in bubbles they are dissolved. The trick is to change the context of the problem, that is, to jump out of the box. This technique has many applications.

We have noticed a number of articles in your publication that concern values and ethics in business, and some people have suggested that business students be required to attend classes in ethics. From our view of the world, sending students to specific courses is a hard box solution and would be ineffective. Ethical behavior is absent from some businesses not because the managers have no ethics (or have the wrong ones) but because the hard "strategy box" does not emphasize them as being valuable. The hard box deals in objectives, and anyone who raises value issues in that context will not survive long.

In contrast, in the "mission bubble" people feel free to talk about values and ethics because there is trust. The problem of the lack of ethical behavior is dissolved.

We have found bubble thinking to be the intellectual equivalent of judo; a person does not resist an attacker but goes with the flow, thereby adding his strength to the other's momentum. Thus when suppliers demanded that their financial exposure to our lack of creditworthiness be reduced, we agreed and suggested that they protect themselves by supplying goods to us on consignment. After all, their own financial analysis showed we couldn't pay them any money! In some cases we actually got consignment deals, and where we didn't the scheme failed because of nervous lawyers (also hard box players) rather than reluctance on the part of the supplier.

Bubble thought structures are characterized by what Edward de Bono calls lateral thinking.[13] The sequential or vertical thought structure is logical and rational; it proceeds through logical stages and depends on a yes-no test at each step. De Bono suggests that in lateral thinking the yes-no test must be suspended, for the purpose is to explore not explain, to test assumptions not conclusions.

We do the same kind of questioning when we do what we call "humming a lot." When confronted with what initially appears to be an unpalatable idea, an effective manager will say "hmm" and wait until the idea has been developed and its implications considered. Quite often, even when an initial idea is out of the question, the fact that we have considered it seriously will lead to a different, innovative solution.

We have found it useful to think of the action opposite to the one we intend taking. When selling businesses we found it helpful to think about acquiring purchasers. This led to deeper research into purchasers' backgrounds and motives and to a more effective packaging and presentation of the businesses to be sold. This approach encourages novel ideas and makes the people who generate them (the entrepreneurs) feel that their ideas, however "dumb," will not be rejected out of hand.

In hard box thought structures, one tends to use conceptual frameworks as lenses, to sit on one side and examine an object on the other. In bubble structures, the frameworks are mirrors reflecting one's own nature and its effect on one's perceptions; object and subject are on the same

---

[13]See Edward de Bono, *The Use of Lateral Thinking* (London: Jonathan Cape, 1967), and *PO: Beyond Yes and No* (New York: Simon and Schuster, 1972).

side. In the hard box, knowledge is facts, from learning; in the bubble, knowledge is wisdom, from experience.

Bubble thought structures are not easily described in words. Language itself is a box reflecting our cultural heritage and emphasizing some features of reality at the expense of others. Part of our struggle during the past three years has been to unlearn many scientific management concepts and develop a new vocabulary. We have come up with some new phrases and words: management by walking around, creative stall, asking dumb questions, jumping out of the box, creating a crisis, humming a lot, and muddling. We have also attached new meanings to old words such as fact and perception, independence and autonomy, hard amd soft, solve and dissolve, and so forth.

THREE YEARS LATER

What we have told you about works in a crisis. And we can well understand your asking whether this approach can work when the business is stable and people lapse back into boxes. We have developed two methods of preventing this lapse.

1. If There Isn't a Crisis, We Create One. One way to stir things up is familiar to anyone who has ever worked in a hard box organization. Intimidation, terror, and the use of raw power will produce all the stress you need. But eventually people run out of adrenalin and the organization is drained, not invigorated.

In a bubble organization, managers dig for opportunities in a much more relaxed manner. During the last three years, for instance, many of our divisions that were profitable and liquid were still in need of strategic overhaul.

During the course of walking around, we unearthed many important issues by asking dumb questions.

The more important of the issues that surface this way offer an opportunity to put a champion (someone who believes in the importance of the issue) in charge of a team of people who can play all the roles required to handle the issue. The champion then sets out with his or her group to go through the incremental development process—developing trust, building both a hard box picture and a shared vision, and, finally, establishing strategy. By the time the strategy is arrived at, the task force disciples have such zeal and sense of mission that they are ready to take the issue to larger groups, using the same process.

Two by-products of asking dumb questions deserve mention. First, when senior management talks to people at all levels, people at all levels start talking to each other. Second, things tend to get fixed before they break. In answering a senior manager's casual question, a welder on the shop floor of a steel fabrication plant revealed that some critical welds had failed quality tests and the customer's inspector was threatening to reject an entire bridge. A small ad hoc task force, which included the inspector (with the customer's permission), got everyone off the hook and alerted top management to a potential weakness in the quality control function.

Applying the principles in other areas takes years to bear fruit. We are now using the process to listen to customers and suppliers. We never knew how to do this before. Now it is clear that it is necessary to create an excuse (crisis) for going to see them, share "secrets," build trust, share a vision, and capture them in your bubble. It's very simple, and early results have been excellent. We call it a soft revolution.

2. Infuse Activities That Some Might Think Prosaic with Real Significance. The focus should be on people first, and always on caring rather than managing. The following approach works in good times as well as bad:

Use a graphic vocabulary that describes what you do.

Share confidential information, personal hopes and fears to create a common vision and promote trust.

Seize every opportunity (open doors, management by walking around, networks) to make a point, emphasize a value, disseminate information, share an experience, express interest, and show you care.

Recognize performance and contribution of as many people as possible. Rituals and ceremonies—retirements, promotions, birthdays—present great opportunities.

Use incentive programs whose main objective is not compensation but recognition.

We have tried to approach things this way, and for us the results have been significant. Now, three years after the crisis first struck our corporation, we are a very different organization. Of our 25 divisions, we have closed 7 and sold 16. Five of the latter were bought by Federal Industries, Ltd. of Winnipeg. Some 860 employees including us, the four members of the management team, have gone to Federal. These divisions are healthy and raring to go. Two divisions remain at York Russel, which has changed its name to YRI-YORK, Ltd.

Now we face new questions, such as how one recruits into a management team. We know that we have to help people grow into the team, and fortunately we find that they flourish in our warm climate. But trust takes time to develop, and the bubble is fragile. The risk is greatest when we have to transplant a senior person from outside, because time pressures may not allow us to be sure we are compatible. The danger is not only to the team itself but also to the person joining it.

Our new framework has given us a much deeper appreciation of the management process and the roles effective general managers play. For example, it is clear that while managers can delegate tasks in the hard box rather easily—perhaps because they can define them—it's impossible to delegate soft bubble activities. The latter are difficult to isolate from each other because their integration takes place in one brain.

Similarly, the hard box general management roles of producer and administrator can be formally taught, and business schools do a fine job of it. The soft roles of entrepreneur and integrator can probably not be taught formally. Instead, managers must learn from mentors. Over time they will adopt behavior patterns that allow them to play the required roles. It would seem, however, that natural ability and an individual's upbringing probably play a much larger part in determining effectiveness in the soft roles than in the hard roles; it is easier to teach a soft bubble player the hard box roles than it is to teach the soft roles to a hard box player.

In the three-year period when we had to do things so differently, we created our own culture, with its own language, symbols, norms, and customs. As with other groups, the acculturation process began when people got together in groups and trusted and cared about each other.[14]

In contrast with our premerger culture, the new culture is much more sympathetic toward and supportive of the use of teams and consensus decision making. In this respect, it would seem to be similar to oriental ways of thinking that place a premium on the same processes. Taoists, for instance, would have no trouble recognizing

---

[14]To explore the current concern with creating strong organizational cultures in North American corporations, see Terrence E. Deal and Alan A. Kennedy *Corporate Cultures* (Reading, Mass.: Addison-Wesley, 1982).

the polarities of the hard box and the soft bubble and the need to keep a balance between the two.[15]

☐ **Heaven** . . . & . . .	◯ **Earth**
☐ *Yang*	◯ *Yin*
☐ *Father*	◯ *Mother*
☐ *Man*	◯ *Woman*

These symbols are instructive. After all, most of us grew up with two bosses: father usually played the hard box parts, while mother played the soft, intuitive, and entrepreneurial roles. The family is the original team, formed to handle the most complex management task ever faced. Of late, we seem to have fired too many of its members—a mistake we can learn from.

TOWARD A MANAGERIAL THEORY OF RELATIVITY

The traditional hard box view of management, like the traditional orientation of physics, is valid (and very useful) only within a narrow range of phenomena. Once one gets outside the range, one needs new principles. In physics, cosmologists at the macro level as well as students of subatomic particles at the micro level use Einstein's theory of relativity as an explanatory principle and set Newton's physics aside.[16] For us, the theory in the bubble is our managerial theory of relativity. At the macro level it reminds us that how management phenomena appear de-

---

[15]For discussion of Tao and some applications, we highly recommend Benjamin Hoff, *The Tao of Pooh* (New York: E. P. Dutton, 1982), p.67; also Allen Watts, *Tao: The Watercourse Way* (New York: Pantheon Books, 1975).

[16]Fritjof Capra, *The Tao of Physics* (London: Fontana Paperbacks, 1983).

pends on one's perspective and biases. At the micro level we remember that all jobs have both hard and soft components.

This latter point is of particular importance to people like us in the service industry. The steel we distribute is indistinguishable from anyone else's. We insist on rigid standards regarding how steel is handled, what reporting systems are used, and so forth. But hard box standards alone wouldn't be enough to set us apart from our competitors. That takes service, a soft concept. And everyone has to be involved. Switchboard operators are in the front line; every contact is an opportunity to share the bubble. Truck drivers and warehouse workers make their own special contribution—by taking pride in the cleanliness of their equipment or by keeping the inventory neat and accessible.

With the box and bubble concept, managers can unlock many of the paradoxes of management and handle the inherent ambiguities. You don't do one or the other absolutely; you do what is appropriate. For instance, the other day in one of our operations the biweekly payroll run deducted what appeared to be random amounts from the sales representatives' pay packets. The branch affected was in an uproar. After taking some hard box steps to remedy the situation, our vice president of human resources seized the opportunity to go out to the branch and talk to the sales team. He was delighted with the response. The sales force saw that he understood the situation and cared about them, and he got to meet them all, which will make future contacts easier. But neither the hard box nor soft bubble approach on its own would have been appropriate. We need both. As one team member put it, "You have to find the bubble in the box and put the box in the bubble." Exactly.

The amazing thing is that the process works so well. The spirit of cooperation among senior managers is intense, and we seem to be getting "luckier" as we go along. When a "magic" event takes place it means that somehow we got the timing just right.[17] And there is great joy in that.

---

[17]Carl Jung developed the concept of synchronicity to explain such events. See, for example, Ira Progoff, *Jung, Synchronicity and Human Destiny—Non-Causal Dimension of Human Experience* (New York: Julian Press, 1973). For an excellent discussion of Jung's work and its relevance to our times, see Laurens van de Post, *Jung and the Story of Our Time* (New York: Random House, 1975).

Three

Managing Our Way to Economic Decline

Robert H. Hayes and
William J. Abernathy

During the past several years American business has experienced a marked deterioration of competitive vigor and a growing unease about its overall economic well-being. This decline in both health and confidence has been attributed by economists and business leaders to such factors as the rapacity of OPEC, deficiencies in government tax and monetary policies, and the proliferation of regulation. We find these explanations inadequate.

They do not explain, for example, why the rate of productivity growth in America has declined both absolutely and relative to that in Europe and Japan. Nor do they explain why in many high-technology as well as mature industries America has lost its leadership position. Although a host of readily named forces—government regulation, inflation, monetary policy, tax laws, labor costs and constraints, fear of a capital shortage, the price of imported oil—have taken their toll on American business, pressures of this sort affect the economic climate abroad just as they do here.

A German executive, for example, will not be convinced by these explanations. Germany imports 95 percent of its oil (we import 50 percent), its government's share of gross domestic product is about 37 percent (ours is about 30 percent), and workers must be consulted on most major decisions. Yet Germany's rate of productivity growth has actually increased since 1970 and recently rose to more than four times ours. In France the situation is similar, yet today that country's productivity growth in manufacturing (despite current crises in steel and textiles) more than triples ours. No modern industrial nation is immune to the problems and pressures besetting U.S. business. Why then do we find a disproportionate loss of competitive vigor by U.S. companies?

Our experience suggests that, to an unprecedented degree, success in most industries today requires an organizational commitment to compete in the marketplace on technological grounds—that is, to compete over the long run by offering superior products. Yet, guided by what they took to be the newest and best principles of management, American managers have increasingly directed their attention elsewhere. These new principles, despite their sophistication and widespread usefulness, encourage a preference for (1) analytic detachment rather than the insight that comes from "hands on" experience and (2) short-term cost reduction rather than long-term development of technological competitiveness. It is this new managerial gospel, we feel, that has played a major role in undermining the vigor of American industry.

American management, especially in the two decades after World War II, was universally admired for its strikingly effective performance. But times change. An approach shaped and refined during stable decades may be ill suited to a world characterized by rapid and unpredictable change, scarce energy, global competition for markets, and a constant need for innovation. This is the world of the 1980s and, probably, the rest of this century.

The time is long overdue for earnest, objective self-analysis. What exactly have American managers been doing wrong? What are the critical weaknesses in the ways that they have managed the technological performance of their companies? What is the matter with the long-unquestioned assumptions on which they have based their managerial policies and practices?

A FAILURE OF MANAGEMENT

In the past, American managers earned worldwide respect for their carefully planned yet highly aggressive action across three different time frames:

Short term—using existing assets as efficiently as possible.

Medium term—replacing labor and other scarce resources with capital equipment.

Long term—developing new products and processes that open new markets or restructure old ones.

The first of these time frames demanded toughness, determination, and close attention to detail; the second, capital and the willingness to take sizable financial risks; the third, imagination and a certain amount of technological daring.

Our managers still earn generally high marks for their skill in improving short-term efficiency, but their counterparts in Europe and Japan have started to question America's entrepreneurial imagination and willingness to make risky long-term competitive investments. As one such observer remarked to us: "The U.S. companies in my industry act like banks. All they are interested in is return on investment and getting their money back. Sometimes they act as though they are more interested in buying other companies than they are in selling products to customers."

In fact, this curt diagnosis represents a growing body of opinion that openly charges American managers with competitive myopia: "Somehow or other, American business is losing confidence in itself and especially confidence in its future. Instead of meeting the challenge of the changing world, American business today is making small, short-term adjustments by cutting costs and by turning to the government for temporary relief. . . . Success in trade is the result of patient and meticulous preparations, with a long period of market preparation before the rewards are available. . . . To undertake such commitments is hardly in the interest of a manager who is concerned with his or her next quarterly earnings reports."[1]

More troubling still, American managers themselves often admit the charge with, at most, a rhetorical shrug of their shoulders. In established businesses, notes one senior vice president of research: "We understand how to market, we know the technology, and production problems are not extreme. Why risk money on new businesses when good profitable low-risk opportunities are on every side?" Says another: "It's much more difficult to come up with a synthetic meat product than a lemon-lime cake mix. But you work on the lemon-lime cake mix because you know exactly what that return is going to be. A synthetic steak is

[1]Ryohei Suzuki, "Worldwide Expansion of U.S. Exports—A Japanese View," *Sloan Management Review*, Spring 1979, p. 1.

going to take a lot longer, require a much bigger invest-ment, and the risk of failure will be greater."[2]

These managers are not alone; they speak for many. Why, they ask, should they invest dollars that are hard to earn back when it is so easy—and so much less risky—to make money in other ways? Why ignore a ready-made situation in cake mixes for the deferred and far less certain prospects in synthetic steaks? Why shoulder the competi-tive risks of making better, more innovative products?

In our judgment, the assumptions underlying these ques-tions are prime evidence of a broad managerial failure—a failure of both vision and leadership—that over time has eroded both the inclination and the capacity of U.S. com-panies to innovate.

Exhibit 1
Growth in Labor Productivity since 1960 (United States and abroad)

| | Average Annual Percent Change | |
	Manufacturing 1960–1978	All Industries 1960–1976
United States	2.8%	1.7%
United Kingdom	2.9	2.2
Canada	4.0	2.1
Germany	5.4	4.2
France	5.5	4.3
Italy	5.9	4.9
Belgium	6.9*	—
Netherlands	6.9*	—
Sweden	5.2	—
Japan	8.2	7.5

*1960–1977.
Source: Council on Wage and Price Stability, *Report on Productivity* (Washington, D.C.: Executive Office of the President, July 1979).

[2]*Business Week* February 16, 1976, p. 57.

Exhibit 2
Growth of Labor Productivity by Sector, 1948–1978

Time Sector	Growth of Labor Productivity (annual average percent)		
	1948–1965	1965–1973	1973–1978
Private business	3.2%	2.3%	1.1%
Agriculture, forestry, and fisheries	5.5	5.3	2.9
Mining	4.2	2.0	−4.0
Construction	2.9	−2.2	−1.8
Manufacturing	3.1	2.4	1.7
Durable goods	2.8	1.9	1.2
Nondurable goods	3.4	3.2	2.4
Transportation	3.3	2.9	0.9
Communication	5.5	4.8	7.1
Electric, gas, and sanitary services	6.2	4.0	0.1
Trade	2.7	3.0	0.4
Wholesale	3.1	3.9	0.2
Retail	2.4	2.3	0.8
Finance, insurance, and real estate	1.0	−0.3	1.4
Services	1.5	1.9	0.5
Government enterprises	−0.8	0.9	−0.7

Note: Productivity data for services, construction, finance, insurance, and real estate are unpublished.
Source: Bureau of Labor Statistics.

FAMILIAR EXCUSES

About the facts themselves there can be little dispute. *Exhibits* 1–4 document our sorry decline. But the explanations and excuses commonly offered invite a good deal of comment.

It is important to recognize, first of all, that the problem is not new. It has been going on for at least 15 years. The rate of productivity growth in the private sector peaked in the mid-1960s. Nor is the problem confined to a few sectors of our economy; with a few exceptions, it perme-

Exhibit 3
National Expenditures for Performance of R&D as a Percent of GNP by Country, 1961–1978*

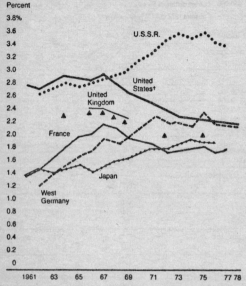

*Gross expenditures for performance of R&D including associated capital expenditures.
†Detailed information on capital expenditures for R&D is not available for the United States. Estimates for the period 1972–1977 show that their inclusion would have an impact of less than one-tenth of 1% for each year.
Note: The latest data may be preliminary or estimates.
Source: *Science Indicators—1978* (Washington, D.C.: National Science Foundation, 1979), p. 6.

ates our entire economy. Expenditures on R&D by both business and government, as measured in constant (non-inflated) dollars, also peaked in the mid-1960s—both in absolute terms and as a percentage of GNP. During the same period the expenditures on R&D by West Germany and Japan have been rising. More important, American spending on R&D as a percentage of sales in such critical research-intensive industries as machinery, professional and scientific instruments, chemicals, and aircraft had dropped by the mid-1970s to about half its level in the early 1960s.

Exhibit 4
Industrial R&D Expenditures for Basic Research, Applied Research, and Development, 1960–1978 (in $ millions)

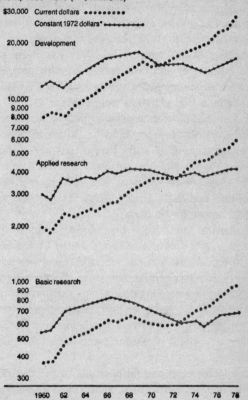

*GNP implicit price deflators used to convert current dollars to constant 1972 dollars.
Note: Preliminary data are shown for 1977 and estimates for 1978.
Source: *Science Indicators—1978*, p. 87.

These are the very industries on which we now depend for the bulk of our manufactured exports.

Investment in plant and equipment in the United States displays the same disturbing trends. As economist Burton

249

G. Malkiel has pointed out: "From 1948 to 1973 the [net book value of capital equipment] per unit of labor grew at an annual rate of almost 3 percent. Since 1973, however, lower rates of private investment have led to a decline in that growth rate to 1.75 percent. Moreover, the recent composition of investment [in 1978] has been skewed toward equipment and relatively short-term projects and away from structures and relatively long-lived investments. Thus our industrial plant has tended to age. . . ."[3]

Other studies have shown that growth in the incremental capital equipment-to-labor ratio has fallen to about one-third of its value in the early 1960s. By contrast, between 1966 and 1976 capital investment as a percentage of GNP in France and West Germany was more than 20 percent greater than that in the United States; in Japan the percentage was almost double ours.

To attribute this relative loss of technological vigor to such things as a shortage of capital in the United States is not justified. As Malkiel and others have shown, the return on equity of American business (out of which comes the capital necessary for investment) is about the same today as 20 years ago, *even after adjusting for inflation*. However, investment in both new equipment and R&D, as a percentage of GNP, was significantly higher 20 years ago than today.

The conclusion is painful but must be faced. Responsibility for this competitive listlessness belongs not just to a set of external conditions but also to the attitudes, preoccupations, and practices of American managers. By their preference for servicing existing markets rather than creating new ones and by their devotion to short-term returns and "management by the numbers," many of them have

[3] Burton G. Malkiel, "Productivity—The Problem Behind the Headlines," HBR May-June 1979, p. 81.

effectively forsworn long-term technological superiority as a competitive weapon. In consequence, they have abdicated their strategic responsibilities.

THE NEW MANAGEMENT ORTHODOXY

We refuse to believe that this managerial failure is the result of a sudden psychological shift among American managers toward a "super-safe, no risk" mind set. No profound sea change in the character of thousands of individuals could have occurred in so organized a fashion or have produced so consistent a pattern of behavior. Instead we believe that during the past two decades American managers have increasingly relied on principles which prize analytical detachment and methodological elegance over insight, based on experience, into the subtleties and complexities of strategic decisions. As a result, maximum short-term financial returns have become the overriding criteria for many companies.

For purposes of discussion, we may divide this *new* management orthodoxy into three general categories: financial control, corporate portfolio management, and market-driven behavior.

Financial Control

As more companies decentralize their organizational structures, they tend to fix on profit centers as the primary unit of managerial responsibility. This development necessitates, in turn, greater dependence on short-term financial measurements like return on investment (ROI) for evaluating the performance of individual managers and management groups. Increasing the structural distance between those entrusted with exploiting actual competitive opportunities and those who must judge the quality of their work virtually guarantees reliance on objectively quantifiable short-term criteria.

Although innovation, the lifeblood of any vital enterprise, is best encouraged by an environment that does not unduly penalize failure, the predictable result of relying too heavily on short-term financial measures—a sort of managerial remote control—is an environment in which no one feels he or she can afford a failure or even a momentary dip in the bottom line.

Corporate Portfolio Management

This preoccupation with control draws support from modern theories of financial portfolio management. Originally developed to help balance the overall risk and return of stock and bond portfolios, these principles have been applied increasingly to the creation and management of corporate portfolios—that is, a cluster of companies and product lines assembled through various modes of diversification under a single corporate umbrella. When applied by a remote group of dispassionate experts primarily concerned with finance and control and lacking hands-on experience, the analytic formulas of portfolio theory push managers even further toward an extreme of caution in allocating resources.

"Especially in large organizations," reports one manager, "we are observing an increase in management behavior which I would regard as excessively cautious, even passive; certainly overanalytical; and, in general, characterized by a studied unwillingness to assume responsibility and even reasonable risk."

Market-Driven Behavior

In the past 20 years, American companies have perhaps learned too well a lesson they had long been inclined to ignore: businesses should be customer oriented rather than product oriented. Henry Ford's famous dictum that the public could have any color automobile it wished as long as the color was black has since given way to its philosophical opposite: "We have got to stop marketing makeable products and learn to make marketable products."

At last, however, the dangers of too much reliance on this philosophy are becoming apparent. As two Canadian researchers have put it: "Inventors, scientists, engineers, and academics, in the normal pursuit of scientific knowledge, gave the world in recent times the laser, xerography, instant photography, and the transistor. In contrast, worshippers of the marketing concept have bestowed upon mankind such products as new-fangled potato chips, feminine hygiene deodorant, and the pet rock. . . ."[4]

The argument that no new product ought to be introduced without managers undertaking a market analysis is common sense. But the argument that consumer analyses and formal market surveys should dominate other considerations when allocating resources to product development is untenable. It may be useful to remember that the initial market estimate for computers in 1945 projected total worldwide sales of only ten units. Similarly, even the most carefully researched analysis of consumer preferences for gas-guzzling cars in an era of gasoline abundance offers little useful guidance to today's automobile manufacturers in making wise product investment decisions. Customers may know what their needs are, but they often define those

---

[4] Roger Bennett and Robert Cooper, "Beyond the Marketing Concept," *Business Horizons*, June 1979, p. 76.

needs in terms of existing products, processes, markets, and prices.

Deferring to a market-driven strategy without paying attention to its limitations is, quite possibly, opting for customer satisfaction and lower risk in the short run at the expense of superior products in the future. Satisfied customers are critically important, of course, but not if the strategy for creating them is responsible as well for unnecessary product proliferation, inflated costs, unfocused diversification, and a lagging commitment to new technology and new capital equipment.

THREE MANAGERIAL DECISIONS

These are serious charges to make. But the unpleasant fact of the matter is that, however useful these new principles may have been initially, if carried too far they are bad for U.S. business. Consider, for example, their effect on three major kinds of choices regularly faced by corporate managers: the decision between imitative and innovative product design, the decision to integrate backward, and the decision to invest in process development.

Imitative vs. Innovative Product Design

A market-driven strategy requires new product ideas to flow from detailed market analysis or, at least, to be extensively tested for consumer reaction before actual introduction. It is no secret that these requirements add significant delays and costs to the introduction of new products. It is less well known that they also predispose managers toward developing products for existing markets and toward product designs of an imitative rather than an innovative nature. There is increasing evidence that market-driven strategies tend, over time, to dampen the general level of innovation in new product decisions.

Confronted with the choice between innovation and imitation, managers typically ask whether the marketplace shows any consistent preference for innovative products. If so, the additional funding they require may be economically justified; if not, those funds can more properly go to advertising, promoting, or reducing the prices of less-advanced products. Though the temptation to allocate resources so as to strengthen performance in existing products and markets is often irresistible, recent studies by J. Hugh Davidson and others confirm the strong market attractiveness of innovative products.[5]

Nonetheless, managers having to decide between innovative and imitative product design face a difficult series of marketing-related trade-offs. *Exhibit* 5 summarizes these trade-offs.

By its very nature, innovative design is, as Joseph Schumpeter observed a long time ago, initially destructive of capital—whether in the form of labor skills, management systems, technological processes, or capital equipment. It tends to make obsolete existing investments in both marketing and manufacturing organizations. For the managers concerned it represents the choice of uncertainty (about economic returns, timing, etc.) over relative predictability, exchanging the reasonable expectation of current income against the promise of high future value. It is the choice of the gambler, the person willing to risk much to gain even more.

Conditioned by a market-driven strategy and held closely to account by a "results now" ROI-oriented control system, American managers have increasingly refused to take

[5]J. Hugh Davidson, "Why Most New Consumer Brands Fail," HBR March-April 1976, p. 117.

Exhibit 5
Trade-Offs between Imitative and Innovative Design for an Established Product Line

Imitative Design	Innovative Design
Market demand is relatively well known and predictable.	Potentially large but unpredictable demand; the risk of a flop is also large.
Market recognition and acceptance are rapid.	Market acceptance may be slow initially, but the imitative response of competitors may also be slowed.
Readily adaptable to existing market, sales, and distribution policies.	May require unique, tailored marketing distribution and sales policies to educate customers or because of special repair and warranty problems.
Fits with existing market segmentation and product policies.	Demand may cut across traditional marketing segments, disrupting divisional responsibilities and cannibalizing other products.

the chance on innovative product/market development. As one of them confesses: "In the last year, on the basis of high capital risk, I turned down new products at a rate at least twice what I did a year ago. But in every case I tell my people to go back and bring me some new product ideas."[6] In truth, they have learned caution so well that many are in danger of forgetting that market-driven, follow-the-leader companies usually end up following the rest of the pack as well.

Backward Integration

Sometimes the problem for managers is not their reluctance to take action and make investments but that, when they do so, their action has the unintended result of reinforcing the status quo. In deciding to integrate backward because of apparent short-term rewards, managers often restrict their ability to strike out in innovative directions in the future.

[6]*Business Week*, February 16, 1976, p.57.

Consider, for example, the case of a manufacturer who purchases a major component from an outside company. Static analysis of production economies may very well show that backward integration offers rather substantial cost benefits. Eliminating certain purchasing and marketing functions, centralizing overhead, pooling R&D efforts and resources, coordinating design and production of both product and component, reducing uncertainty over design changes, allowing for the use of more specialized equipment and labor skills—in all these ways and more, backward integration holds out to management the promise of significant short-term increases in ROI.

These efficiencies may be achieved by companies with commoditylike products. In such industries as ferrous and nonferrous metals or petroleum, backward integration toward raw materials and supplies tends to have a strong, positive effect on profits. However, the situation is markedly different for companies in more technologically active industries. Where there is considerable exposure to rapid technological advances, the promised value of backward integration becomes problematic. It may provide a quick, short-term boost to ROI figures in the next annual report, but it may also paralyze the long-term ability of a company to keep on top of technological change.

The real competitive threats to technologically active companies arise less from changes in ultimate consumer preference than from abrupt shifts in component technologies, raw materials, or production processes. Hence those managers whose attention is too firmly directed toward the marketplace and near-term profits may suddenly discover that their decision to make rather than buy important parts has locked their companies into an outdated technology.

Further, as supply channels and manufacturing operations become more systematized, the benefits from attempts to "rationalize" production may well be accompanied by unanticipated side effects. For instance, a company may find itself shut off from the R&D efforts of various independent suppliers by becoming their competitor. Similarly, the commitment of time and resources needed to master technology back up the channel of supply may distract a company from doing its own job well. Such was the fate of Bowmar, the pocket calculator pioneer, whose attempt to integrate backward into semiconductor production so consumed management attention that final assembly of the calculators, its core business, did not get the required resources.

Long-term contracts and long-term relationships with suppliers can achieve many of the same cost benefits as backward integration without calling into question a company's ability to innovate or respond to innovation. European automobile manufacturers, for example, have typically chosen to rely on their suppliers in this way; American companies have followed the path of backward integration. The resulting trade-offs between production efficiencies and innovative flexibility should offer a stern warning to those American managers too easily beguiled by the lure of short-term ROI improvement. A case in point: the U.S. auto industry's huge investment in automating the manufacture of cast-iron brake drums probably delayed by more than five years its transition to disc brakes.

Process Development

In an era of management by the numbers, many American managers—especially in mature industries—are reluctant to invest heavily in the development of new manufacturing processes. When asked to explain their reluctance, they tend to respond in fairly predictable ways. "We can't afford to design new capital equipment for just our own manufacturing needs" is one frequent answer. So is: "The capital equipment producers do a much better job, and they can amortize their development costs over sales to many companies." Perhaps most common is: "Let the others experiment in manufacturing; we can learn from their mistakes and do it better."

Each of these comments rests on the assumption that essential advances in process technology can be appropriated more easily through equipment purchase than through in-house equipment design and development. Our extensive conversations with the managers of European (primarily German) technology-based companies have convinced us that this assumption is not as widely shared abroad as in the United States. Virtually across the board, the European managers impressed us with their strong commitment to increasing market share through internal development of advanced process technology—even when their suppliers were highly responsive to technological advances.

By contrast, American managers tend to restrict investments in process development to only those items likely to reduce costs in the short run. Not all are happy with this. As one disgruntled executive told us: "For too long U.S. managers have been taught to set low priorities on mechanization projects, so that eventually divestment appears to be the best way out of manufacturing difficulties. Why?

"The drive for short-term success has prevented managers from looking thoroughly into the matter of special manufacturing equipment, which has to be invented, developed, tested, redesigned, reproduced, improved, and so on. That's a long process, which needs experienced, knowledgeable, and dedicated people who stick to their jobs over a considerable period of time. Merely buying new equipment (even if it is possible) does not often give the company any advantage over competitors."

We agree. Most American managers seem to forget that, even if they produce new products with their existing process technology (the same "cookie cutter" everyone else can buy), their competitors will face a relatively short lead time for introducing similar products. And as Eric von Hippel's studies of industrial innovation show, the innovations on which new industrial equipment is based usually originate with the user of the equipment and not with the equipment producer.[7] In other words, companies can make products more profitable by investing in the development of their own process technology. Proprietary processes are every bit as formidable competitive weapons as proprietary products.

THE AMERICAN MANAGERIAL IDEAL

Two very important questions remain to be asked: (1) Why should so many American managers have shifted so strongly to this new managerial orthodoxy? and (2) Why are they not more deeply bothered by the ill effects of those principles on the long-term technological competitiveness of their companies? To answer the first question, we must take a look at the changing career patterns of American managers during the past quarter century; to answer the second, we must understand the way in which they have come to regard their professional roles and responsibilities as managers.

The Road to the Top
During the past 25 years the American manager's road to the top has changed significantly. No longer does the

[7]Eric von Hippel, "The Dominant Role of Users in the Scientific Instrument Innovation Process," MIT Sloan School of Management Working Paper 75–764, January 1975.

typical career, threading sinuously up and through a corporation with stops in several functional areas, provide future top executives with intimate hands-on knowledge of the company's technologies, customers, and suppliers.

Exhibit 6 summarizes the currently available data on the shift in functional background of newly appointed presidents of the 100 largest U.S. corporations. The immediate significance of these figures is clear. Since the mid-1950s there has been a rather substantial increase in the percentage of new company presidents whose primary interests and expertise lie in the financial and legal areas and not in production. In the view of C. Jackson Grayson, president of the American Productivity Center, American management has for 20 years "coasted off the great R&D gains made during World War II, and constantly rewarded executives from the marketing, financial, and legal sides of the business while it ignored the production men. Today [in business schools] courses in the production area are almost nonexistent."[8]

In addition, companies are increasingly choosing to fill new top management posts from outside their own ranks. In the opinion of foreign observers, who are still accustomed to long-term careers in the same company or division, "High-level American executives . . . seem to come and go and switch around as if playing a game of musical chairs at an Alice in Wonderland tea party."

Far more important, however, than any absolute change in numbers is the shift in the general sense of what an aspiring manager has to be "smart about" to make it to the top. More important still is the broad change in attitude such trends both encourage and express. What has developed, in the business community as in academia, is a preoccupation with a false and shallow concept of the

[8]*Dun's Review*, July 1978, p. 39.

Exhibit 6
Changes in the Professional Origins of Corporate Presidents (percent changes from baseline years [1948–52] for 100 top U.S. companies)

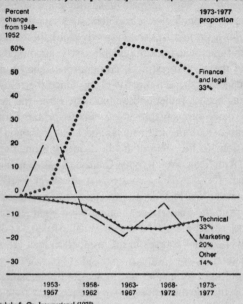

Source: Golightly & Co. International (1978).

professional manager, a "pseudoprofessional" really—an individual having no special expertise in any particular industry or technology who nevertheless can step into an unfamiliar company and run it successfully through strict application of financial controls, portfolio concepts, and a market-driven strategy.

The Gospel of Pseudo-Professionalism

In recent years, this idealization of pseudo-professionalism has taken on something of the quality of a corporate religion. Its first doctrine, appropriately enough, is that neither industry experience nor hands-on technological expertise counts for very much. At one level, of course, this doctrine helps to salve the conscience of those who lack them. At another, more disturbing level it encourages the faithful to make decisions about technological matters simply as if they were adjuncts to finance or marketing decisions. We do not believe that the technological issues facing managers today can be meaningfully addressed without taking into account marketing or financial considerations; on the other hand, neither can they be resolved with the same methodologies applied to these other fields.

Complex modern technology has its own inner logic and developmental imperatives. To treat it as if it were something else—no matter how comfortable one is with that other kind of data—is to base a competitive business on a two-legged stool, which must, no matter how excellent the balancing act, inevitably fall to the ground.

More disturbing still, true believers keep the faith on a day-to-day basis by insisting that as issues rise up the managerial hierarchy for decision they be progressively distilled into easily quantifiable terms. One European manager, in recounting to us his experiences in a joint venture with an American company, recalled with exasperation that ''U.S. managers want everything to be simple. But sometimes business situations are not simple, and they cannot be divided up or looked at in such a way that they become simple. They are messy, and one must try to understand all the facets. This appears to be alien to the American mentality.''

The purpose of good organizational design, of course, is to divide responsibilities in such a way that individuals have relatively easy tasks to perform. But then these differentiated responsibilities must be pulled together by sophisticated, broadly gauged integrators at the top of the managerial pyramid. If these individuals are interested in but one or two aspects of the total competitive picture, if their training includes a very narrow exposure to the range of functional specialties, if—worst of all—they are devoted simplifiers themselves, who will do the necessary integration? Who will attempt to resolve complicated issues rather than try to uncomplicate them artificially? At the strategic level there are no such things as pure production problems, pure financial problems, or pure marketing problems.

Merger Mania

When executive suites are dominated by people with financial and legal skills, it is not surprising that top management should increasingly allocate time and energy to such concerns as cash management and the whole process of corporate acquisitions and mergers. This is indeed what has happened. In 1978 alone there were some 80 mergers involving companies with assets in excess of $100 million each; in 1979 there were almost 100. This represents roughly $20 billion in transfers of large companies from one owner to another—two-thirds of the total amount spent on R&D by American industry.

In 1978 *Business Week* ran a cover story on cash management in which it stated that "the 400 largest U.S. companies together have more than $60 billion in cash— almost triple the amount they had at the beginning of the 1970s." The article also described the increasing attention devoted to—and the sophisticated and exotic techniques used for—managing this cash hoard.

There are perfectly good reasons for this flurry of activity. It is entirely natural for financially (or legally) trained managers to concentrate on essentially financial (or legal) activities. It is also natural for managers who subscribe to the portfolio "law of large numbers" to seek to reduce total corporate risk by parceling it out among a sufficiently large number of separate product lines, businesses, or technologies. Under certain conditions it may very well make good economic sense to buy rather than build new plants or modernize existing ones. Mergers are obviously an exciting game; they tend to produce fairly quick and decisive results, and they offer the kind of public recognition that helps careers along. Who can doubt the appeal of the titles awarded by the financial community; being called a "gunslinger," "white knight," or "raider" can quicken anyone's blood.

Unfortunately, the general American penchant for separating and simplifying has tended to encourage a diversification away from core technologies and markets to a much greater degree than is true in Europe or Japan. U.S. managers appear to have an inordinate faith in the portfolio law of large numbers—that is, by amassing enough product lines, technologies, and businesses, one will be cushioned against the random setbacks that occur in life. This might be true for portfolios of stocks and bonds, where there is considerable evidence that setbacks *are* random. Businesses, however, are subject not only to random setbacks such as strikes and shortages but also to carefully orchestrated attacks by competitors, who focus all their resources and energies on one set of activities.

Worse, the great bulk of this merger activity appears to have been absolutely wasted in terms of generating economic benefits for stockholders. Acquisition experts do not necessarily make good managers. Nor can they increase the value of their shares by merging two companies any better than their shareholders could do individually by buying shares of the acquired company on the open market (at a price usually below that required for a takeover attempt).

There appears to be a growing recognition of this fact. A number of U.S. companies are now divesting themselves of previously acquired companies; others (for example, W.R. Grace) are proposing to break themselves up into relatively independent entities. The establishment of a strong competitive position through in-house technological superiority is by nature a long, arduous, and often unglamorous task. But it is what keeps a business vigorous and competitive.

THE EUROPEAN EXAMPLE

Gaining competitive success through technological superiority is a skill much valued by the seasoned European (and Japanese) managers with whom we talked. Although we were able to locate few hard statistics on their actual practice, our extensive investigations of more than 20 companies convinced us that European managers do indeed tend to differ significantly from their American counterparts. In fact, we found that many of them were able to articulate these differences quite clearly.

In the first place, European managers think themselves more pointedly concerned with how to survive over the long run under intensely competitive conditions. Few markets, of course, generate price competition as fierce as in the United States, but European companies face the remorseless necessity of exporting to other national markets or perishing.

The figures here are startling: manufactured product exports represent more than 35 percent of total manufacturing sales in France and Germany and nearly 60 percent in the Benelux countries, as against not quite 10 percent in the United States. In these export markets, moreover, European products must hold their own against "world class'' competitors, lower-priced products from developing countries, and American products selling at attractive devalued dollar prices. To survive this competitive squeeze, European managers feel they must place central emphasis on producing technologically superior products.

Further, the kinds of pressures from European labor unions and national governments virtually force them to take a consistently long-term view in decision making. German managers, for example, must negotiate major decisions at the plant level with worker-dominated works councils; in turn, these decisions are subject to review by supervisory boards (roughly equivalent to American boards of directors), half of whose membership is worker elected. Together with strict national legislation, the pervasive influence of labor unions makes it extremely difficult to change employment levels or production locations. Not surprisingly, labor costs in Northern Europe have more than doubled in the past decade and are now the highest in the world.

To be successful in this environment of strictly constrained options, European managers feel they must employ a decision-making apparatus that grinds very fine—and very deliberately. They must simply outthink and outmanage their competitors. Now, American managers also have their strategic options hedged about by all kinds of restrictions. But those restrictions have not yet made them as conscious as their European counterparts of the long-term implications of their day-to-day decisions.

As a result, the Europeans see themselves as investing more heavily in cutting-edge technology than the Americans. More often than not, this investment is made to create new product opportunities in advance of consumer demand and not merely in response to market-driven strategy. In case after case, we found the Europeans striving to develop the products and process capabilities with which to lead markets and not simply responding to the current demands of the marketplace. Moreover, in doing this they seem less inclined to integrate backward and more likely to seek maximum leverage from stable, long-term relationships with suppliers.

Having never lost sight of the need to be technologically competitive over the long run, European and Japanese managers are extremely careful to make the necessary arrangements and investments today. And their daily concern with the rather basic issue of long-term survival adds perspective to such matters as short-term ROI or rate of growth. The time line by which they manage is long, and it has made them painstakingly attentive to the means for keeping their companies technologically competitive. Of course they pay attention to the numbers. Their profit margins are usually lower than ours, their debt ratios higher. Every tenth of a percent is critical to them. But they are also aware that tomorrow will be no better unless they constantly try to develop new processes, enter new markets, and offer superior—even unique—products. As one senior German executive phrased it recently, "We look at rates of return, too, but only after we ask 'Is it a good product?' "[9]

CREATING ECONOMIC VALUE

Americans traveling in Europe and Asia soon learn they must often deal with criticism of our country. Being forced to respond to such criticism can be healthy, for it requires rethinking some basic issues of principle and practice.

We have much to be proud about and little to be ashamed of relative to most other countries. But sometimes the

[9]*Business Week,* March 3, 1980, p. 76.

criticism of others is uncomfortably close to the mark. The comments of our overseas competitors on American business practices contain enough truth to require our thoughtful consideration. What is behind the decline in competitiveness of U.S. business? Why do U.S. companies have such apparent difficulties competing with foreign producers of established products, many of which originated in the United States?

For example, Japanese televisions dominate some market segments, even though many U.S. producers now enjoy the same low labor cost advantages of offshore production. The German machine tool and automotive producers continue their inroads into U.S. domestic markets, even though their labor rates are now higher than those in the United States and the famed German worker in German factories is almost as likely to be Turkish or Italian as German.

The responsibility for these problems may rest in part on government policies that either overconstrain or undersupport U.S. producers. But if our foreign critics are correct, the long-term solution to America's problems may not be correctable simply by changing our government's tax laws, monetary policies, and regulatory practices. It will also require some fundamental changes in management attitudes and practices.

It would be an oversimplification to assert that the only reason for the decline in competitiveness of U.S. companies is that our managers devote too much attention and energy to using existing resources more efficiently. It would also oversimplify the issue, although possibly to a lesser extent, to say that it is due purely and simply to their tendency to neglect technology as a competitive weapon.

Companies cannot become more innovative simply by increasing R&D investments or by conducting more basic research. Each of the decisions we have described directly affects several functional areas of management, and major conflicts can only be reconciled at senior executive levels. The benefits favoring the more innovative, aggressive option in each case depend more on intangible factors than do their efficiency-oriented alternatives.

Senior managers who are less informed about their industry and its confederation of parts suppliers, equipment suppliers, workers, and customers or who have less time to consider the long-term implications of their interactions are likely to exhibit a noninnovative bias in their choices. Tight financial controls with a short-term emphasis will also bias choices toward the less innovative, less technologically aggressive alternatives.

The key to long-term success—even survival—in business is what it has always been: to invest, to innovate, to lead, to create value where none existed before. Such determination, such striving to excel, requires leaders—not *just* controllers, market analysts, and portfolio managers. In our preoccupation with the braking systems and exterior trim, we may have neglected the drive trains of our corporations.

Four

Marks and Spencer, Ltd.

The principles on which the business was founded do not change. The original ideas have been expanded to conform to the changing requirements of a more knowledgeable and discerning public—a public which has broadened to include wider strata of the community.

In the course of the years, we have built up three great assets:

1. The good will and confidence of the public.
2. The loyalty and devotion of management and staff throughout the system.
3. The confidence and cooperation of our suppliers.

This case was prepared by Ms. Christine Harris (under the direction of Professor Joseph L. Bower) as the basis for class discussion rather than to illustrate either effective or ineffective handling of an administrative situation. This revision was prepared by Mr. Mark B. Fuller.

Copyright © 1975 by the President and Fellows of Harvard College Harvard Business School case 375–358.

The principles upon which the business is built are:

1. To offer our customers a selective range of high-quality, well-designed and attractive merchandise at reasonable prices.
2. To encourage our suppliers to use the most modern and efficient techniques of production and quality control dictated by the latest discoveries in science and technology.
3. With the cooperation of our suppliers, to enforce the highest standard of quality control.
4. To plan the expansion of our stores for the better display of a widening range of goods and for the convenience of our customers.
5. To foster good human relations with customers, suppliers and staff.

These five tenets constituted the fundamental operating principles of Marks and Spencer, according to Lord Marks of Broughton, Chairman of the firm from 1916 to 1964. Applying them, Marks and Spencer (M&S) had achieved outstanding success. By 1974, M&S was the largest retail organization in the United Kingdom. Each week more than thirteen million customers made purchases at the firm's 251 stores which offered some 700 food and 3,000 nonfood (primarily textile) items. Textiles supplied 71 percent of M&S sales in 1974; food 27 percent, and exports 2 percent. The company accounted for 12 percent of British consumer expenditures for clothing and footwear and held over one-third of the market in women's lingerie and men's underwear.

Despite the disappointing British economic situation, Marks and Spencer prospered in 1974. While national income declined 2 percent and inflation rose 15 percent–18 percent, M&S posted record sales of $1,422,109,000. Pretax profit climbed 10 percent to $180,538,000 (see

Exhibit 1). While sales/square foot for Britain's top retailers averaged $180 per year, Marks and Spencer's reached $260. The company's Marble Arch outlet in London achieved sales/square foot of $1,000, earning it a listing in *Guinness' Book of World Records* as the most profitable store in the world.

A board of 22 executives managed M&S from the firm's offices in Baker Street, London. Buying, merchandising, distribution, quality control and finance were centralized in the Baker Street headquarters. Marks and Spencer sold all of its merchandise under the exclusive "St. Michaels" brand name. The company owned no production facilities, relying instead on a broad network of suppliers from whom it ordered some $25 million worth of goods each week.

M&S's major competitors included a supermarket chain with food sales nearly twice M&S's; two retailing firms which imitated M&S but sold cheaper, lower quality goods; and an "American" style department store which emphasized more fashion-oriented goods at lower prices and quality.

History of M&S: The Early Years

The business principles enunciated by Lord Marks originated in the experiences of his father, Michael Marks, the founder of M&S. In 1884, the elder Marks, a Polish Jew, began visiting the town markets of Northern England, setting up stalls which featured the sign, "Don't Ask the Price—It's a Penny." The slogan proved so popular that Marks adopted the penny price in all his stalls. The simplicity of the single fixed price allowed Marks to give up keeping accounts and inspired him to search continually for goods as varied and excellent as could be sold for a penny. High turnover counterbalanced the low profit margins.

Exhibit 1

MARKS AND SPENCER, LTD.
Profit and Loss Account
For the Years Ended March 31, 1973, and 1974
(£ 000)

	1974	1973
Gross store sales	$591,570	$511,934
Export sales	13,583	10,370
Net sales	605,153	522,304
Operating profit	76,825	70,036
Taxation	39,900	24,900
Profit after taxation	36,925	45,136
Extraordinary Item:		
Surplus on disposal of fixed assets	2,383	176
	39,308	45,312
Dividends	19,008	21,388
Undistributed surplus	$20,300	$23,924
Earnings per share	11.4 p	13.9 p

MARKS AND SPENCER, LTD.
Balance Sheet
As of March 31, 1974
(£ 000)

Assets	1974	1973
Current assets:		
Inventory	$31,472	$29,638
Cash and short-term deposits	18,400	44,612
Debtors and prepayments	10,502	8,150
Tax reserve certificates	–	4,000
Total current assets	60,434	86,400
Fixed assets:		
Properties	221,895	182,710
Fixtures and equipment	19,825	15,668
Total assets	$304,364	$284,830

Liabilities		
Current liabilities:		
Creditors and accrued charges	$28,055	$29,971
Corporation tax	28,237	23,359
Dividends (interim payable and final proposed)	12,255	21,283
Total current liabilities	68,547	74,613
Long-term liability:		
Deferred taxation	18,400	13,100
Debenture stock	45,000	45,000
Total long-term liabilities	63,400	58,100

Net worth		
Shareholders' interest	172,417	152,117
Total liabilities and net worth	$304,364	$284,830

Exhibit 1 (concluded)
10-Year Statement—Year Ended March 31

	1965*	1966	1967	1968	1969	1970	1971*	1972	1973	1974
						(£ 000)				
Turnover†	208,636	226,135	242,954	268,607	299,672	338,843	390,915	438,600	522,304	605,153
Operating Profit	27,506	29,618	30,659	33,871	38,123	43,705	50,115	53,766	70,036	76,825
Profit after Taxation	12,706	18,268	18,959	20,121	21,773	26,005	31,215	34,416	45,136	36,925
Corporation Tax Rate	N.C.	40%	40%	42.5%	45%	42.5%	40%	40%	40%	52%
Earnings per Share	N.C.	5.6p	5.8p	6.2p	6.7p	8.0p	9.6p	10.6p	13.9p	11.4p‡
Dividend Payments to Shareholders	9,258	9,928	9,950	10,266	10,609	11,928	13,904	15,528	17,826	19,008
Retained Profit	3,246	4,322	2,461	2,536	3,667	5,747	8,220§	9,132	23,924	17,917§
Depreciation	1,844	1,993	2,177	2,488	2,987	3,534	4,177	4,620	5,055	5,464
Ordinary Share Capital and Reserves	105,468	109,790	112,251	114,788	118,455	123,152	127,711	136,843	150,767	171,067
Total Sales Area (square feet – 000)	3,337	3,471	3,635	3,929	4,214	4,408	4,708	4,944	5,059	5,489

N.C. = Not comparable
*53 weeks.
†Turnover for the year ended March 31, 1974, is shown after deduction of V.A.T. For the purpose of comparison, turnover figures for previous years have been shown after deduction of purchase tax.
‡Earnings per share are not comparable by reason of the change in basis of taxation.
§Excluding surplus on disposal of assets: 1971—£2,393,000
1974—£2,383,000

Marks' business flourished and, in 1894, he took Thomas Spencer into partnership. By 1903, when Spencer retired, the company boasted 40 branches. In that year Marks and Spencer, Ltd. was formed, with control entirely in Marks and Spencer family hands, and the headquarters was moved to Manchester, which possessed a pleasant Jewish society. Spencer died in 1905; Michael Marks in 1908. After Marks' death, control of M&S temporarily passed out of family hands.

The Years 1914–1939

When the founder's son, Simon Marks (later Lord Marks) regained control of the firm in 1914, it was a national chain with 140 branches. While only 10 percent were in market halls, M&S maintained its traditional policies of open display, easy accessibility to goods, and self-selection. Management also strove to make M&S a place where employees were happy and proud to work. Each store had a manageress in charge of training and a heated room in which the staff could eat and relax.

With the accession of Simon Marks, a strong family influence returned to M&S. Simon exercised overall direction while his brother-in-law, Israel Sieff (later Lord Sieff) took charge of buying and merchandising. After their deaths, their descendants continued to dominate M&S into the 1970s (see Exhibit 2).[1] Two outside influences also had profound impact on M&S in the decade after 1914: first, Chaim Weizmann, the brilliant chemist and famous Zionist leader, encouraged Marks and Sieff in commitments which became cornerstones of the modern M&S. In addition to introducing the pair to Zionism, Weizmann interested them in the applications and benefits of new technologies and

[1] In 1975, M&S had no outside directors.

inspired them to regard their business as a social service to both customers and employees. Secondly, a 1924 visit to the U.S. allowed Simon Marks to study American chain stores. He returned to England determined to transform M&S into a chain of "super stores" featuring continuous merchandise flow and a central organization acutely sensitive to consumer needs.

Exhibit 2
Management at Marks and Spencer, 1894–1975

1894— Partnership between Michael Marks and Thomas Spencer.

1905— Thomas Spencer dies.

1908— Michael Marks dies. Control of M&S leaves family hands.

1914— Simon Marks (later Lord Marks) assumes control of M&S. His brother-in-law, Israel Sieff (later Lord Sieff) becomes responsible for buying and merchandising.

1964— Lord Marks dies; Lord Sieff becomes Chairman.

1968— Lord Sieff relinquishes chairmanship to his brother, J. Edward Sieff, and becomes President.

1972— Lord Sieff dies.

1973— J. Edward Sieff relinquishes chairmanship to Israel's son, Sir Marcus, and becomes President.

M&S went public in 1926 and within ten years had a branch in every major town. Enhanced staff amenities accompanied this rapid growth. The welfare department, founded in 1933, supervised a variety of employee facilities and expanded medical and dental services which included chiropody (especially significant to salespeople who spent hours standing). A pension plan was initiated in 1936.

Changes also occurred in M&S's relations with its suppliers. In 1928, Marks and Spencer registered the "St. Michael" brand name (honoring M&S's founder) and became the first department store in the U.K. to set for itself the goal of selling only "own-brand" merchandise. To assure the highest product quality, M&S insisted on close cooperation with suppliers and stressed the use of technological advances in materials and production processes. In 1928 M&S's large orders enabled the company to overcome traditional wholesale opposition and place orders directly with producers. Food purchases, upon which management imposed extremely strict standards, followed a similar pattern.

The Years 1945–1955

In the decade following the war, M&S's sales rose 450 percent and pretax profits 351 percent. The St. Michael brand gradually emerged on all products and became increasingly identified in consumers' minds with quality and value. Concentrating on a limited product range, M&S developed a dominant position in many textile lines.

Sales growth led to store modernization and expansion. After postwar controls were abolished in the 1950s, growth accelerated rapidly.

Table 1
Growth in Marks and Spencer, Ltd. 1946–1974

	Sales* (000)	Profits (000)	Number of Stores	Total Store Space (000/sq. ft.)
1946	£ 19,693	£ 2,027	224	1,407
1955	108,375	9,168	234	2,461
1968	282,308	33,871	241	3,939
1974	571,650	76,825	251	5,489

*Including exports. Food sales ranged from 14 percent of total sales (1957) to 27 percent (1974).

Operation Simplification (1956)

On February 16, 1956, Lord Marks, Chairman of M&S, was presented with a budget which exceeded the previous year's by millions of pounds. He reacted strongly to the increases and launched a companywide campaign to eliminate the burgeoning load of paperwork which appeared chiefly responsible for rising overhead. As Lord Marks remarked to Israel Sieff, "It's not a law of business growth that administrative costs continue to increase. Anyway, if things go on like this, we shall be selling women's blouses at £10 apiece." The campaign, known as "Operation Simplification," aimed at liberating staff, management, and supporting services from paperwork so that they could focus on one task: increasing sales in pounds sterling.

The general principles of Operation Simplification were:

1. *Sensible approximation:* The price of perfection is prohibitive; approximation often suffices and costs less;
2. *Exception reporting:* Events generally occur as arranged, and only exceptions need to be reported;
3. *"Never legislate for exceptions"*: Detailed manuals are unnecessary (M&S went from 13 manuals to 2), and local decision-making enhances willingness to assume responsibility;
4. *Decategorization:* Those below management and supervisory levels are more useful in a "general staff" category than as specialists;
5. *People can and need to be trusted:* Eliminating checks and controls saves time and money, while improving staff self-confidence and sense of responsibility. Management control is more effectively exercised by selective spot checks.

Lord Marks set a goal of allowing store staff, management, and support services to focus on one task—increasing sales in pounds sterling. The new system made senior executives responsible for profitability. They determined one markup target for food and another for textiles. With margins thus standardized, the selectors focused on finding goods of acceptable quality that would turn over rapidly. Stores then worked to use space and customers in ways to achieve maximum sales of the selected goods.

To insure the effectiveness of the system, Lord Marks enlisted the personal support of head office managers who then assumed responsibility for improving efficiency in their areas. The campaign, which culminated in a symbolic bonfire of old records, eliminated 26 million pieces of paper per year—120 tons—and reduced the 32,000-person staff by 10,000. The abolition of countless forms and routines freed senior managers to leave their desks and get personally involved in their departments. Commenting on the drive for simplicity, Lord Sieff wrote:

> Both the executives and the merchandisers of the department should *probe* into the goods in the stores *with seeing eyes and a critical mind*. The department supervisor and the salesgirl are his best sources of information. To depend on statistics is to asphyxiate the dynamic spirit of the business.

Lord Sieff described the process as:

> The method whereby the interested and inquiring mind of the executive and his colleagues penetrates beneath the surface of things and discovers the facts.

The emphasis on "probing" became an integral part of the M&S management philosophy. Brian Howard, Director of Foods, illustrated the merits of "probing":

We get concerned when statistics get on paper because they hide things. For example, suppose I had a report on sales at a store that showed for a day:

	Beginning Stock	Sales	Ending Stock
Item A	100	100	0
Item B	50	20	30

I might conclude that sales of A to B were 5:1 and act accordingly. But if I looked after lunch, I might find that the sales for the morning showed:

	Beginning Stock	Sales	Ending Stock
Item A	100	100	0
Item B	50	10	40

I have to ask the store manager to learn that the proper order is more like 10:1. That's why we distrust statistics and value "probing."

Simplicity remained a touchstone for Marks and Spencer management in the 1970s. In 1974 M&S inaugurated a "Good Housekeeping" campaign to limit paperwork. "Probing" continued to occupy an important place. It was conducted not only at the head office but also, especially, in the stores. All senior executives frequented stores as often as possible, many stopping on their way home from work. In 1974 only 10 of M&S's 251 stores failed to receive a visit from a senior board member.

Every weekend, each director received a hamper of M&S food to use. In addition, he was expected to wear M&S clothes. Both policies allowed executives to monitor product quality personally. On Saturdays, each board member and senior executive toured two or three stores. Managers frequently encountered other executives in stores when "probing." For example, a researcher accompanied Brian Howard on a Saturday tour of the Uxbridge store. Over coffee Howard assembled a textile sales manager, junior executives in food and textiles, a food technologist and the store manager. All were headed for other stores. As a head office employee remarked about the directors:

> They work 60 hours during the week, they visit stores on Saturday and they talk about it on Sunday. They live, eat and breathe M&S.

During the Saturday visits, executives spent a great deal of time talking with employees. The following is an excerpt from a 1974 store tour conducted by the Chairman, Sir Marcus Sieff, and Brian Howard:

> Staines was a small store but did £40,000/week. We arrived around 9:15 and were greeted by one of the supervisors. The store traffic seemed brisk but the staff manageress thought it a little below normal.
>
> A very young food department supervisor was asked to take us around. She was flustered but did her best to answer questions. It was easy to see what was meant by the necessity at M&S of being able to give straight, clear answers. Brian Howard expected her to know her numbers and her situation. There were problems of short produce deliveries and he wanted them described. He also offered comments on store layout.
>
> Later the staff manageress took us around upstairs. The warehouse space floor was spotless. The atmosphere was one of easy-going efficiency and competence.
>
> Leaving Staines, Mr. Howard drove on to the Reading store to meet Sir Marcus Sieff. Sir Marcus led his party around the store. All that he was wearing that day, except his shoes—slacks, shirt, sweater, and jacket—

were available on the racks in the store. His questions dealt entirely with merchandise and people. What was moving? The store manager answered from memory with current sales numbers representing percentage comparison with previous weeks and years. Department managers added comments.

The discussion was candid. Of a shirt, "Here's one of our mistakes. Have you reduced this?"

"Yes, but it still isn't moving. We'll have to take it down another pound."

"Why isn't there a price notice?" to a young sales supervisor.

"We just got these this morning, Chairman, and the sign is being made."

"We buy this from Burlington. We've ordered 2 million yards of this fabric so far. It's moving very well."

Looking at a child's snowsuit jacket at £6.25 (approximately $15.00). "Is that our price? We've *got* to get a less expensive range. Our customers can't afford that." Everyone had his pad from the chairman down and all took their own notes.

"Did your boss come in to work today?" to a warehouse foreman whose wife worked as a sales clerk. "Yes, Chairman." "How is Mary?" "She's well, thank you."

On our tour of the lunchroom and offices, he asked for the hairdresser by name. "She's the queen of Reading," and gave numerous directives—"I want 'switch the lights out please' signs near the doors whenever the switches aren't near the door. They have to learn we have a balance of payments problems. When do our window lights go off?" "6:30." "When do we close?" "6." "I want them off at 6."

Driving to his home for lunch, Sir Marcus commented on what he had learned.

"Some lines we like don't move—like this jacket. We have to find out why. We have a problem in having enough stock for the period after New Year's without carrying too much inventory. And that store has some good people. They're doing a good job."

Other Developments at M&S

1. Personnel Point 5 of the General Principles of *Operation Simplification* reemphasized Marks and Spencer's traditional commitment to the well-being of its employees. M&S implemented this commitment by establishing company-financed social and recreational clubs at Baker Street and in each store and by upgrading medical and pension benefits. When Lord Sieff succeeded to the chairmanship in 1964, he reiterated the company's concern,

> M&S started with people. We (Lord Marks and I) both felt that making people happy was the great thing in life. So, when we got into the stores, we automatically thought in these lines. For instance, we found that the girls were going without lunch when they were broke or busy. So we put in lunchrooms and saw to it that they got time to eat their meals.

A 1969 speech by Managing Director (later Chairman) Sir Marcus Sieff reflected similar sentiments:

> The guiding light of business enterprise is attention to human relations within the business. Firms, like our own, which study human relations—labor relations, and industrial relations, they are called in some places—are

often asked to supply people to lecture on the subject. It is very difficult. How can you tell people to do things which you know they are not doing because they are the way they are? You cannot get the good will of the people who work for you by changing words such as "canteen" into "dining room," "navvy" to "worker," "office boy" to "junior clerk," and so on, or even just by paying higher wages. In the last analysis, good labor relations come from workers approving the kind of people they believe their employers to be.

Good human relations can only develop if top management believes in its importance and then sees that such a philosophy is dynamically implemented. . . . They must come in a sensible way which we have found brings in response with few exceptions from all grades of staff. This response expresses itself in loyalty to the firm's cooperation with management, greater labor stability and a willing acceptance of new and more modern methods. The majority of workers under such conditions take pride in doing a good job. All this results in greater productivity and higher profits. This enables management to provide all those facilities which make for contented and hard-working staff, and to pay better wages based on genuinely increased productivity.

Management designed the M&S personnel organization to implement the philosophy of concern (see Exhibit 3). In each outlet, a store personnel executive oversaw the training, movement and welfare of the store's staff. The job of the head office personnel executive was similar but somewhat less structured due to the close relationships between headquarter's top executives and staff. Of particular importance was the post of pension and welfare executive who not only ran M&S's pension plan, but also looked after retired M&S employees. Retired employees remained attached to a particular store from which the company provided various services, including a free medical plan and periodic lunches. The pension plan itself, long non-contributory, provided well above average benefits.

Concerning these policies Sir Marcus commented:

> The word *welfare* has an old-fashioned sound reminiscent of the Victorian era, but I do not know a better one to replace it. People do have troubles, and it is a fundamental part of a good staff policy to be able unobtrusively and, above all, speedily to give help and advice when needed.

M&S also offered current employees a rich and varied program of free activities, including river boat trips, table tennis, bowling and concert tickets. Of these amenities Sir Marcus said:

> They should be of such a nature that executives are pleased to take advantage of them. . . . If the facilities are not good enough for top management, then they are not good enough for staff whatever the grade.

By 1972 annual welfare costs at M&S exceeded £4.5 million.

Ultimate responsibility for the company's personnel and welfare policies rested with a Welfare Committee of nine senior managers. The committee, which met weekly, handled those cases which exceeded local store authority or which required a "common handwriting." Decisions of the committee were never questioned.

Marks and Spencer's emphasis on family atmosphere and employee welfare resulted in a distinctive work environment. An employee described M&S's "house rules" as follows:

1. The first thing to remember is that it is a *family* business. Because we're a family business, we care for people. It's a paternal business. How does that affect the professional? You have to receive your inoculation. If you get a violent reaction, you'd better go. And then you grow with the business. It comes back to a recruitment policy. We have to get them young and train them ourselves.

2. You can't be a loner. You have to be part of the team.

3. You have to spread your decisions around. Some in-house decisions are "I don't like it." You learn to accept a decision and wait your time to come back with it.

4. You have to learn how to handle people in an ordinary, decent way.

5. Nobody succeeds who can't talk clearly and simply to the management.

II. Marketing Marks and Spencer's marketing philosophy, like its personnel policy, developed from traditional antecedents. The late Lord Sieff[2] summarized it thus:

The future of the business depends on quick imaginative study of what the people need—not of what the public can be persuaded to buy. . . . Only in supplying real needs will a business flourish in the long term. Only by giving the people what on reflection they continue to want will a business earn the respect of the customer, which is essential to anything more durable than a cheapjack's overnight success. So long as Marks and Spencer continues to study what the people need, and efficiently produce it by means of a staff humanely organized, we can meet any economic trend and . . . challenge. . . .

[2]Israel Sieff.

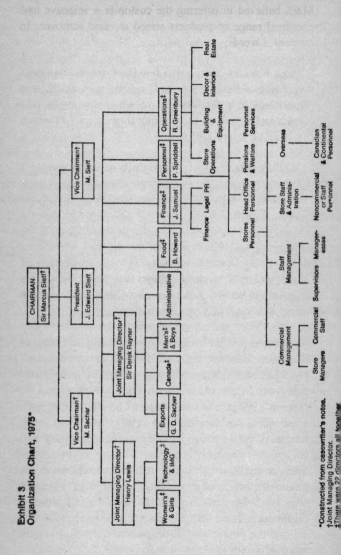

Exhibit 3
Organization Chart, 1975*

*Constructed from casewriter's notes.
†Joint Managing Director.
‡There were 22 directors all together.

M&S believed in offering the customer a selective and streamlined range of products aimed at rapid turnover. In Lord Sieff's words:

> In each section there are a few lines which do a large percentage of the business and, generally speaking, it is these items, the development of which merit our first consideration. It is no use wasting time on articles which can have no future.

The 3,000 item range of textile products included women's clothing and lingerie, men's clothing and underwear, children's clothing, footwear, domestic furnishings, floor coverings, accessories and toiletries. Among the 700 food offerings were bakery goods, confectionaries, produce, poultry and meat, dairy products, beverages and frozen foods. Articles selected typically offered the consumer very high quality at moderate, rather than low, prices. This combination of quality and price encouraged customers to associate M&S with "value for money."

Though M&S had always attempted to maintain a policy of one markup percentage for all merchandise, the range of markups had been expanding. Markups for food ranged from 18 percent to 24 percent with a target of 23 percent; textiles from 26 percent to 33 percent with a target of 30 percent. In 1974, the Annual Report announced that margins had been "deliberately and substantially" cut, with "attendant loss of profit" to counteract rising prices and costs.

M&S never held sales and reduced merchandise for clearance purposes only. It did little advertising (.3 percent of sales vs. 2–3 percent in the U.S.) and that was limited to information (i.e., new product line). Executives believed that the products sold themselves and relied largely on word of mouth to tell their story.

Sales within the store were for cash only. Although customers could centralize purchases for purposes of check writing, M&S honored no credit cards. Executives believed that credit only increased costs.

The company provided no fitting rooms, but maintained a liberal refund policy. M&S accepted virtually all returns on face value, thus eliminating customers' anxieties.

President J. Edward Sieff summarized M&S's basic marketing principles as follows:

1. We do what's best for our suppliers, staff and customers; and
2. We get better at it all the time.

III. Production and Product Line Organization

It is easy enough to test goods when they are made. What is more important is to be sure they will be well made from the start. What we want to have is process control and testing at the point of production.

Lord Marks, 1960

Although M&S did not manufacture the goods it sold, it was often responsible for 75-90 percent of a supplier's output. The company worked closely with the approximately 175 food and 400 nonfood independents providing St. Michael merchandise to M&S specifications. Indeed, according to Brian Howard:

Management at M&S is concerned with a flow that begins with the manufacture of synthetic fibers or the import of raw goods and ends with what we hope is a steady movement of merchandise across store counters.

Supplier relationships often stretched back thirty years or

more allowing many suppliers to share in M&S's growth. In 1975, the company employed over 250 scientists, engineers and support staff who worked in teams with merchandising departments and suppliers to develop product specifications and monitor product quality. Suppliers manufactured goods according to an M&S-planned schedule and held them until the company requested delivery to specific stores, at which time M&S accepted title.

Responsibility for handling the flow from suppliers to M&S rested with the merchandise teams (see Exhibit 4). Within the *textiles division*, two subdivisions existed, each headed by a *managing director*. One director supervised men's and boys' wear, home furnishings, footwear, accessories, and new products; the other, women's and girls' wear. Reporting to the managing director of each subdivision were one or more *senior executives*, each of whom had charge of one or more product lines handled by the division. Each line was further subdivided into segments overseen by *junior executives* (e.g., menswear subdivisions included knitwear and outerwear). Junior executives, in turn, supervised *selectors* responsible for developing merchandise ranges and *merchandisers* responsible for sales estimates, production, packaging, and distribution.

The food division, though more centralized, adhered to the same basic philosophies and procedures as textiles. Each product group within the food division had a selector and merchandiser with the same responsibilities as in the textile division. Merchandise teams tested new items with recipes and tasting panels. Product shelf life frequently required a shorter time span for food division operations than for textiles.

At the store level, food operations differed slightly from textiles. Store staff, responsible for determining the merchandise they desired, prepared weekly lists of stock on hand that indicated what they wanted delivered on each day of the following week. The merchandisers who controlled distribution edited these orders. After the individual store orders were submitted, a computer, programmed weekly with the production capacity and location of each supplier, generated a production plan for each supplier and geographical area. The merchandise was subsequently ordered. All food orders were transported to the stores via depots operated by independent contractors. Perishable goods were delivered daily. Each product bore a clear sell-out date and it was the responsibility of the merchandise and store staffs to monitor the freshness of the food continually. In addition to testing all new products and resampling trial lines, M&S staff randomly selected items from stores and brought them to the laboratory for inspection.

Merchandising began with semiannual estimates for the coming season, including budgets for sale, stock and production. Merchandisers, selectors, and merchandise executives held joint responsibility for estimates. The board of directors calculated the total estimate for the company and for each major decision. All estimates were made *exclusively* in pounds sterling.

Senior executives monitored sales performance personally and by means of reports. Of particular interest was the Stock Checking List Summary which was used in both foods and textiles and circulated weekly to the directors (see Exhibit 5). Most merchandise executives believed that the basics needed monitoring, while fashion items would "take care of themselves." Senior management was reluctant to accept external conditions as justification for results below plan. Generally, if department sales were unsatisfactory, internal procedures were evaluated first. Senior management constantly monitored departments when performance was smooth and eased up in the face of difficult problems. The reasoning was that good performance deteriorated easily, if not continually pressured.

Exhibit 4
Organization of the Textiles Division for Men's, Boys', Home Furnishings, Footwear, Accessories, and New Products, Including Detailed Organization for Men's Wear

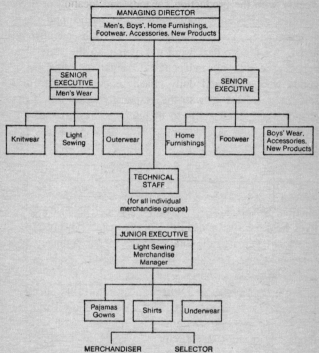

Source: Researcher's notes.

Exhibit 5
Stock Checking List, Summary

This Year FIVE Week(s) Ending December 30. 1974
Last Year FIVE Week(s) Ending December 31. 1973

C.L. Item	Article	Selling Price £	Sales £	Stock £	On Order £	Stock at Mfrs. (Including Warehouses) £	Production Planned next 8 Weeks	
					5 WEEKS		This Period	
	KNEE NYLON SOCKS							
62A/B	NYLON							
62A/B	White	22p 35p	226319	245968	38938	260000	370000	
62C	Colours	22p 25p	22123	26529	1016	10000	75000	
62D 64	Grey/Beige	22p 35p	15234 35p	24685	1203	5000	70000	
	WOOL/NYLON							
56	T.O.T.	44p 49p	41817	39758	586	20000	50000	
63	St. Top	33p 44p	48885	55146	1386	45000	50000	
	ORLON/NYLON							
61	Plain	30p 40p	30905	10180	420	25000	40000	
59	Pattern	40p 49p	77388	30577	2185	5000		
	TOTAL KNEE HIGH SOCKS		462471	432845	45734	370000	655000	
81/82 83/84	Heavyweight Tights	ALL	148960	162994	14395	10000		C.L. Reduced
77	Girls' One Size Tights	23p	24607	7783				
65/66 72	Boys' Socks	24p 45p	20112					
45/47/48 52/55/58 68/98	Experimental & Unseasonable	ALL	42542	138793	53703	375000	290000	
	TOTAL FULL SELLING PRICE		698692	742413	113832	755000	945000	
	Reduced	ALL	28542	75303				
	GRAND TOTAL		727234	817716	113832	755000	945000	
	Stock Target 28th Dec. 1974			750000		750000		
	Estimated Intake for Period £780,000							

The Chairman	Sir Derek Rayner	Mr. G. D. Sacher	Mr. A. S. Orion	Mr.
The President	Mr. H. B. Freeman	Mr. S. J. Sacher	Mr. C. V. Silver	Mr.
Mr. M. M. Sacher	Mr. L. R. Goodman	Mr. J. Salisse	Mr. I. A. Frodsham	
Mr. M. D. Sieff	Mr. R. Greenbury	Mr. D. Susman	Mr. J. Gardiner	
Mr. H. M. Lewis	Mr. J. A. Rishworth	Mr. B. J. Lynch	Mr. B. Harries	

		2 WEEKS		Last Period		Last Year		5 WEEKS	
No. of Stores	Sales £	Stock £	On Order £	Stock at Mfrs. (Including Warehouses) £	Sales £	Stock £	Selling Price £	Remark
	53764	210470	131998	320000	189116	191386	18p 29p	
	8485	31076	5840	5000	36595	42063	18p 29p	
	3635	41002	5367	10000	15806	55012	22p 32p	
	14149	39167	19864	15000	38672	63445	35p 40p	
	14829	41252	30460	45000	41315	43567	28p 37p	
	8768	56510	16114	30000	60851	104163	27p 35p	
200	32407	92217	21707	15000	31601	37063	37p 45p	
	136037	511694	231350	440000	413836	536699		
3/12/74	52735	178273	69730	70000	198133	98655	55p 70p	
140	6803	17504	6137	10000				
	5622	32840	2549	20000	45595	74419	27p 45p	
	2561	67240	7633	305000	18277	88555	ALL	
	203758	807551	317399	875000	675601	796328		
	334	2343			8931	8152	ALL	
	204092	809894	317399	875000	684532	804480		

IV. Store Divisional Organization In 1974 M&S had 251 stores, divided into 11 *divisions*, each under a *corporate director* with responsibility for store operations, building and equipment, transportation, packaging, and real estate. Twelve *divisional superintendents*, covering regional groups of stores, acted as Baker Street's field representatives and helped store managers as needed. The *store managers* were the senior line managers in each store and were held responsible by the board for implementing its policies.

In practice, the store manager concentrated on sales. Relieved of responsibility for profit margins and usually ignorant of individual margins, managers strove to increase volume, control store expenses, monitor turnover, eliminate "counter cloggers" and insure adequate stock in fast-moving items. The *staff manageress* was responsible for staff selection, training, assignment, development and welfare. Most store managers were men, but some women had recently been promoted to that position.

The dual authority structure was designed to instill a "family spirit" in each store. In effect, stores were run by a "father" and "mother." M&S felt it very important to develop and maintain a family spirit in every store. The manager and manageress of a *new* store always had comparable experience in other stores and were expected to achieve a family spirit within six months.

The typical store in 1973 had a manager, assistant manager, staff manageress, 2–3 department managers, warehouse manager, cashier, 10 department supervisors, and 150 general staff. All managerial staff received training in company stores. By age 30, however, most staff and line managers embarked on different career paths, with staff people centralized at headquarters (see Exhibit 6).

The *sales assistant* occupied one of the most important positions in the company. Assigned to specific departments and attired in identical uniforms, sales assistants monitored product quality, kept stock plentiful and neat, operated the cash registers, and assisted customers. They had authority to replenish stock and reject goods which seemed of poor quality or inappropriate for the department. However, rejection of a range was seldom exercised.

A Look at a Store

The researchers toured a large downtown London store. The tour began in the overwhelmingly clean and tidy stock and receiving area. Merchandise was received on conveyor belts, spot counted, and immediately put into stock. A large, spotless area, used for food stock and storage, included freezers and cold storage rooms. Unique baskets enabled stacking so that food products would not be damaged.

Staff amenities included medical room and nurse, with periodic visits from a physician, dentist, and chiropodist; one-room infirmary; hairdressing salon (charge 75¢) where women were served lunch under the dryers; cloakroom with security lockers; shower and bathroom facilities; staff refrigerator; recreation room; and staff dining room. The dining room provided lunches, coffee, and afternoon tea— the charge for all three was 25¢ per day. The food compared favorably with that served in executive dining rooms.

The main sales floor was arranged to reflect shopping behavior rather than production process, e.g., knitwear was separated into men's, women's, and children's. Except for area identification signs, there were no graphics or displays. Merchandise was displayed on tables and garment racks.

The food department had separate check-out, but no barriers to the department store. All food was packaged in see-through containers. Many shelves were completely empty because M&S ordered only a 1-day supply, plus minimum stock for the next day. When shelf life expired, unsold goods were available to staff at half price or less.

Movement of both textiles and foods was continuously monitored by the store manager. He remarked, "By 12:00

Exhibit 6
Marks & Spencer Organization for Store Operation

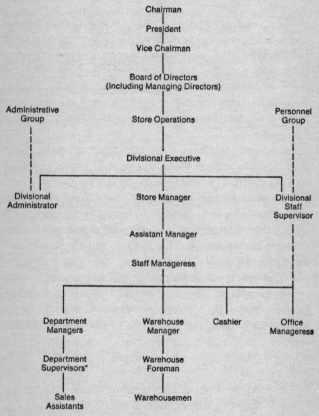

*Present only in larger stores, but in some instances numbering 10.

noon I know the fastest moving item in the store. It's my job to move that merchandise and make sure we get enough of it. The major problem I face is if I can't get what I know to be the best, what will I settle for as next best?''

V. Finance According to John Samuel, Financial Officer, M&S's financial policy aimed to provide sufficient resources for capital development, retained earnings and dividends. The board determined the specific amounts to be committed. A pretax profit goal of 10 to 10.5 percent and expense level of about 12 percent together implied need for about a 25 percent gross profit margin. Only senior board members dealt with profitability, but even they regarded profit as a required residual, and focused on sales volume and expenses in pounds sterling. They tried to balance food and clothing sales as related to margins and overall volume. Store-level goals were set in terms of sales and expenses, while merchandising and buying dealt with production and distribution cost and quality.

Despite growth, major percentage relationships changed little over time. For example, expenses remained 11–12 percent of sales from 1970 to 1974. Samuel indicated that M&S's size minimized the effects of change and eliminated the threat of violent shifts.

The company made every effort to finance its continual growth internally. Although dividend payout was high, Samuel reported a ''massive scaling down of proportions paid out to the shareholders in order to finance continued growth.''

During the period of domestic expansion, M&S also built up exports to 159 retailers in 41 countries, who operated St. Michael shops in departments stocked exclusively with M&S merchandise. In 1974 exports rose 31 percent to $31,920,050. The company was also beginning to move directly into foreign markets. In 1972, a 50 percent joint venture was formed with People's Department Stores of Canada, under the name, ''St. Michael Shops of Canada.'' Major developments were also underway for France (two stores) and Belgium (one store). Although these operations required local borrowing, retained earnings remained the major source of investment funds for both Canadian and European expansion.

In recent years the company's freedom in financial matters had been increasingly circumscribed by government actions. These included:

1. Raising the corporate tax rate from 40 percent to 52 percent in 1974;
2. Mandating, under the provisions of the Counter-Inflation Act of 1973, that the gross equivalent of ordinary dividends declared in 1973 could not exceed those of the previous year by more than 5 percent.
3. Forcing all retailers to reduce gross margins by 10 percent in the spring of 1974.

The Marks and Spencer Management Style

A week at Baker Street began with an 8:30 A.M. meeting in the chairman's office. Generally eight or nine of the senior members met daily with the chairman, M&S's chief operational director. The members most frequently in attendance included the President, J. Edward Sieff; the Vice Chairmen, and Joint Managing Directors, M. Sacher and Michael Sieff; Joint Managing Directors, Henry Lewis and Sir Derek Rayner; and Directors, R. Greenbury, W.B. Howard and G.D. Sacher.

As he entered the chairman's office, each member received sales and stock figures for the previous week. The chairman generally started the meeting by relating a particular incident he had observed during the previous several days. He frequently spoke for several minutes on one or two particular problems and how they related to the business. General comments were then interchanged by all present. The chairman then went around the room and asked each director if he had anything he wished to discuss, starting with the Vice Chairman, Michael Sacher. The following excerpts are from a meeting held on January 15, 1975.

Sir Marcus:	We are not taking our markdowns fast enough or sharp enough.
Henry Lewis:	That's related to some problems we discussed yesterday. The production cutoff date is not in adequate control. We must be able to learn from production sheets so we don't make mistakes. Production changes and cutoffs should be noted for reference next year.
Sir Marcus:	If you go away from the principle, it costs you more than you gain 9 times out of 10.
Brian Howard:	We are moving further into computers in food. From July 1975 to November 1975, stores will be converted from a daily indent (order) system to a weekly system. The computer then translates the weekly ordering into daily projections. It reduces paperwork and by 1976, the stores probably won't be ordering at all. It's going to take a lot of training to get people to think in total terms. The one system will, however, simplify the stores' life.
J. Edward Sieff:	I want to make a plea for self-restraint in cloth buying on price points.

	There's no point in buying more expensive fabrics. We are only interested in the desirability of the article. Once we see the retail price in print, it qualifies the cost price, which doesn't necessarily represent value. We should ask ourselves, "Is it better, of more value, and better quality?"
Sir Marcus:	I think the president is absolutely right. It's a matter of self-restraint. Anything else, Teddy (J. Edward)?
J. Edward Sieff:	I ran across a fabric yesterday, 5–8. I think it's inferior. I hear our people saying it's lousy. It may be an achievement for technology but not for women. And ICI (major fabric supplier) is pushing it.
Sir Marcus:	Are we telling them?
Michael Sacher:	We have a meeting Thursday.
Sir Marcus:	We must be frank with our suppliers.
J. Edward Sieff:	We must be frank with ourselves.
Sir Derek Rayner:	I've been trying to work our priority stores for 1975. Over two-thirds of the sales will come from 95 stores. We need good stock composition of basic merchandise. Can we carry both basic merchandise in all stores and specialized lines in selected stores?

*****

Michael Sacher:	I'm concerned about two operations in the stores—training of the cashiers and methods of filling up the displays. For £45 million of goods, we handle £180 million at Marble Arch. We accept too much of this and take too many things for granted.

We handle everything four times before it gets to the customer.

R. Greenbury: I have set up a team to look at the handling of bread and crisps (potato chips).

J. Edward Sieff: Anything to learn from Safeway or Migros (grocery chains)?

Sir Marcus: Let's ask them. Or Sainsbury. They'll tell us. No need to invent everything ourselves.

R. Greenbury: I've asked them.

Sir Marcus: O.K., but let's *do* something. I don't want to see the perfect solution.

*****

On Mondays only, after the 8:30 A.M. meeting, those meeting with the chairman proceeded to a conference room for the 10 A.M. meeting of all directors and senior executives. A total of approximately 25–30 men gathered around a long table. The meeting was conducted in the same manner as the 8:30 A.M. meeting. The chairman began with several points and each executive present was called on to contribute observations or problems. The following are excerpts of the January 30 meeting:

Sir Marcus: Henry Lewis and I visited 9 of Nottingham Manufacturing factories (the largest M&S supplier). They are in outstanding operation but they have failed to innovate in the design area. However, they had no criticism of our criterion in this respect. Also, they were making a line of ladies' nylons, 3 in a package, for 75p that was not making enough money for them. They asked us if we really wanted them to make lines at a substantial loss. We said "certainly not" and we cancelled the line.

My second point is that we brought back goods that were of appalling quality—not poor in make, but in conception. Are we sufficiently self-critical—are our standards high enough—do we probe enough in our eating and wearing? You must see that it applies to you—we've got to be critical.

Another point concerns customers' criticism and complaints. Ninety-four percent of them are replied to by me within a maximum of 48 hours. This procedure should apply around this table. It is a job for the senior members—not the subordinate member. "A soft answer turneth away wrath."

****

J. Edward Sieff: I've heard complaints about hosiery that doesn't stay up. We must look at the technicians' role. We are not calling on our technicians sufficiently. Secondly, I'd like to talk about our taste, which should be one of classic simplicity. We give too much credibility to gimmicks that we see in foreign fairs. I know the young people want the showy goods, but we must draw the balance. What are the parameters of taste?

Sir Marcus: Decent taste, reasonably up-to-date taste.

****

Michael Sieff: The opening of Paris—we have very poor stock conditions. The outstanding orders aren't being filled. I want to know what's happening. Next, markdowns. The trial reports and evaluations are important. We must be cautious to avoid markdowns.

Thirdly, price increases. Some of our margins have been increased to 32–33 percent, which makes up for the budget line of 24 percent. To talk to the stores about margin is difficult. Should we bring in margin? It may not be wise.

Michael Sacher: Their job is to sell whatever they've got at whatever price, including the reduced items. I don't think they should be told.

****

Sir Derek Rayner: We must take action to clear. Down to half price. Also, the spring goods, we are short of sizes and have stockouts. We should study checking lists for balance.

****

Henry Lewis: Some stores still have an October range. Merchandise and garment development must be worked on.

****

John Levy:[3] Our packaging for dark colored clothes

[3]Senior executive—Transport and Packaging.

is inadequate. People can't see the color. We are working on a flip-top package to expose half the garment in order for the customer to handle it.

****

Sir Marcus: I received a letter from the Wolverhampton store about our plan for extension there. As you know, we cancelled plans to extend the operation. The letter was written by departmental supervisors asking for an extension of their store. It's a very well written letter. Let me read it to you (reads the letter). I think we should look into the situation again.[4]

At the conclusion of the general meeting, many directors and senior executives met with their respective groups. Senior directors often joined such gatherings. At a food meeting attended by a researcher, one of the vice chairmen came in and threw a package of rhubarb crumble on the table. He scathingly commented on the poor taste and consistency of the dish:

This is the most disgusting thing I have ever had the pleasure of serving to guests. The rhubarb was unripe and overcooked—it was inedible. Also, the product is overpackaged. We should take a closer look at our packaging policies.

Elsewhere at Baker Street, a constant parade of people

[4]Sir Marcus noted in March 1975 that the supervisors' letter led to an investment of over £1 million.

went in and out of offices. Standard procedure was to knock and immediately enter, without awaiting a response. The object was to project an open-door policy; often the visitor would get an answer to a question and leave. Outside each door was an "engaged" sign that could be lit from the occupant's desk when he didn't want to be disturbed.

Executives were constantly available to anyone who wanted to work with them. In each office and in the halls, was a light with four colors (much like a traffic light). Each board member and senior executive was assigned a combination of colors. These lights flashed whenever someone wanted to reach an executive who was not in his office. Those without a light combination carried pocket "bleepers."

Most executives' offices featured two phones. One could be used for any purpose. The other was answered by an operator; the executive told the operator whom he was looking for, hung up, and was called back when the party was located. Thus, no executive, unless off the premises, was out of reach of anyone who wanted to see or talk with him.

Concerns about the Future

The management of M&S were figures of considerable public importance, well known in the business community. Asked about the future, the chairman spoke of his concern for the economic future of M&S and the nation.

We believe that if we guard the standards of our goods, improve our systems and look after both our staff and our customers, we shall continue to grow and to make profits.

We need profits, after paying taxes:

1. To improve the pay and working conditions of our staff

and to take care of them during retirement. The high morale and productivity of our staff owes much to these factors, most of them take pride in working for a successful business which is quality oriented;
2. To have funds for investment in the development of the business, which is clearly desired by our many customers;
3. To pay a proper dividend to our 240,000 shareholders, which include many small savers, individual pensioners and pension funds.

Marks and Spencer has over the years, under a private enterprise system, made a significant contribution to the economic life of the country and has helped to raise the standard of living. We doubt whether we could have achieved this under any other system.

Sir Marcus was particularly upset with inept government interventions in business. When asked what these actions would mean to his basic strategy of expansion in Britain, he commented:

First we have to be concerned with our liquidity. We will not spend our reserves. The result is whereas we were going to spend £40 million/year to upgrade our stores, we're now going to spend £20 million. We have to preserve our position.

The consequences will not be important in the short term. But as a pattern they will hurt Britain severely in three to four years' time.

A particularly clear expression of Sir Marcus' views was made in a corporate statement issued on October 8, 1974, two days before the 1974 Parliamentary elections. The statement made headlines in all Britain's major papers.

Retailing performs a major role in the chain of production and distribution. We cooperate with whatever government is in office, but some Ministers and their advisers do not seem to appreciate the significant contribution which a healthy and competitive retail industry can make in stemming the rise in the cost of living. We are not helped in this task by misguiding interference.

Corporation tax takes more than half our profits. The Government criticizes the private sector for its failure to invest but it omits to explain that much investment is financed out of profits. If our profits are subject to politically motivated restrictions and massively reduced, confidence is eroded, and investment on which the maintenance of employment and the future prosperity of the country depends slows down.

The remaining profit (after tax and dividends) is retained in the business to finance its future growth. Present Government policy has substantially reduced the money available for such development in the immediate future.

Michael Sacher, Vice Chairman, commented on some of the firm's internal issues and problems:

What has always astounded me is how few people have learned the simple principles on which we operate. I think we have carved a market out here which is quality goods at lower prices. As long as we stick to that we'll be okay, as long as the younger people learn the principles of the business. You have to have a clear policy where you upgrade areas in which you are weak and stay out of the caviar business. The board can help here but there are so many things distracting us from being shopkeepers: bombs, the government and so on. But we implement by generalizing from the particular. That is how you teach young people.

I always try to pick out one thing and then work on it. Take frozen canneloni; it's a new line that I think will move very well. People like canneloni and it's hard to make. Someone else suggested spaghetti. The housewife can make perfectly good spaghetti with ease, why should we? It just requires a bit of common sense. It's no good developing a slip department if everyone's wearing pants.

Researcher:	Isn't it inevitable that you sell the spaghetti as well?
Michael Sacher:	No, I don't think so. We don't believe in a high degree of specialization and it has always been our practice to move selectors around the business. So much of selection is taste, feel, and common sense.
	I was going to say something else, also immodest, and it's true of other senior colleagues. You have to become expert in a wide variety of activities: selecting goods, feel for merchandise, know what's coming, principles of building, and rudimentary technological questions.
Michael Sacher:	I heard a lecture in Israel about tomatoes, so I know something about them. I've been shown cell sections of frozen material, so I can ask why our beans and sprouts have such lassitude. I've acquired enough garbage to ask technological questions that they can't throw out.
	In the end, the decision has to be

taken by management, not the experts. And you have to be humble. I just try to take a jolly good look at everything that's been here a long time in the same place. Repotting is healthy managerially if not horticulturally.

I do see problems: you can't help but lean on the strengths that you have. Take Teddy. He has an astronomic knowledge of textiles and he applies himself. His taste is not perfect, but he knows what an M&S range should be. He's done a wonderful job in his new role.
The family is a binding force in another way. Members of the family can talk to each other in a candid way that I find extremely difficult to discover with professional managers. It happens with some, but it takes time.

Researcher: How much does great wealth have to do with it?

Michael Sacher: Well, there is something to that. We know what good taste is. We see fashion as it emerges and whether it lasts. I once suggested that we send our selectors to the Caribbean for the winter holiday to see what is being worn.

Another problem is that most of our executives have joined us straight from the university. It compels you

> to have a series of graded courses outside the university. Not so much what they learn, but they can test themselves against peers. My generation had the war in which to measure themselves.

Senior members of the board agreed that the major question facing M&S concerned the proper rate of expansion in Britain, and the moves into the Common Market and Canada. Sir Marcus articulated reasons for the moves:

> First, as an opportunity for more profit. Given the deteriorating situation in Britain we think Canada can become very important for us. Second, as a chance to expand British exports. And finally, should things be really bad, it's a lifeline for us abroad.

Five

The Ten Commandments for Managing a Young Growing Business
Steven C. Brandt

1 **Limit the number of primary participants to people who can consciously agree upon and contribute directly to that which the enterprise is to accomplish, for whom, by when.** There are many reasons people become involved in young, growing companies as owners, investors, or key employees. The broad range of satisfactions sought runs from an opportunity for personal expression on one end of the spectrum to capital gains on the other. Unless there is compatibility between what each primary participant wants out of the business, debilitating conflict is likely to ensue. The process of trying to consciously agree on the purpose of the enterprise is often difficult and revealing.

2 **Define the business of the enterprise in terms of what is to be bought, precisely by whom, and why.** Businesses are organs of society that perform tasks associated with providing most goods and services the public decides it wishes to own and use. Under this capitalistic system, a business can prosper to the extent it performs its particular tasks effectively and efficiently within the law. The nature of the tasks to be performed usually changes over time as those served change. The successful company predicts and responds to its chosen customers' needs. Customers, therefore, define the business. At all times, some customers are growing in their ability to buy; others are declining. The astute manager ascertains which is which.

3 Concentrate all available resources on accomplishing two or three specific, operational objectives within a given time period. Enterprises have finite resources. A smaller company achieves competitive advantage when playing for limited, explicit gains in a marketplace of its own choosing. Specialization breeds an organization sensitive to opportunities and quick to act. But any advantage withers if follow-through is weak. It will be weak if resources are dissipated. Resource dilution is a sure formula for mediocrity, a state of being that aspiring growth businesses cannot afford.

4 Prepare and work from a written plan that delineates who in the total organization is to do what, by when. Until committed to paper, intentions are seeds without soil, sails without wind, mere wishes which render communication within an organization inefficient, understanding uncertain, feedback inaccurate, and execution sporadic. Without execution, there is no payoff. The process of committing plans to paper is easy to postpone under the press of day-to-day events. In the absence of a document, fully coordinated usage of the resources of the business is unlikely. Each participant travels along a different route toward a destination of his or her own choosing. Decisions are made independently, without a map. Time is lost; energy squandered.

5 **Employ key people with proven records of success at doing what it is the enterprise requires done.** People do what they like; they like what they know. Experience adds depth to knowledge. The best indicator of how a person will perform in the future is how he or she has done in the past in the same or related activity. Criteria for selecting key people is dictated by the plans, the blueprints, for the business. A brickmason is not needed to construct a wooden building. The plans reflect the operational objectives and the intentions of the primary participants. The interests and capabilities of a new person must harmonize with both.

6 **Reward individual performance that exceeds agreed upon standards.** Performance above the perfunctory level is a discretionary matter for each employee. Most people have alternative, off-the-job ways of utilizing excess energy or talent. Channeling such excess into activity beneficial to the business requires a tailored approach to each individual. A manager must first insure that there is understanding of the minimum results to be achieved. Then, for performance above the minimums, forms of compensation important to the performer—or in some cases, teams of performers—must be utilized.

7 **Expand methodically from a profitable base toward a balanced business.** Optimism is both the poison and the antidote of the growth company manager. It may

315

be possible to accomplish all things, but not simultaneously. With limited resources, sequential growth over time is the judicious prescription for prosperity. Seek logical, incremental extensions of existing activities, but avoid a growth for growth's sake psychology. Bigger is not automatically better; more is not necessarily merrier. Make managing a competitive advantage. Increase customer dependency on the enterprise. Economic success can breed more of the same and/or other returns for the primary participants. Money is the traditional reward; life style considerations are becoming more widespread.

8 **Project, monitor, and conserve cash and credit capability.** Cash flow is the blood of a growth business. A company's ability to continue is determined daily, not at year end; by the contents of the checking account rather than the financial statement. Keeping money in hand or readily available for both planned and unplanned events is not only prudent but necessary in unsettled times. Cultivation of financial sources is an enduring duty.

9 **Maintain a detached point of view.** Managing a growing business requires unyielding dedication that can consume the body, impair the senses, and warp the mind. Such effects are harmful to the individual and the enterprise. Clinical objectivity is the only preventative. Growth implies and entails risk. Risk begets failures as well as successes. Wide perspective gained through non-business experience or study helps one endure the pressures and accept with equanimity the results, good and bad, of business decisions.

10 **Anticipate incessant external change by continuously**

testing adopted business plans for their consistency with the realities of the world marketplace. The past will not come again. Neither isolation nor insulation from tomorrow is possible. The problems of the times are the opportunities of the times, as always, but the strings attached are multiplying. Governments, domestic and foreign, will increasingly affect the conduct of business. Despair is of little value. Vigilance is.

Index

321

323

About the Author

Steven C. Brandt is currently Senior Lecturer in Management at the Stanford University Graduate School of Business. Since 1971 he has combined teaching with research and managing activities involving a variety of domestic and international companies.

Dr. Brandt is an experienced CEO and director, and he is the author of *Entrepreneuring: Ten Commandments for Building a Growth Organization*, also available in a Mentor edition, and *Strategic Planning in Emerging Companies*. In addition, he has published articles in leading national magazines, and he regularly speaks on entrepreneuring and related subjects.